THE WORKS OF
CHARLES DARWIN

Volume 17. *Various contrivances by which orchids are fertilized*

THE WORKS OF
CHARLES DARWIN

EDITED BY
PAUL H. BARRETT & R. B. FREEMAN
ADVISOR: PETER GAUTREY

VOLUME
17

THE VARIOUS CONTRIVANCES BY WHICH ORCHIDS ARE FERTILIZED BY INSECTS

NEW YORK UNIVERSITY PRESS
WASHINGTON SQUARE, NEW YORK

Published in 1988 in the U.S.A. by New York University Press

Washington Square, New York, NY 10003

LIBRARY OF CONGRESS

Library of Congress Cataloging-in-Publication Data

Darwin, Charles, 1809–1882.
  The various contrivances by which orchids
are fertilized by insects.

(The works of Charles Darwin ; v. 17)
   Includes index.
   ISBN 0–8147–1806–X
   1. Orchids—Reproduction. 2. Pollination
by insects. I. Title. II. Series: Darwin,
Charles, 1809–1882. Works. 1987 ; v. 17.
QH365.A1 1987 vol. 17 575 s   88–22493
[QK495.064]   [584′.15041662]

Printed in Great Britain at the
University Press, Cambridge

INTRODUCTION TO VOLUME SEVENTEEN

The Various Contrivances by which Orchids are Fertilized by Insects. [Second edition] 1877. Freeman 801.

Most of Darwin's books after the publication of *On the Origin of Species* were in support of particular aspects of his evolutionary theories and this is the first of them. The first edition (Freeman 800) came out in 1862 with the longer title *On the various contrivances by which British and foreign orchids are fertilized by insects, and the good effects of intercrossing.* Down House is in good orchid country and he had also gathered material from the Royal Botanic Gardens at Kew and from commercial firms particularly that of James Veitch and his son at Chelsea.

A French translation of the first edition was to be published in 1870. Darwin had collected so much new material by this time that he wanted to incorporate it in this translation. He put his notes together and had them published in an article which appeared in 1869 in the *Annals and Magazine of Natural History* Vol. 4, pages 141–59. The first edition of 1862 has one other peculiarity; it is bound in a ribbed plum coloured cloth; all the rest of Darwin's works published by John Murray up to the turn of the century, including the second edition of this work, are in dark green. The second edition of 1877 is the only other one. It is reproduced here because of its more complete character, and because it illustrates Darwin's habit of continuing studies in many fields.

*On the Fertilization of Orchids
by Insects*

THE

VARIOUS CONTRIVANCES

BY WHICH

ORCHIDS ARE FERTILISED BY INSECTS.

By CHARLES DARWIN, M.A., F.R.S., &c.

SECOND EDITION, REVISED.

WITH ILLUSTRATIONS.

LONDON:

JOHN MURRAY, ALBEMARLE STREET.

1877.

[*The right of Translation is reserved.*]

PREFACE

TO THE SECOND EDITION

The first edition of this work was published early in the year 1862, and has been for some time out of print. During the two or three years after its appearance I received, through the kindness of various correspondents in different parts of the world, a large number of letters, especially from Fritz Müller in South Brazil, communicating to me many new and curious facts, and calling my attention to some errors. Various memoirs on the fertilization of orchids have also since been published, and I have myself examined several new and striking forms. A large amount of matter has thus been accumulated; but the present volume would be rendered much too long if the whole were introduced. I have, therefore, selected only the more interesting facts, and have given a brief abstract of the several published papers. The work has thus been remodelled; and the additions and corrections are so numerous that I have found it impossible to follow my usual plan of giving a list of them. I have, however, / appended, in chronological order, the titles of all the papers and books on the fertilization of the Orchideae which have been published since the appearance of the first edition of the present book. Finally, I will remark that any reader who wishes merely to see how wonderfully complex and perfect are the adaptations for the fertilization of these plants had better read chapter VII on the Catasetidae. The account of their structure and of the action of the several parts will, I think, be intelligible, if he will first glance at the explanation of the terms given at the close of the Introduction. /

LIST OF PAPERS AND BOOKS BEARING ON THE FERTILIZATION
OF THE ORCHIDEAE, WHICH HAVE BEEN PUBLISHED SINCE THE
APPEARANCE OF THE FIRST EDITION OF THIS WORK IN 1862,
ARRANGED IN CHRONOLOGICAL ORDER

Bronn, H. G. *Charles Darwin, über die Einrichtungen zur Befruchtung britischer und ausländischer Orchideen*, with an Appendix by the Translator on *Stanhopea devoniensis*. Stuttgart, 1862

Gray, Asa On *Platanthera (Habenaria)* and *Gymnadenia* in 'Enumeration of Plants of the Rocky Mountains', *American Journal of Science and Arts, Second Series*, vol. xxxiv, No. 101, September, 1862, p. 33

Gray, Asa On *Platanthera hookeri*, in a review of the first edition of the present work, *American Journal of Science and Arts*, vol. xxxiv, July, 1862, p. 143

Anderson, J. 'Fertilization of Orchids', *Journal of Horticulture and Cottage Gardener*, 21 April, 1863, p. 287

Gosse, P. H. 'Microscopic Observation on some Seeds of Orchids', *Journal of Horticulture and Cottage Gardener*, 21 April, 1863, p. 287

Gray, Asa On *Platanthera (Habernaria) flava* and *Gymnadenia tridentata*, *American Journal of Science and Arts*, vol. xxxvi, September, 1863, p. 292

Journal of Horticulture and Cottage Gardener 17 March, 1863, p. 206. 'On Orchid Cultivation, Cross-breeding, and Hybridising'

Scudder, J. H. On *Pogonia ophioglossoides, Proceedings of the Boston Society of Natural History*, vol. ix, April, 1863

Treviranus 'Ueber Dichogamie nach C. C. Sprengel und Ch. Darwin. § 3. Orchideen', *Botanische Zeitung*, No. 2, 1863, p. 9 /

Treviranus 'Nachträgliche Bemerkungen über die Befruchtung einiger Orchideen', *Botanische Zeitung*, No. 32, 1863, p. 241 /

Trimen, R. 'On the Fertilization of *Disa grandiflora*, Linn.', *Journal of Linnean Society, Botany*, vol. vii, 1863, p. 144

West of Scotland Horticultural Magazine 'Fertilization of Orchids', September, 1863, p. 65

Crüger 'A few Notes on the Fecundation of Orchids, and their Morphology', *Journal of Linnean Society, Botany*, vol. viii, No. 31, 1864, p. 127

Scott, J. 'On the Individual Sterility and Cross-impregnation of certain Species of Oncidium', *Journal of Linnean Society*, vol. viii, No. 31, 1864, p. 162

Moggridge, J. Traherne 'Observations on some Orchids of the South of France', *Journal of Linnean Society, Botany*, vol. viii, No. 32, 1865, p. 256

Trimen, R. 'On the Structure of *Bonatea speciosa*, Linn., with reference to its Fertilization', *Journal of Linnean Society*, vol. ix, 1865, p. 156

Rohrbach, P. 'Ueber *Epipogium gmelini*', *Gekrönte Preisschrift*, Göttingen, 1866

Delpino *Sugli Apparecchi della Fecondazione nelle Piante antocarpee*, Florence, 1867

Hildebrand, F. *Die Geschlechter-Vertheilung bei den Pflanzen*, Leipzig, 1867, p. 51, *et seq.*

Hildebrand, F. 'Frederigo Delpino's Beobachtungen über die Bestäubungsvorrichtungen bei den Phanerogamen', *Botanische Zeitung*, No. 34, 1867, p. 265

Moggridge, J. Traherne On *Ophrys, Flora of Mentone*, 1867 (?), Plates 43–5

Weale, J. P. Mansel 'Notes on the Structure and Fertilization of the Genus Bonatea, with a special description of a species found at Bedford, South Africa', *Journal of Linnean Society, Botany*, vol. x, 1867, p. 470

Hildebrand 'Notizen über die Geschlechtsverhältnisse brasilianischer Pflanzen. Aus einem Briefe von Fritz Müller', *Botanische Zeitung*, No. 8, 1868, p. 113 /

Müller, Fritz 'Ueber Befruchtungserscheinungen bei Orchideen', *Botanische Zeitung*, No. 39, 1868, p. 629

Müller, Hermann 'Beobachtungen an westfälishen Orchideen', *Verhandlungen des nat. Vereins für Pr. Rheinl. u. Westf.* 1868 and 1869

Darwin, Charles 'Notes on the Fertilization of Orchids', *Annals and Magazine of Natural History*, September, 1869

Delpino *Ulteriori Osservazioni sulla Dicogamia nel Regno vegetale, Parte prima*, Milan, 1868–9, pp. 175–8

Moggridge, J. Traherne 'Ueber *Ophrys insectifera*, L. (part)', *Verhandlungen der Kaiserl. Leop. Carol. Akad. (Nova Acta)*, vol. xxxv, 1869

Müller, Fritz 'Ueber einige Befruchtungserscheinungen', *Botanische Zeitung*, No. 14, 1869, p. 224

Müller, Fritz 'Umwandlung von Staubgefässen in Stempel bei Begonia. Uebergang von Zwitterblüthigkeit in Getrenntblüthigkeit bei Chamissoa. Triandrische Varietät eines monandrischen Epidendrum', *Botanische Zeitung*, No. 10, 1870, p. 149

Weale, J. P. Mansel 'Note on a Species of Disperis found on the Kageberg, South Africa', *Journal of Linnean Society, Botany*, vol. xiii, 1871, p. 42

Weale, J. P. Mansel 'Some Observations on the Fertilization of *Disa macrantha*', *Journal of Linnean Society*, vol. xiii, 1871, p. 45

Weale, J. P. Mansel 'Notes on some Species of Habenaria found in South Africa', *Journal of Linnean Society*, vol. xiii, 1871, p. 47

Cheeseman, T. F. 'On the Fertilization of the New Zealand Species of Pterostylis', *Transactions of the New Zealand Institute*, vol. v, 1873, p. 352

Müller, Hermann *Die Befruchtung der Blumen durch Insekten*, Leipzig, 1873, pp. 74–86

Cheeseman, T. F. 'On the Fertilization of *Acianthus cyrtostilis*', *Transactions of the New Zealand Institute*, vol. vii, 1874 (issued 1875), p. 349 /

Müller, Hermann 'Alpine Orchids adapted to Cross-fertilization by Butterflies', *Nature*, 31 December, 1874

Delpino *Ulteriori Osservazioni sulla Dicogamia nel Regno vegetale*, Parte seconda, fasc. ii, Milan, 1875, pp. 149–50

Lubbock, Sir J. *British Wild Flowers*, London, 1875, pp. 162–75

Fitzgerald, R. D. *Australian Orchids*, Part I, 1875, Part II, 1876, Sydney, New South Wales /

CONTENTS

INTRODUCTION   [1–5] 1

CHAPTER I

Ophreae

Structure of the flower of *Orchis mascula* – Power of movement of the pollinia – Perfect adaptation of the parts in *Orchis pyramidalis* – Other species of Orchis and of some closely allied genera – On the insects which visit the several species, and on the frequency of their visits – On the fertility and sterility of various orchids – On the secretion of nectar, and on insects being purposely delayed in obtaining it

[6–44] 5

CHAPTER II

Ophreae continued

Fly and Spider Ophrys – Bee Ophrys, apparently adapted for perpetual self-fertilization, but with paradoxical contrivances for intercrossing – *Herminium monorchis*, attachment of the pollinia to the front legs of insects – *Peristylus viridis*, fertilization indirectly effected by nectar secreted from three parts of the labellum – *Gymnadenia conopsea*, and other species – Habenaria or *Platanthera chlorantha* and *bifolia*, their pollinia attached to the eyes of Lepidoptera – Other species of Habenaria – Bonatea – Disa – Summary on the powers of movement in the pollinia

[45–79] / 31

CHAPTER III

Arethuseae

Cephalanthera grandiflora; rostellum aborted; early penetration of the pollen-tubes; case of imperfect self-fertilization; cross-fertilization effected by insects which gnaw the labellum – *Cephalanthera ensifolia* – Pogonia – Pterostylis and other Australian orchids with the labellum sensitive to a touch – Vanilla – Sobralia   [80–92] 56

CHAPTER IV

Neotteae

Epipactis palustris; curious shape of the labellum and its importance in the fructification of the flower – other species of Epipactis – Epipogium – *Goodyera repens* – *Spiranthes autumnalis*; perfect adaptation by which the pollen of a younger flower is carried to the stigma of an older flower on another plant – *Listera ovata*; sensitiveness of the rostellum; explosion of viscid matter; action of insects; perfect adaptation of the several organs – *Listera cordata* – *Neottia nidus-avis*; its fertilization effected in the same manner as in Listera – Thelymitra, self-fertile   [93–127] 65

CHAPTER V

Malaxeae and Epidendreae

Malaxis paludosa – Masdevallia, curious closed flowers – Bolbophyllum, labellum kept in constant movement by every breath of air – Dendrobium, contrivance for self-fertilization – Cattleya, simple manner of fertilization – Epidendrum – Self-fertile Epidendreae   [128–48] / 90

CHAPTER VI

Vandeae

Structure of the column and pollinia – Importance of the elasticity of the pedicel; its power of movement – Elasticity and strength of the caudicles – Calanthe with lateral stigmas, manner of fertilization – *Angraecum sesquipedale*, wonderful length of nectary – Species with the entrance into the stigmatic chamber much contracted, so that the pollen-masses can hardly be inserted – Coryanthes, extraordinary manner of fertilization   [149–77] 105

CHAPTER VII

Vandeae continued – *Catasetidae*

Catasetidae, the most remarkable of all orchids – The mechanism by which the pollinia of Catasetum are ejected to a distance and are transported by insects – Sensitiveness of the horns of the rostellum – Extraordinary difference in the male, female, and hermaphrodite forms of *Catasetum tridentatum* – *Mormodes ignea*, curious structure of the flowers; ejection of the pollinia – *Mormodes luxata* – *Cycnoches ventricosum*, manner of fertilization   [178–225] 125

CHAPTER VIII

Cypripedeae – homologies of the flowers of orchids

Cypripedium, differs much from all other orchids – Labellum in the form of a slipper with two small orifices by which insects can escape – Manner of fertilization by small bees of the genus Andrena – Homological nature of the several parts of the flowers of the Orchideae – Wonderful amount of modification which they have undergone   [226–46] / 159

CHAPTER IX

Gradation of organs, etc – Concluding remarks

Gradation of organs, of the rostellum, of the pollen-masses – Formation of the caudicle – Genealogical affinities – Secretion of nectar – Mechanism of the movement of the pollinia – Uses of the petals – Production of seed – Importance of trifling details of structure – Cause of the great diversity of structure in the flowers of orchids – Cause of the perfection of the contrivances – Summary on insect-agency – Nature abhors perpetual self-fertilization   [247–93] 174

INDEX   [294–300] / 207

LIST OF WOODCUTS

1. *Orchis mascula* [8] 7
2. *Orchis mascula* pollinia of [12] 9
3. *Orchis pyramidalis* [18] 13
4. Moth's head and proboscis, with attached pollinia [31] 21
5. *Ophrys muscifera* [46] 32
6. *Ophrys aranifera* [50] 34
7. *Ophrys arachnites* [51] 35
8. *Ophrys apifera* [53] 36
9. *Peristylus viridis* [62] 43
10. *Gymnadenia conopsea* [65] 45
11. *Habenaria chlorantha* [69] 48
12. Pollinia of *Habenaria chlorantha* and *bifolia* [74] 51
13. *Cephalanthera grandiflora* [81] 57
14. *Pterostylis longifolia* [87] 61
15. *Epipactis palustris* [94] 66
16. *Epipactis latifolia* [101] 71
17. *Spiranthes autumnalis* [107] 75
18. *Listera ovata* [116] 81
19. *Malaxis paludosa* [130] 92
20. *Masdevallia fenestrata* [136] 96
21. *Dendrobium chrysanthum* [139] 98
22. Cattleya [144] 101
23. Diagram illustrative of the structure of the Vandeae [150] 106
24. Pollinia of Vandeae [154] 108
25. Pollinium of Ornithocephalus [160] / 112
26. *Calanthe masuca* [161] 113
27. *Coryanthes speciosa* [174] 123
28. *Catasetum saccatum* [182] 128
29. *Catasetum saccatum* [183] 129
30. *Catasetum tridentatum* [194] 136
31. Monachanthus and Myanthus [199] 140

32. *Mormodes ignea* [209] 147
33. *Cycnoches ventricosum* [222] 156
34. *Cycnoches ventricosum* section through bud [223] 157
35. Cypripedium [227] 160
36. Transverse section of flower of an orchid [236] 166
37. Rostellum of Catasetum [256] 180
38. Disc of *Gymnadenia conopsea* [272] 191

P.S.   I am much indebted to Mr G. B. Sowerby for the pains which he has taken in making the diagrams as intelligible as possible. /

INTRODUCTION

The object of the following work is to show that the contrivances by which orchids are fertilized, are as varied and almost as perfect as any of the most beautiful adaptations in the animal kingdom; and, secondly, to show that these contrivances have for their main object the fertilization of the flowers with pollen brought by insects from a distinct plant. In my volume *On the Origin of Species* I gave only general reasons for the belief that it is an almost universal law of nature that the higher organic beings require an occasional cross with another individual; or, which is the same thing, that no hermaphrodite fertilizes itself for a perpetuity of generations. Having been blamed for propounding this doctrine without giving ample facts, for which I had not sufficient space in that work, I wish here to show that I have not spoken without having gone into details.

I have been led to publish this little treatise separately, as it is too large to be incorporated with any other subject. As orchids are universally acknowledged to rank among the most singular and most / modified forms in the vegetable kingdom, I have thought that the facts to be given might lead some observers to look more curiously into the habits of our several native species. An examination of their many beautiful contrivances will exalt the whole vegetable kingdom in most persons' estimation. I fear, however, that the necessary details are too minute and complex for anyone who has not a strong taste for Natural History. This treatise affords me also an opportunity of attempting to show that the study of organic beings may be as interesting to an observer who is fully convinced that the structure of each is due to secondary laws, as to one who views every trifling detail of structure as the result of the direct interposition of the Creator.

I must premise that Christian Konrad Sprengel, in his curious and valuable work, *Das entdeckte Geheimniss der Natur*, published in 1793, gave an excellent outline of the action of the several parts in the genus Orchis; for he well knew the position of the stigma, and he discovered

1

that insects were necessary to remove the pollen-masses.[1] But he overlooked many curious contrivances – a consequence, apparently, of his belief that the stigma generally receives pollen from the same flower. Sprengel, likewise, has partially described the structure of Epipactis; but in the case of Listera he entirely misunderstood the remarkable phenomena characteristic of that genus, which has been well described by Dr Hooker in the *Philosophical Transactions* / for 1854. Dr Hooker has given a full and accurate account, with drawings, of the structure of the parts; but from not having attended to the agency of insects, he did not fully understand the object gained. Robert Brown,[2] in his celebrated paper in the *Linnean Transactions*, expresses his belief that insects are necessary for the fructification of most orchids; but adds, that the fact of all the capsules on a dense spike not infrequently producing seed, seems hardly reconcilable with this belief: we shall hereafter find that this doubt is groundless. Many other authors have given facts and expressed their belief, more or less fully, on the necessity of insect-agency in the fertilization of orchids.

In the course of the following work I shall have the pleasure of expressing my deep obligation to several gentlemen for their unremitting kindness in sending me fresh specimens, without which aid this work would have been impossible. The trouble which several of my kind assistants have taken has been extraordinary: I have never once expressed a wish for aid or for information which has not been granted me, as far as possible, in the most liberal spirit.

EXPLANATION OF TERMS

In case anyone should look at this treatise who has never attended to botany, it may be convenient to explain the meaning of the common terms used. In most flowers the stamens, or male organs, surround in a ring the one or more female organs, called the pistils. In all common orchids there is only one well-developed stamen, which is confluent with the pistils, and they / form together the *column*. Ordinary stamens

[1] Delpino has found (*Ult. Osservazioni sulla Dicogamia*, Part ii, 1875, p. 150) a memoir by Waetcher, published in 1801 in Roemer's *Archiv für die Botanik*, vol. ii, p. 11, which apparently has remained unknown to everyone else. In this memoir Waetcher, who does not seem to have been acquainted with Sprengel's work, shows that insects are necessary for the fertilization of various orchids, and describes well the wonderful structure of Neottia.

[2] *Linnean Transactions*, 1833, vol. xvi, p. 704.

consist of a filament, or supporting thread (rarely seen in British orchids), which carries the anther; and within the anther lies the pollen or male vivifying element. The anther is divided into two cells, which are very distinct in most orchids, so much so as to appear in some species like two separate anthers. The pollen in all common plants consists of fine granular powder: but in most orchids the grains cohere in masses, which are often supported by a very curious appendage, called the *caudicle*. This part and all the other organs will hereafter be more fully described and figured under the head of the first species, *orchis mascula*. The pollen-masses, with their caudicles and other appendages, are called the *pollinia*.

Orchids properly have three pistils or female organs, united together, the upper and anterior surfaces of two of which form the two stigmas. But the two are often completely confluent, so as to appear as one. The stigma is penetrated in the act of fertilization by long tubes, emitted by the pollen-grains, which carry the contents of the grains down to the ovules or young seeds in the ovarium.

The upper stigma is modified into an extraordinary organ, called the *rostellum*, which in many orchids presents no resemblance to a true stigma. When mature it either includes or is altogether formed of viscid matter. In many species the pollen-masses are firmly attached to a portion of the exterior membrane, which, when insects visit the flowers, is removed, together with the pollen-masses. This removable portion consists in most British orchids merely of a small piece of membrane, with a layer or ball of viscid matter underneath, and I shall call it the '*viscid disc*'; but in many exotic species the portion removed is so / large and so important, that one part must be called, as before, the viscid disc, and the other part the *pedicel* of the rostellum, to the end of which the pollen-masses are attached. Authors have called that portion of the rostellum which is removed, the 'gland' or 'retinaculum', from its apparent function of retaining the pollen-masses in their places. The pedicel, or prolongation of the rostellum, to which in many exotic species the pollen-masses are attached, seems generally, to have been confounded, under the name of caudicle, with the true caudicle of the pollen-masses, though their nature and origin are totally different. The part of the rostellum which is left after the removal of the discs and viscid matter, is sometimes called the 'bursicula', or 'fovea', or 'pouch'. But it will be found convenient to avoid all these terms, and to call the whole modified stigma the rostellum – sometimes adding an adjective to define its shape; that portion of the rostellum which is removed with the pollen-masses being called the *viscid disc*, together in some cases with the *pedicel*.

Lastly, the three outer divisions of the flower are called *sepals*, and form the calyx; but, instead of being green, as in most common flowers, they are generally coloured, like the three inner divisions or *petals* of the flower. In almost all the species, one of the petals, which is properly the upper one, is larger than the others and stands on the lower side of the flower, where it offers a landing-place for insects, having been carried round by the twisting of the ovarium. It is called the lower lip or *labellum*, and often assumes most singular shapes. It secretes nectar for the sake of attracting insects, and is often produced into a spur-like nectary. /

CHAPTER I

OPHREAE

Structure of the flower of *Orchis mascula* – Power of movement of the pollinia – Perfect adaptation of the parts in *Orchis pyramidalis* – Other species of Orchis and of some closely allied genera – On the insects which visit the several species, and on the frequency of their visits – On the fertility and sterility of various orchids – On the secretion of nectar, and on insects being purposely delayed in obtaining it.

Throughout the following volume I have followed, as far as I conveniently could, the arrangement of the Orchideae given by Lindley. The British species belong to five of his tribes, the Ophreae, Neotteae, Arethuseae, Malaxeae, and Cypripedeae, but the two latter tribes contain each only a single genus. Various British and foreign species belonging to the several tribes are described in the first eight chapters. The eighth also contains a discussion on the homologies of the flowers of the Orchideae. The ninth chapter is devoted to miscellaneous and general considerations.

The Ophreae include most of our common British species, and we will begin with the genus Orchis. The reader may find the following details rather difficult to understand; but I can assure him, if he will have patience to make out the first case, the succeeding ones will be easily intelligible. The accompanying diagrams (fig. 1, p. 8) show the relative position of the more important organs in the flower of the Early Orchis (*O. mascula*). The sepals and the petals have been removed, excepting the labellum with its nectary. The / nectary is shown only in the side view (*n*, fig. A); for its enlarged orifice is almost hidden in shade in the front view (B). The stigma (*s*) is bilobed, and consists of two almost confluent stigmas; it lies under the pouch-formed rostellum (*r*). The anther (*a*, in B and A) consists of two rather widely separated cells, which are longitudinally open in front: each cell includes a pollen-mass or pollinium.

A pollinium removed out of one of the two anther-cells is represented by fig. C; it consists of a number of wedge-formed packets of pollen-grains (see fig. F, in which the packets are forcibly separated), united together by excessively elastic, thin threads. These threads become confluent at the lower end of each pollen-mass, and compose the straight elastic caudicle (c, C). The end of the caudicle is firmly attached to the viscid disc (d, C), which consists (as may be seen in the section of the pouch-formed rostellum, fig. E) of a minute oval piece of membrane, with a ball of viscid matter on its underside. Each pollinium has its separate disc; and the two balls of viscid matter lie enclosed together (fig. D) within the rostellum.

The rostellum is a nearly spherical, somewhat pointed projection (r, figs A and B) overhanging the two almost confluent stigmas, and must be fully described, as every detail of its structure is full of significance. A section through one of the discs and balls of viscid matter is given (fig. E); and a front view of both viscid discs within the rostellum (fig. D) is likewise given. This latter figure (D) probably best serves to explain the structure of the rostellum; but it must be understood that the front lip is here considerably depressed. The lowest part of the anther is united to the back of the rostellum, as may be seen in fig. B. At an early period of growth the rostellum / consists of a mass of polygonal cells, full of brownish matter, which cells soon resolve themselves into two balls of extremely viscid semi-fluid matter, void of structure. These viscid masses are slightly elongated, almost flat on the top, and convex below. They lie quite free within the rostellum (being surrounded by fluid), except at the back, where each viscid ball adheres to a small portion or disc of the exterior membrane of the rostellum. The ends of the two caudicles are strongly attached externally to these two little discs of membrane.

The membrane forming the whole exterior surface of the rostellum is at first continuous; but as soon as the flower opens the slightest touch causes it to rupture transversely in a sinuous line, in front of the anther-cells and of the little crest or fold of membrane (see fig. D) between them. This act of rupturing makes no difference in the shape of the rostellum, but converts the front part into a lip, which can be depressed easily. This lip is represented considerably depressed in fig. D, and its edge is seen (fig. B), in the front view. When the lip is thoroughly depressed, the two balls of viscid matter are exposed. Owing to the elasticity of the hinder part, the lip or pouch, after being pressed down, springs up again and encloses the two viscid balls.

I will not affirm that the rupturing of the exterior membrane of the rostellum never takes place spontaneously; and no doubt the

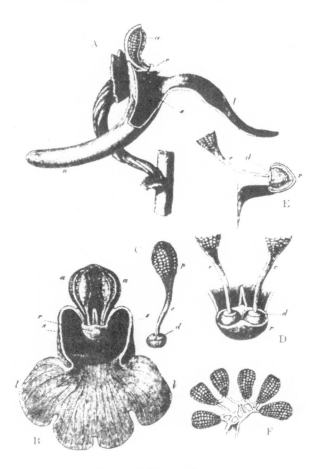

Fig. 1 *Orchis mascula*

a. anther, consisting of two cells, *r.* rostellum, *s.* stigma, *l.* labellum, *n.* nectary, *p.* pollen-mass, *c.* caudicle of pollinium, *d.* viscid disc of pollinium

A. Side view of flower, with all the petals and sepals cut off except the labellum, of which the near half is cut away, as well as the upper portion of the near side of the nectary
B. Front view of flower, with all sepals and petals removed, except the labellum
C. One pollinium, showing the packets of pollen-grains, the caudicle, and viscid disc
D. Front view of the caudicles of both pollinia with the discs lying within the rostellum, its lip being depressed
E. Section through one side of the rostellum, with the included disc and caudicle of one pollinium, lip not depressed
F. Packets of pollen-grains, tied together by elastic threads, here extended. (Copied from Bauer) /

7

membrane is prepared for rupture by having become very weak along defined lines; but several times I saw the act ensue from an excessively slight touch – so slight that I conclude that the action is not simply mechanical, but, for the want of a better term, may be called vital. We shall hereafter meet with other cases, in which the slightest / touch or the vapour of chloroform causes the exterior membrane of the rostellum to rupture along certain defined lines.

At the same time that the rostellum becomes transversely ruptured in front, it probably (for it was impossible to ascertain this fact from the position of the parts) ruptures behind in two oval lines, thus separating and freeing from the rest of the exterior surface of the rostellum the two little discs of membrane, to which the two caudicles are attached externally, and to which the two balls of viscid matter adhere internally. The line of rupture is thus very complex, but strictly defined.

As the two anther-cells are open longitudinally in front from top to bottom, even before the flower expands, it follows that as soon as the rostellum is properly ruptured from the effects of a slight touch, its lip can be depressed easily, and, the two little discs of membrane being already separate, the two pollinia now lie absolutely free, but are still embedded in their proper places. So that the packets of pollen and the caudicles still lie within the anther-cells; the discs still form part of the rostellum, but are separate; and the balls of viscid matter still lie concealed within the rostellum.

Now let us see in the case of *Orchis mascula* (fig. 1) how this complex mechanism acts. Suppose an insect to alight on the labellum, which forms a good landing-place, and to push its head into the chamber (see side view, A, or front view, B), at the back of which lies the stigma (s), in order to reach with its proboscis the end of the nectary; or, which does equally well to show the action, push very gently a sharply-pointed common pencil into the nectary. Owing to the pouch-formed rostellum projecting into the gangway of the nectary. / It is scarcely possible that any object can be pushed into it without the rostellum being touched. The exterior membrane of the rostellum then ruptures in the proper lines, and the lip or pouch is easily depressed. When this is effected, one or both of the viscid balls will almost infallibly touch the intruding body. So viscid are these balls that whatever they touch they firmly stick to. Moreover the viscid matter has the peculiar chemical quality of setting, like a cement, hard and dry in a few minutes' time. As the anther-cells are open in front, when the insect withdraws its head, or when the pencil is withdrawn, one pollinium, or both, will be withdrawn, firmly cemented to the object, projecting up like horns, as shown (fig. 2) by the upper figure, A. The firmness of the attachment

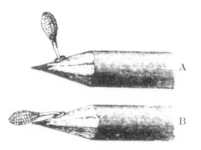

Fig. 2
A. Pollen-mass of *O. mascula*, when first attached
B. Pollen-mass of *O. mascula*, after the act of depression

of the cement is very necessary, for if the pollinia were to fall sideways or backwards they could never fertilize the flower. From the position in which the two pollinia lie in their cells, they diverge a little when attached to any object. Now suppose that the insect flies to another flower, or let us insert the pencil (A, fig. 2), with the attached pollinium into / the same or into another nectary: by looking at the diagram (fig. 1, A) it will be evident that the firmly attached pollinium will be simply pushed against or into its old position, namely, into the anther-cell. How then can the flower be fertilized? This is effected by a beautiful contrivance: though the viscid surface remains immovably affixed, the apparently insignificant and minute disc of membrane to which the caudicle adheres is endowed with a remarkable power of contraction (as will hereafter be more minutely described), which causes the pollinium to sweep through an angle of about ninety degrees, always in one direction, viz., towards the apex of the proboscis or pencil, in the course of thirty seconds on an average. The position of the pollinium after the movement is shown at B in fig. 2. After this movement, completed in an interval of time which would allow an insect to fly to another plant,[1] it will be seen, by turning to the diagram

[1] Dr H. Müller (*Die Befruchtung der Blumen durch Insekten*, 1873, p. 84) has timed humble-bees at work on the spikes of flowers of *Orchis mascula*, and finds that this statement is correct.

9

(fig. 1, A), that, if the pencil be inserted into the nectary, the thick end of the pollinium now exactly strikes the stigmatic surface.

Here again comes into play another pretty adaptation, long ago noticed by Robert Brown.[2] The stigma is very viscid, but not so viscid as when touched by a pollinium to pull the whole off an insect's head or off a pencil, yet sufficiently viscid to break the elastic threads (fig. 1, F) by which the packets of pollen-grains are tied together, and leave some of them on the stigma. Hence a pollinium attached to an insect or to a pencil can be applied to many stigmas, and will fertilize all. I have often seen the / pollinia of Orchis pyramidalis adhering to the proboscis of a moth, with the stump-like caudicles alone left, all the packets of pollen having been left glued to the stigmas of the successively visited flowers.

One or two other little points must be noticed. The balls of viscid matter within the pouch-formed rostellum are surrounded with fluid; and this is very important, for, as already mentioned, the viscid matter sets hard when exposed to the air for a very short time. I have pulled the balls out of their pouches, and found that they had entirely lost the power of adhesion after a few minutes. Again, the little discs of membrane, the movement of which, as causing the movement of the pollinia, is so absolutely indispensable for the fertilization of the flower, lie at the upper and back surface of the rostellum, and are closely enfolded and thus kept damp within the bases of the anther-cells; and this is very necessary, as an exposure of about thirty seconds causes the movement of depression to take place; but as long as the disc is kept damp, the pollinia remain ready for action whenever removed by an insect.

Lastly, as I have shown, the pouch, after being depressed, springs up to its former position; and this is likewise of great service; for if this action did not take place, and an insect after depressing the lip failed to remove the two viscid balls, or if it removed one alone, then in the first case both, and in the second case one would be left exposed to the air; consequently one or both would quickly lose all adhesiveness, and the pollinium would be rendered absolutely useless. That with many kinds of orchids insects often remove only one of the two pollinia at a time is certain; it is even probable that they generally remove only one, for the lower and older / flowers almost always have both pollinia removed, whilst the younger flowers close beneath the buds, which will

---

[2] *Transactions of the Linnean Society*, vol. xvi, p. 731.

have been seldomer visited, have frequently only one pollinium removed. In a spike of *Orchis maculata*, I found as many as ten flowers, chiefly the upper ones, which had only one pollinium removed; the other pollinium being still in its proper place with the lip of the rostellum well closed up; so that all the mechanism was perfect for its subsequent removal by some other insect.

When the first edition of this book was published, I had not seen any insects visiting the flowers of the present species; but a friend watched some plants, and saw them visited by several humble-bees, apparently *Bombus muscorum*; and Dr H. Müller[3] has seen four other species of Bombus at work. He caught ninety-seven specimens, and of these thirty-two had pollinia attached to their heads.

The description now given of the action of the organs in *Orchis mascula* applies to *O. morio, fusca, maculata*, and *latifolia*. These species present slight and apparently co-ordinated differences in the length of their caudicles, in the direction of the nectary, in the shape and position of the stigma, but they are not worth detailing. In all, the pollinia when removed from the anther-cells undergo the curious movement of depression, which is so necessary to place them in a right position on an insect's head for striking the stigmatic surface of another flower. Six species of humble-bees, the hive-bee and two other kinds have been seen by H. Müller and myself visiting the flowers of *Orchis morio*. On some of the / hive-bees from ten to sixteen pollen-masses adhered; to the head of *Eucera longicornis* eleven, to the head of *Osmia rufa* several, and several to the bare surface close above the mandibles of *Bombus muscorum*. H. Müller has seen twelve different kinds of bees visiting the flowers of *O. latifolia*, which are also visited by Diptera. My son George oberved for some time plants of *O. maculata*, and saw many specimens of a fly (*Empis livida*) inserting their proboscides into the nectary; and subsequently the same fact was observed by me. He brought home six specimens of this *Empis*, with pollinia attached to their spherical eyes, on a level with the bases of the antennae. The pollinia had undergone the movement of depression, and stood a little above and parallel to the proboscis; hence they were in a position excellently adapted to strike the stigma. Six pollinia were thus attached to one specimen, and three to another. My son also saw another and smaller species (*Empis pennipes*) inserting its proboscis into the nectary; but this species did not act so well or so regularly as the other in fertilizing the flowers.

[3] *Die Befruchtung, etc.*, p. 84.

One specimen of this latter *Empis* had five pollinia, and a second had three pollinia, attached to the dorsal surface of its convex thorax. H. Müller has seen two other genera of Diptera at work on this orchis, with pollinia attached to the front part of their bodies; and on one occasion he saw a humble-bee visiting the flowers.[4]

We now come to *Orchis* (subgenus, *Anacamptis*) *pyramidalis*, one of the most highly organized species / which I have examined, and which is ranked by several botanists as a distinct genus. The relative position of the parts (fig. 3) is here considerably different from what it is in *O. mascula* and its allies. There are two quite distinct rounded stigmatic surfaces (*s, s,* A) placed on each side of the pouch-formed rostellum. This latter organ, instead of standing some height above the nectary, is brought down (see side view B) so as to overhang and partially to close its orifice. The antechamber to the nectary, formed by the union of the edges of the labellum to the column, which is large in *O. mascula* and its allies, is here small. The pouch-formed rostellum is hollowed out on the underside in the middle: it is filled with fluid. The viscid disc is single and of the shape of a saddle (figs C and E); it carries on its nearly flat top or seat the two caudicles of the pollinia, the ends of which firmly adhere to its upper surface. Before the membrane of the rostellum ruptures, the saddle-formed disc can be clearly seen to be continuous with the rest of the surface. The disc is partially hidden and kept damp (which is of great importance) by the overfolding bases of the two anther-cells. It consists of several layers of minute cells, and is therefore rather thick; it is lined beneath with a layer of highly adhesive matter, which is formed within the rostellum. It corresponds strictly to the two minute, oval, separate discs to which the two caudicles of *O. mascula* and its allies are attached.

When the flower opens and the rostellum has become symmetrically ruptured, either from a touch or spontaneously (I know not which), the slightest pressure depresses the lip, that is, the lower and bilobed portion of the exterior membrane of the rostellum, which projects into the mouth of the nectary. / When the lip is depressed, the under and viscid surface of the disc, still remaining in its proper place, is uncovered, and is almost certain to adhere to the touching object. Even a human hair, when pushed into the nectary, is stiff enough to depress

---

[4] M. M. Girard caught a longicorn beetle, *Strangalia atra*, with a tuft of the pollen-masses of this Orchis attached to the front of its mouth: *Annales de la Soc. Entomolog. de France*, vol. ix, 1869, p. xxxi.

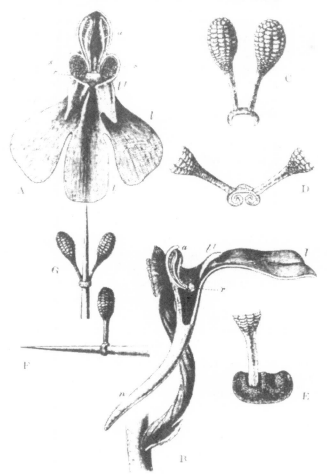

Fig. 3 *Orchis pyramidalis*

a. anther, *s, s.* stigma, *r.* rostellum, *l.* labellum, *l'.* guiding plate on the labellum, *n.* nectary

A. Front view, with all the sepals and petals removed, except the labellum
B. Side view, with all the sepals and petals removed, with the labellum longitudinally bisected, and with the near side of the upper part of the nectary cut away
C. The two pollinia attached to the saddle-shaped viscid disc
D. The disc after the first act of contraction, with no object seized
E. The disc seen from above, and flattened by force, with one pollinium removed; showing a depression in its surface, by which the second movement of the pollinium is effected
F. The pollinia removed by the insertion of a needle into the nectary, after the saddle has clasped the needle by the first act of contraction
G. The same pollinia after the second movement and their consequent depression /

13

the lip or pouch; and the viscid surface of the saddle adheres to it. If, however, the lip be pushed only slightly, it springs back and recovers the underside of the saddle.

The perfect adaptation of the parts is well shown by cutting off the end of the nectary and inserting a bristle at that end; consequently in a reversed direction to that in which moths insert their proboscides; and it will be found that the rostellum may easily be torn or penetrated, but that the saddle is rarely or never caught. When the saddle together with the pollinia is removed on a bristle, the underlip instantly curls closely inwards, and leaves the orifice of the nectary more open than it was before; but whether this is of much service to the moths which frequent the flowers, and consequently to the plant, I will not pretend to decide.

Lastly, the labellum is furnished with two prominent ridges (*l'*, figs A, B), sloping down to the middle and expanding outwards like the mouth of a decoy; these ridges serve to guide any flexible body, like a fine bristle or hair, into the minute and rounded orifice of the nectary, which, small as it already is, is partly choked up by the rostellum. This contrivance of the guiding ridges may be compared to the little instrument sometimes used for guiding a thread into the fine eye of a needle.

Now let us see how these parts act. Let a moth insert its proboscis (and we shall presently see how frequently the flowers are visited by Lepidoptera) / between the guiding ridges of the labellum, or insert a fine bristle, and it is conducted safely to the minute orifice of the nectary, and can hardly fail to depress the lip of the rostellum; this being effected, the bristle comes into contact with the now naked and sticky under surface of the suspended saddle-formed disc. When the bristle is removed, the saddle with the attached pollinia is removed. Almost instantly, as soon as the saddle is exposed to the air, a rapid movement takes place, and the two flaps curl inwards and embrace the bristle. When the pollinia are pulled out by their caudicles, by a pair of pincers, so that the saddle has nothing to clasp, I observed that the flaps curled inwards so as to touch each other in nine seconds (see fig. D), and in nine more seconds the saddle was converted by the flaps curling still more inwards into an apparently solid ball. The proboscides of the many moths which I have examined, with the pollinia of this Orchis attached to them, were so thin that the tips of the flaps just met on the underside. Hence a naturalist, who sent me a moth with several saddles attached to its proboscis, and who did not know of this movement, very naturally came to the extraordinary conclusion that the moth had cleverly bored through the exact centres of the so-called sticky glands of some orchid.

Of course this rapid clasping movement helps to fix the saddle upright on the proboscis, which is very important; but the viscid matter setting hard rapidly would probably suffice for this end, and the real object gained by the clasping or curling movement is the divergence of the pollinia. The pollinia, being attached to the flat top or seat of the saddle, project at first straight up and nearly parallel to each other; / but as the flat top curls round the cylindrical and thin proboscis, or round a bristle, the pollinia necessarily diverge. As soon as the saddle has clasped the bristle and the pollinia have diverged, a second movement commences, which action, like the last, is exclusively due to the contraction of the saddle-shaped disc of membrane, as will be more fully described in the ninth chapter. This second movement is the same as that in *O. mascula* and its allies, and causes the divergent pollinia, which at first projected at right angles to the needle or bristle (see fig. F), to sweep through an angle of nearly ninety degrees towards the tip of the needle (see fig. G), so as to become depressed and finally to lie in the same plane with the needle. In three specimens, this second movement was effected in from thirty to thirty-four seconds after the removal of the pollinia from the anther-cells, and therefore in about fifteen seconds after the saddle had clasped the bristle.

The use of this double movement becomes evident if a bristle with pollinia attached to it, which have diverged and become depressed, be pushed between the guiding ridges of the labellum into the nectary of the same or another flower (compare figs A and G); for the two ends of the pollen-masses will be found now to have acquired such a position that the end of the one strikes against the stigma on the one side, and the end of the other at the same moment strikes against the stigma on the opposite side. The secretion on the stigmas is so viscid that when the pollinia are withdrawn, the elastic threads by which the packets of pollen are bound together are ruptured; and some dark-green grains may be seen, even by the naked eye, remaining on the two white stigmatic surfaces. I have shown this little experiment to several / persons, and all have expressed the liveliest admiration at the perfection of the contrivance by which this orchid is fertilized.

As in no other plant, or indeed in hardly any animal, can adaptations of one part to another, and of the whole to other organisms widely remote in the scale of nature, be named more perfect than those presented by this Orchis, it may be worth while briefly to sum them up. As the flowers are visited both by day and night-flying Lepidoptera, it is not fanciful to believe that the bright-purple tint (whether or not specially developed for this purpose) attracts the day-fliers, and the strong foxy odour the night-fliers. The upper sepal and two upper petals form a hood protecting the anther and stigmatic surfaces from the weather. The labellum is developed into a long nectary in order to attract Lepidoptera, and we shall presently give reasons for suspecting that the nectar is purposely so lodged that it can be sucked only slowly (very differently from what occurs in most other plants), in order to give time for the viscid matter on the underside of the saddle to set hard and dry. He who will insert a fine and flexible bristle into the expanded mouth of the flower between the sloping ridges on the labellum, will not doubt that they serve as guides and effectually prevent the bristle or proboscis from being inserted obliquely into the nectary. This latter circumstance is of manifest importance, for, if the proboscis were inserted obliquely, the saddle-formed disc would become attached obliquely, and after the compounded movement of the pollinia they would not strike the two lateral stigmatic surfaces.

Then we have the rostellum partially closing the mouth of the nectary, like a trap placed in a run for / game; and the trap so complex and perfect, with its symmetrical lines of rupture forming the saddle-shaped disc above, and the lip of the pouch below; and, lastly, this lip so easily depressed that the proboscis of a moth can hardly fail to uncover the viscid disc and adhere to it. But if this fails to occur, the elastic lip rises and covers again the viscid surface, so as to keep it damp. The viscid matter within the rostellum is attached to the saddle-shaped disc alone, and is surrounded by fluid, so that it does not set hard till the disc is withdrawn. The upper surface of the saddle, with the attached caudicles, is also kept damp by the bases of the anther-cells, until it is withdrawn, and then the curious clasping movement instantly commences, causing the pollinia to diverge, followed by the movement of depression, which movements together are exactly fitted to cause the ends of the two pollen-masses to strike the two stigmatic surfaces. These stigmatic surfaces are not so sticky as to tear off the whole pollinium from the proboscis of the moth, but by rupturing the elastic threads to secure a few packets of pollen, leaving plenty for other flowers.[5]

[5] The late Professor Treviranus has confirmed (*Botanische Zeitung*, 1863, p. 241) all my observations, but points out two unimportant inaccuracies in the drawing which I have given.

But let it be observed that, although the moth probably takes a considerable time to suck the nectar of a flower, yet the movement of depression in the pollinia does not commence (as I know by trial) until they are fully withdrawn; nor will the movement be completed, and the pollinia properly placed for striking the stigmatic surfaces, until about half a minute has elapsed, which will give ample time for the moth to / fly to another plant, and thus effect a union beween two distinct individuals.

Orchis ustulata[6] resembles *O. pyramidalis* in some important respects, and differs from it in others. The labellum is deeply channelled, and the channel which replaces the guiding ridges of *O. pyramidalis* leads to the small triangular orifice of the short nectary. The upper angle of the triangle is overhung by the rostellum, the pouch of which is rather pointed below. In accordance with this position of the rostellum, close to the mouth of the nectary, the stigma is double and lateral. This species shows in an interesting manner how easily two distinct stigmas, like those of *O. pyramidalis*, might be converted into a single one, by becoming at first slightly lobed like that of *O. mascula*, and then acquiring its present structure. For directly beneath the rostellum there is a narrow transverse rim, formed of true stigmatic tissue, which connects together the two lateral stigmas; so that if this rim were widened, the two stigmas would be converted into a single transverse one. Conversely a single stigma might thus easily be converted into a double one. The pollinia undergo the usual movement of depression, and in acquiring this position the two diverge slightly, so as to be ready to strike the two lateral stigmas.

Orchis (subgenus *Himantoglossum*) *hircina*. A fine specimen of this extremely rare British plant, the Lizard Orchis, with its curious elongated labellum, was sent me by Mr Oxenden. The two pollinia arise from a single almost square disc; and when / they are removed from their cells, they do not diverge, but become depressed, sweeping through an angle of ninety degrees, in about thirty seconds. They are then in a proper position for striking the single large stigma which lies beneath the rostellum. In the case of *O. pyramidalis* we have seen that the depression of the two pollinia is effected by the contraction of the disc in front of each, two furrows or valleys being there formed; whilst with the present species, the whole front of the disc contracts or sinks

[6] I am greatly indebted to Mr G. Chichester Oxenden of Broome Park for fresh specimens of this Orchis, and for his never-tiring kindness in supplying me with living plants, and information regarding many of the rarer British orchids.

down, the front part being thus separated from the hinder part by an abrupt step.

Aceras[7] (*Orchis*) *anthropophora*. The caudicles of the pollinia are unusually short; the nectary consists of two minute rounded depressions in the labellum; the stigma is transversely elongated; and lastly the two viscid discs lie so close together within the rostellum that they affect each other's outline. This latter fact is worth notice, as a step towards the two becoming absolutely confluent, as in the following species of Aceras, in *O. pyramidalis* and *hircina*. Nevertheless, in Aceras a single pollinium is sometimes removed by insects, though more rarely than with the other species of Orchis.

Aceras (*Orchis*) *longibracteata*. Mr Moggridge has given an interesting account, together with a figure, of this plant which grows in the South of France.[8] The pollinia are attached to a single viscid disc. When they are removed they do not diverge as in *O. pyramidalis*, but converge and then undergo the / movement of depression. The most remarkable point about this species is that insects seem to suck nectar out of minute open cells in the honeycombed surface of the labellum. The flowers are visited by various hymenopterous and dipterous insects; and the author saw the pollinia attached to the forehead of a large bee, the *Xylocopa violacea*.

Neotinea (*Orchis*) *intacta*. Mr Moggridge sent me from North Italy living specimens of this very rare British plant, which, as he informed me, is remarkable from producing seeds without the aid of insects. When insects were carefully excluded by me, almost all the flowers produced capsules. Their fertilization follows from the pollen being extremely incoherent, so as to fall spontaneously on the stigma. Nevertheless a short nectary is present, the pollinia possess small viscid discs, and all the parts are so arranged that, if insects were to visit the flowers, the pollen-masses would almost certainly be removed and carried to another flower, but not so effectually as with most other orchids.

Serapias cordigera, an inhabitant of the South of France, has been described by Mr Moggridge in the paper just referred to. The pollinia are attached to a single viscid disc; when first withdrawn, they are bent backwards, but soon afterwards move forwards and downwards in the usual manner. As the stigmatic cavity is narrow, the pollinia are guided into it by two guiding plates.

---

[7] The separation of this genus is entirely artificial. It is a true Orchis, but with a very short nectary. Dr Weddell has described (*Annales des Sc. Nat.*, 3 ser. Bot. vol. xviii, p. 6) the occurrence of numerous hybrids naturally produced, between this Aceras and *Orchis galeata*.

[8] *Journ. Linn. Soc. Bot.*, vol. viii, 1865, p. 256. He gives also a figure of *Orchis hircina*.

Nigritella angustifolia. This Alpine species is said by Dr H. Müller[9] to differ from all ordinary orchids in the ovarium not being twisted; so that the labellum stands on the upper side of the flower, and insects / alight on the opposite sepals and petals. As a consequence of this, when a butterfly inserts its proboscis into the narrow entrance of the nectary, the viscid discs become attached to the lower surface of the proboscis, and the pollinia afterwards move upwards, instead of as in all other orchids downwards. They are then in the proper position for striking the stigma of the next flower which is visited. Dr Müller remarks that the flowers are frequented by an extraordinary number of butterflies.

I have now described the structure of most of the British and of a few foreign species in the genus Orchis and its close allies. All these species, with the exception of the Neotinea, require the aid of insects for their fertilization. This is obvious from the fact that the pollinia are so closely embedded in the anther-cells, and the ball of viscid matter in the pouch-formed rostellum, that they cannot be shaken out by violence. We have also seen that the pollinia do not assume the proper position for striking the stigmatic surface until some time has elapsed; and this indicates that they are adapted to fertilize, not their own flowers, but those on a distinct plant. To prove that insects are necessary for the fertilization of the flowers, I covered up a plant of *Orchis morio* under a bell-glass, before any of its pollinia had been removed, leaving three adjoining plants uncovered; I looked at the latter every morning, and daily found some of the pollinia removed, till all were gone with the exception of those in a single flower low down on one spike, and of those in one or two flowers on the summits of all the spikes, which were never removed. But it should be observed that when only a very few flowers remain open on the summits of the spikes, these are no longer conspicuous, / and would consequently be rarely visited by insects. I then looked at the perfectly healthy plant under the bell-glass, and it had, of course, all its pollinia in the anther-cells. I tried an analogous experiment with specimens of *O. mascula* with the same result. It deserves notice that the spikes which had been covered up, when subsequently left uncovered, never had their pollinia carried away by insects, and did not, of course, set any seed, whereas the adjoining plants produced plenty of seed. From this fact it may be inferred that there is a proper season for each kind of Orchis, and that insects cease their visits after the proper season has passed.

[9] *Nature*, 31 December, 1874, p. 169.

With many of the hitherto mentioned species, and with several other European kinds, the sterility of the flowers, when protected from the access of insects, depends solely on the pollen-masses not coming into contact with the stigma. This has been proved to be the case by Dr Hermann Müller, who, as he informs me, applied the pollen-masses of *Orchis pyramidalis* (44), *fusca* (6), *militaris* (14), *variegata* (3), *coriophora* (6), *morio* (4), *maculata* (18), *mascula* (6), *latifolia* (8), *incarnata* (3), *Ophrys muscifera* (8), *Gymnadenia conopsea* (14), *albida* (8), *Herminium monorchis* (6), *Epipogon aphyllus* (2), *Epipactis latifolia* (14), *palustris* (4), *Listera ovata* (5), and *Cypripedium calceolus* (2), to their own stigmas, and full-sized capsules, containing seeds in appearance good, were formed. The numbers placed after the names of the species show how many flowers were tried in each case. These facts are remarkable, because Mr Scott and Fritz Müller[10] have proved / that various exotic species, both in this country and in their native homes, invariably fail to yield seed-capsules, when the flowers are fertilized with their own pollen.

From the observations already given, and from what will hereafter be shown with respect to Gymnadenia, Habenaria, and some other species, it is a safe generalization[11] that species with a short and not very narrow nectary are fertilized by bees[12] and flies; whilst those with a much elongated nectary, or one having a very narrow entrance, are fertilized by butterflies or moths, these being provided with long and thin proboscides. We thus see that the structure of the flowers of orchids and that of the insects which habitually visit them, are correlated in an interesting manner – a fact which has been amply proved by Dr H. Müller to hold good with many of the Orchideae and other kinds of plants.

With respect to *Orchis pyramidalis*, which possesses, as we have seen, an elongated nectary, Mr Bond was so kind as to send me a large number of Lepidoptera, out of which I selected twenty-three species,

[10] An abstract of their observations is given in my *Variation of Animals and Plants under Domestication*, chap. xvii, 2nd edit. vol. ii, p. 114.

[11] Some remarks to this effect were given in my *Notes on the Fertilisation of Orchids*, in *Annals and Mag. of Nat. Hist.*, September, 1869, p. 2.

[12] M. Ménière (in *Bull. Bot. Soc. de France*, vol. i, 1854, p. 370) says he saw in Dr Guépin's collection, bees collected at Saumur with the pollinia of orchids attached to their heads; and he states that a person who kept bees near the Jardin de la Faculté (at Toulouse?) complained that his bees returned from the garden with their heads charged with yellow bodies, of which they could not free themselves. This is good evidence how firmly the pollinia are attached. There is, however, nothing to show whether the pollinia in these cases belonged to the genus Orchis or to some other genus of the family.

enumerated in the following list, with the pollinia of this orchid, which can easily be recognized, attached to their proboscides. /

Polyommatus alexis
Lycaena phlaeas
Arge galathea
Hesperia sylvanus
Hesperia linea
Syrichthus alveolus
Anthrocera filipendulae
Anthrocera trifolii[13]
Lithosia complana
Leucania lithargyria (two specimens)
Caradrina blanda
Caradrina alsines

Agrotis cataleuca
Eubolia mensuraria (two specimens)
Hadena dentina
Heliothis marginata (two specimens)
Xylophasia sublustris (two specimens)
Euclidia glyphica
Toxocampa pastinum
Melanippe rivaria
Spilodes palealis
Spilodes cinctalis
Acontia luctuosa

A large majority of these moths and butterflies had two or three pairs of pollinia attached to them, and invariably to the proboscis. The Acontia had seven pair (fig. 4), and the Caradrina no less than eleven pair! The proboscis of this latter moth presented an extraordinary arborescent appearance. The saddle-formed discs, each bearing a pair of pollinia, adhered to the proboscis, one before the other, with perfect symmetry; and this follows from the moth having always inserted its proboscis into the nectary in exactly the same manner, owing to the presence of the guiding plates on the labellum. The unfortunate Caradrina, with its proboscis thus encumbered, could hardly have reached the extremity of the nectary, and would soon have / been starved to death. Both these moths must have sucked many more than the seven and eleven flowers, of which they bore the trophies, for the earlier attached pollinia had lost much of their pollen, showing that they had touched many viscid stigmas.

Fig. 4   Head and proboscis of *Acontia luctuosa* with seven pair of pollinia of *Orchis pyramidalis* attached to the proboscis

[13] I am indebted to Mr Parfitt for an examination of this moth, which is mentioned in the *Entomologist's Weekly Intelligencer*, vol. ii, p. 182, and vol. iii, p. 3, 3 October, 1857. The pollinia were erroneously thought to belong to *Ophrys apifera*. The pollen had changed from its natural green colour to yellow; on washing it, however, and drying it, the green tint returned.

The above list proves that many different species of Lepidoptera visit the same kind of Orchis. The *Hadena dentina* also frequents Habenaria. Probably all the orchids provided with elongated nectaries are visited indifferently by many kinds of moths. Whether any of the British orchids are fertilized exclusively by special insects confined to certain localities is very doubtful; but we shall hereafter see that *Epipactis latifolia* seems to be fertilized by wasps alone. I have twice observed plants of *Gymnadenia conopsea*, which had been transplanted into a garden many miles from its native home, with nearly all their pollinia removed. Mr Marshall of Ely[14] has made the same observation on similarly transplanted specimens of *O. maculata*. On the other hand fifteen plants of *Ophrys muscifera* had not one pollen-mass there removed. *Malaxis paludosa* was placed in a bog about two miles from that in which it naturally grew; and it had most of its pollinia immediately removed.

The list which follows serves to show that insects in most cases perform the work of fertilization effectually. But the list by no means gives a fair idea how effectually it is done; for I have often found nearly all the pollinia removed, but kept an exact record only in exceptional cases, as may be seen by the appended remarks. Moreover, in most cases, the pollinia which / had not been removed were in the upper flowers beneath the buds, and many of these would probably have been subsequently carried away. I have often found an abundance of pollen on the stigmas of flowers which had not their own pollinia removed, showing that they had been visited by insects. In many other cases the pollinia had been removed, but no pollen had been as yet left on the stigmas.

In the second lot of *O. morio*, in the list, we see the injurious effects of the extraordinary cold and wet season of 1860 on the visits of insects, and, consequently, on the fertilization of this orchid, very few seed-capsules having been produced.

I have examined spikes of *O. pyramidalis* in which every single expanded flower had its pollinia removed. The forty-nine lower flowers of a spike from Folkestone (sent me by Sir Charles Lyell) actually produced forty-eight fine seed-capsules; and of the sixty-nine lower flowers in three other spikes, seven alone had failed to produce

---

[14] *Gardener's Chronicle*, 1861, p. 73. Mr Marshall's communication was in answer to some remarks of mine on this subject previously published in the *Gardener's Chronicle*, 1860, p. 528.

	Number of flowers with both or one pollinium removed. Flowers lately open excluded.	Number of flowers with only one pollinium removed. These flowers are included in the column to the left.	Number of flowers with neither pollinium removed.
Orchis morio, 3 small plants, N. Kent	22	2	6
Orchis morio, 38 plants, N. Kent. These plants were examined after nearly 4 weeks of extraordinarily cold and wet weather in 1860; and therefore under the most unfavourable circumstances	110	23	193
Orchis pyramidalis, 2 plants, N. Kent and Devonshire	39	..	8
Orchis pyramidalis, 6 plants from 2 protected valleys, Devonshire	102	..	66
Orchis pyramidalis, 6 plants from a much exposed bank, Devonshire	57	..	166
Orchis maculata, 1 plant, Staffordshire. Of the 12 flowers which had not their pollinia removed, the greater number were young flowers under the buds	32	6	12
Orchis maculata, 1 plant, Surrey	21	5	7
Orchis maculata, 2 plants, N. and S. Kent	28	17	50
Orchis latifolia, 9 plants from S. Kent, sent me by the Rev. B. S. Malden. The flowers were all mature	50	27	119
Orchis fusca, 2 plants, S. Kent. Flowers quite mature, and even withered	8	5	54
Aceras anthropophora, 4 plants, S. Kent	63	6	34

capsules. These facts show how well moths and butterflies perform their office of marriage-priests.[15]

The third lot of *O. pyramidalis* in the above list grew on a steep grassy bank, overhanging the sea near Torquay, and where there were no bushes or other shelter for Lepidoptera; being surprised how few pollinia had been removed, though the spikes were old and very many of the lower flowers withered, I gathered, for comparison, six other spikes from two bushy and sheltered valleys, half a mile on each side of the exposed bank; these spikes were certainly younger, and would probably have had several more of their pollinia removed; but in their present

[15] In the summer of 1875, which was a very wet one, I gathered 6 unusually fine spikes of *O. pyramidalis*. These bore 302 flowers, excluding 14 which were still fully expanded and capable of being fertilized; and on this occasion only 119 flowers produced capsules, 183 having failed to do so. 6 spikes of *O. maculata* bore 187 flowers, of which 82 produced capsules, 105 having failed.

condition we see how much more frequently they had been visited by moths, and consequently fertilized, than those growing on the much exposed bank. The Bee Ophrys and *O. pyramidalis* grow mingled together in many parts of England; and they did so here, but the Bee Ophrys, instead of being, as usual, the rarer species, was here / much more abundant than *O. pyramidalis*. No one would readily have suspected that one chief reason of this difference probably was, that the exposed situation was unfavourable to Lepidoptera, and therefore to the seeding of *O. pyramidalis*; whereas, as we shall hereafter see, the Bee Ophrys is independent of insects.

Many spikes of *O. latifolia* were examined, because, being familiar with the usual state of the closely allied *O. maculata*, I was surprised to find in nine nearly withered spikes (as may be seen in the list) how few pollinia had been removed. In one instance, however, *O. maculata* had been even worse fertilized; for seven spikes with 315 flowers, produced only forty-nine seed-capsules – that is, on an average only seven capsules on each spike. In this case the plants formed larger beds than I had ever before seen; and I imagine that there were too many flowers for the insects to visit and fertilize all of them. On some other plants of *O. maculata* growing at no great distance, above thirty capsules had been produced by each spike.

Orchis fusca offers a still more curious case of imperfect fertilization. I examined ten fine spikes from two localities in South Kent, sent to me by Mr Oxenden and Mr Malden: most of the flowers on these spikes were partly withered, with the pollen mouldy even in the uppermost flowers; we may therefore infer that no more pollinia would have been removed. I examined all the flowers only in two spikes, on account of the trouble from their withered condition, and the result may be seen in the list, namely, fifty-four flowers with both pollinia in place, and only eight with one or both removed. In this orchid, and in *O. latifolia*, neither of which had been sufficiently visited by insects, there were more flowers with one pollinium than with both removed. I casually examined many / flowers in the other spikes of *O. fusca*, and the proportion of pollinia removed was evidently not greater than in the two in the list. The ten spikes bore altogether 358 flowers, and, in accordance with the few pollinia removed, only eleven capsules had been formed: five of the ten spikes produced not a single capsule; two spikes had only one, and one had as many as four capsules. As corroborating what I have before said with respect to pollen being often found on the stigmas of flowers which retain their own pollinia, I may add that, of the eleven flowers which had produced capsules, five had both pollinia still within their now withered anther-cells.

From these facts the suspicion naturally arises that *O. fusca* is so rare a species in Britain from not being sufficiently attractive to insects, and to its not producing a sufficiency of seed. C. K. Sprengel[16] noticed, that in Germany *O. militaris* (ranked by Bentham as the same species with *O. fusca*) is likewise imperfectly fertilized, but more perfectly than our *O. fusca*; for he found five old spikes bearing 138 flowers which had set thirty-one capsules; and he contrasts the state of these flowers with those of *Gymnadenia conopsea*, in which almost every flower produces a capsule.

An allied and curious subject remains to be discussed. The existence of a well-developed spur-like nectary seems to imply the secretion of nectar. But Sprengel, a most careful observer, thoroughly searched many flowers of *O. latifolia* and *morio*, and could never find a drop of nectar; nor could Krünitz[17] find nectar / either in the nectary or on the labellum of *O. morio, fusca, militaris, maculata,* or *latifolia*. I have looked to all our common British species and could find no trace of nectar; I examined, for instance, eleven flowers of *O. maculata*, taken from different plants growing in different districts, and taken from the most favourable position on each spike, and could not find under the microscope the smallest bead of nectar. Sprengel calls these flowers '*Scheinsaftblumen*', or sham-nectar producers; he believes that these plants exist by an organized system of deception, for he well knew that the visits of insects were indispensable for their fertilization. But when we reflect on the incalculable number of plants which have lived during a great length of time, all requiring that insects should carry the pollen-masses from flower to flower in each generation; and as we further know from the number of the pollen-masses attached to their proboscides, that the same insects visit a large number of flowers, we can hardly believe in so gigantic an imposture. He who believes in Sprengel's doctrine must rank the sense or instinctive knowledge of many kinds of insects, even bees, very low in the scale. To test the intellect of moths and butterflies I tried the following little experiment, which ought to have been tried on a larger scale. I removed a few already-opened flowers on a spike of *O. pyramidalis*, and then cut off about half the length of the nectaries of the six next non-expanded flowers. When all the flowers were nearly withered, I found that

[16] *Das entdeckte Geheimniss*, etc. p. 404.
[17] Quoted by J. G. Kurr in his *Untersuchungen über die Bedeutung der Nektarian*, 1833, p. 28. See also *Das entdeckte Geheimniss*, p. 403.

thirteen of the fifteen upper flowers with perfect nectaries had their pollinia removed, and two alone had their pollinia still in the anther-cells; of the six flowers with their nectaries cut off, three had their pollinia removed, and three were still in place; and this indicates / that moths do not go to work in a quite senseless manner.[18]

Nature may be said to have tried this same experiment, but not quite fairly; for *Orchis pyramidalis*, as shown by Mr Bentham,[19] often produces monstrous flowers without a nectary, or with a short and imperfect one. Sir C. Lyell sent me several spikes from Folkestone with many flowers in this condition: I found six without a vestige of a nectary, and their pollinia had not been removed. In about a dozen other flowers, having either short nectaries, or with the labellum imperfect, the guiding ridges being either absent or developed in excess and rendered foliaceous, the pollinia in one alone had been removed, and the ovarium of another flower was swelling. Yet I found that the saddle-formed discs in these eighteen flowers were perfect, and that they readily clasped a needle when inserted in the proper place. Moths had removed the pollinia, and had thoroughly fertilized the perfect flowers on the same spikes; so that they must have neglected the monstrous flowers, or, if visiting them, the derangement in the complex mechanism of the parts had hindered the removement of the pollinia, and prevented their fertilization.

Notwithstanding these several facts I still suspected that nectar must be secreted by our common orchids, / and I determined to examine *O. morio* rigorously. As soon as many flowers were open, I began to examine them for twenty-three consecutive days: I looked at them after hot sunshine, after rain, and at all hours: I kept the spikes in water, and examined them at midnight, and early the next morning: I irritated the nectaries with a bristle, and exposed them to irritating vapours: I took flowers which had lately had their pollinia removed by insects, of which fact I had independent proof on one occasion by

---

[18] Kurr (*Bedeutung der Nektarien*, 1833, p. 123) cut off the nectaries of fifteen flowers of *Gymnadenia conopsea*, and they did not produce a single capsule: he also treated in the same manner fifteen flowers of *Platanthera* or *Habenaria bifolia*, and these set only five capsules; but then it should be observed that the nectaries of both these orchids contain free nectar. He also cut off the corolla, leaving the nectary, of forty flowers of *Orchis morio*; and these set no capsules; and this case shows that insects are guided to the flowers by the corolla. Sixteen flowers of Platanthera treated in the same manner bore only one capsule. Similar experiments made by him on Gymnadenia seem to me open to doubt.

[19] *Handbook of the British Flora*, 1858, p. 501.

finding grains of some foreign pollen within the nectary; and I took other flowers, which judging from their position on the spike, would soon have had their pollinia removed; but the nectary was invariably quite dry. After the publication of the first edition of this work, I one day saw various kinds of bees visiting repeatedly the flowers of this same orchid, so that this was evidently the proper time to examine their nectaries; but I failed to detect under the microscope even the minutest drop of nectar. So it was with the nectaries of *O. maculata* at a time when I repeatedly saw flies of the genus Empis keeping their proboscides inserted into them for a considerable length of time. *Orchis pyramidalis* was examined with equal care with the same result, for the glittering points within the nectary were absolutely dry. We may therefore safely conclude that the nectaries of the above-named orchids neither in this country nor in Germany ever contain nectar.

Whilst examining the nectaries of *O. morio* and *maculata*, and especially of *O. pyramidalis* and *hircina*, I was surprised at the degree to which the inner and outer membranes forming the tube or spur were separated from each other – also at the delicate nature of the inner membrane, which could be penetrated very easily – and, lastly, at the quantity of fluid contained / between the two membranes. So copious is this fluid, that, after cutting off the extremities of the nectaries of *O. pyramidalis*, and gently squeezing them on glass under the microscope, such large drops of fluid exuded from the cut ends, that I concluded that at last I had found nectaries which contained nectar; but when I carefully made, without any pressure, a slit along the upper surface of other nectaries from the same plants, and looked into them, their inner surfaces were quite dry.

I then examined the nectaries of *Gymnadenia conopsea* (a plant ranked by some botanists as a true Orchis) and of *Habenaria bifolia*, which are always full of nectar up to one-third or two-thirds of their length. The inner membrane presented the same structure and was covered with papillae as in the foregoing species; but there was a plain difference in the inner and outer membranes being closely united, instead of being in some degree separated from each other and charged with fluid. I was therefore led to conclude that insects penetrate the lax inner membrane of the nectaries of the above-named orchids, and suck the copious fluid between the two membranes. This was a bold hypothesis; for at the time no case was known of insects penetrating with their delicate proboscides even the laxest membrane. But I have now heard from Mr Trimen, that at the Cape of Good

27

Hope moths and butterflies do much injury to peaches and plums by puncturing their unbroken skins. In Queensland, Australia, a moth, the *Ophideres fullonica*, bores through the thick rind of the orange with its wonderful proboscis, provided with formidable teeth.[20] There is therefore not the least difficulty in believing that Lepidoptera with their delicate proboscides, and bees / with their much stronger ones, could penetrate with ease the soft inner membrane of the nectaries of the above-named orchids. Dr H. Müller is also convinced[21] that insects puncture the thickened bases of the standard petals of the Laburnum,[22] and perhaps the petals of some other flowers, so as to obtain the included fluid.

The various kinds of bees which I saw visiting the flowers of *Orchis morio* remained for some time with their proboscides inserted into the dry nectaries, and I distinctly saw this organ in constant movement. I observed the same fact with Empis in the case of *O. maculata*; and on afterwards opening several of the nectaries, I occasionally detected minute brown specks, due as I believe to the punctures made some time before by these flies. Dr H. Müller, who has often watched bees at work on several species of Orchis, the nectaries of which do not contain any free nectar, fully accepts my view.[23] On the other hand, Delpino still maintains that Sprengel is right, and that insects are continually deceived by the presence of a nectary, though this contains no nectar.[24] His belief is founded chiefly on a statement by Sprengel that insects soon find out that it is of no use to visit the nectaries of these orchids, as shown by their fertilizing only the / lower and first opened flowers. But this statement is completely contradicted by my observations previously given, from which it follows that very many of the upper flowers are fertilized; for instance, on a spike of

[20] My son Francis has described and figured this organ in the *Q. Journal of Microscopical Science*, vol. xv, 1875, p. 385.

[21] *Die Befruchtung*, etc., p. 235.

[22] Treviranus confirms (*Bot. Zeitung*, 1863, p. 10) a statement made by Salisbury, that when the filaments in the flowers of another leguminous plant, Edwardsia, fall off, or when they are cautiously separated, a large quantity of *sweet* fluid flows from the points of separation; and as beforehand there was no trace of any such fluid, it must have been contained, as Treviranus remarks, within the cellular tissue. I may add an apparently similar, but really distinct case, namely, the presence of nectar in several monocotyledonous plants (as described by Ad. Brongniart in *Bull. Soc. Bot. de France*, vol. i, 1854, p. 75) between the two walls (feuillets) which form the divisions of the ovarium. But the nectar in this case is conducted to the outside by a channel; and the secreting surface is homologically an exterior surface.

[23] *Die Befruchtung*, p. 84.

[24] *Ult. Osservazioni sulla Dicogamia*, 1875, p. 121.

O. pyramidalis with between fifty and sixty flowers, no less than forty-eight had their pollinia removed. Nevertheless, as soon as I learnt that Delpino still believed in Sprengel's view, I selected during the unfavourable season of 1875 six old spikes of *O. maculata*, and divided each into halves, so as to observe whether many more capsules were produced by the lower than by the upper half. This certainly was not always the case; for in some of the spikes no difference could be detected between them; in others there were more capsules in the lower, while in others there were more in the upper half. A spike of *O. pyramidalis* examined in the same manner produced twice as many capsules in the upper as in the lower half. Bearing in mind these facts and others before given, it appears to me incredible that the same insect should go on visiting flower after flower of these orchids, although it never obtains any nectar. Insects, or at least bees, are by no means destitute of intelligence. They recognize from a distance the flowers of the same species, and keep to them as long as they can. When humble-bees have bitten holes through the corolla, as they often do, so as to reach the nectar more easily, hive-bees immediately perceive what has been done and take advantage of the perforations. When flowers having more than a single nectary are visited by many bees, so that the nectar is exhausted in most of them, the bees which afterwards visit such flowers insert their proboscides only into one of the nectaries, and if they find this exhausted, they instantly pass on to another flower. Can it be believed that bees which / show this much intelligence, should persevere in visiting flower after flower of the above-named orchids, and in keeping their proboscides in constant movement for some time within the nectaries, in the hope of obtaining nectar which is never present? This, as I have said, seems to me utterly incredible.

It has been shown how numerous and beautiful are the contrivances for the fertilization of orchids. We know that it is of the highest importance that the pollinia, when attached to the head or proboscis of an insect, should be fixed symmetrically, so as not to fall either sideways or backwards. We know that in the species as yet described the viscid matter of the disc sets hard in a few minutes when exposed to the air, so that it would be a great advantage to the plant if insects were delayed in sucking the nectar, time being thus allowed for the disc to become immovably affixed. It is manifest that insects must be delayed by having to bore through several points of the inner membrane of the nectary, and to suck the nectar from the intercellular spaces; and we can thus understand why the nectaries of the above-named species of Orchis do not contain free nectar, but secrete it internally between the two membranes.

The following singular relation supports this view in a striking manner. I have found free nectar within the nectaries of only five British species of Ophreae, namely, in *Gymnadenia conopsea* and *albida*, in *Habenaria bifolia* and *chlorantha*, and in *Peristylus* (or *Habenaria*) *viridis*. The first four of these species have the viscid surfaces of the discs of their pollinia naked or not enclosed within pouches, and the viscid matter does not rapidly set hard when exposed to the air, as if it did, it would immediately have been rendered useless; and this shows that it must differ in chemical / nature from that in the foregoing species of Orchis. But to make sure of this fact I removed the pollinia from their anther-cells, so that the upper as well as the under surfaces of the viscid discs were freely exposed to the air; in *Gymnadenia conopsea* the disc remained sticky for two hours, and in *Habenaria chlorantha* for more than twenty-four hours. In *Peristylus viridis* the viscid disc is covered by a pouch-formed membrane, but this is so minute that botanists have overlooked it. I did not, when examining this species, see the importance of ascertaining exactly how soon the viscid matter set hard; but I copy from my notes the words written at the time: 'disc remains sticky for some time when removed from its little pouch'.

Now the meaning of these facts is clear: as the viscid matter of the discs of these five latter species is so adhesive that it serves to attach the pollinia firmly to the insects which visit the flowers, without setting hard, there would be no use in the insects being delayed by having to bore holes at several points through the inner membrane of the nectaries; and in these five species, and in these alone, we find copious nectar ready stored for rapid suction in open nectaries. On the other hand, whenever the viscid matter sets hard by exposure for a short time to the air, it would manifestly be advantageous to the plant, if insects were delayed in obtaining the nectar; and in all such species the nectar is lodged within intercellular spaces, so that it can be obtained only by the inner membrane being penetrated at several points, and this will require time. If this double relation is accidental, it is a fortunate accident for the plants; but I cannot believe it to be so, and it appears to me one of the most wonderful cases of adaptation which has ever been recorded. /

CHAPTER II

OPHREAE *continued*

Fly and Spider Ophrys – Bee Ophrys, apparently adapted for perpetual self-fertilization, but with paradoxical contrivances for intercrossing – *Herminium monorchis*, attachment of the pollinia to the front legs of insects – *Peristylus viridis*, fertilization indirectly effected by nectar secreted from three parts of the labellum – *Gymnadenia conopsea*, and other species – Habenaria or *Platanthera chlorantha* and *bifolia*, their pollinia attached to the eyes of Lepidoptera – Other species of Habenaria – Bonatea – Disa – Summary on the powers of movement in the pollinia.

The genus Ophrys differs from Orchis chiefly in having separate pouch-formed rostella,[1] instead of the two being confluent.

In *Ophrys muscifera*, or the Fly Ophrys, the chief peculiarity is that the caudicle of the pollinium (B, fig. 5) is doubly bent. The nearly circular piece of membrane, to the underside of which the ball of viscid matter adheres, is of considerable size, and forms the summit of the rostellum. It is thus freely exposed / to the air, instead of lying almost hidden at the base of the anther, as in Orchis, and thus kept damp. Nevertheless, when a pollinium is removed, the caudicle bends downwards in the course of about six minutes, and, therefore, at an unusually slow rate; the upper end still remaining curved. I formerly thought that it was incapable of any movement, but have been convinced by Mr T. H. Farrer of my error. The ball of viscid matter is bathed in fluid within the pouch formed by the lower half of the

---

[1] It is not correct to speak of two rostella, but the inaccuracy may be forgiven from its convenience. The rostellum strictly is a single organ, formed by the modification of the dorsal stigma and pistil; so that in Ophrys the two pouches, the two viscid discs, and the space between them together form the true rostellum. Again, in Orchis I have spoken of the pouch-formed organ as the rostellum, but strictly the rostellum includes the little crest or fold of membrane (see B in fig. 1) projecting between the bases of the anther-cells. This folded crest (sometimes converted into a solid ridge) corresponds with the smooth surface lying between the two pouches in Ophrys, and owes its protuberant and folded condition in Orchis to the two pouches having been brought together and rendered confluent. This modification will be more fully explained in a future chapter.

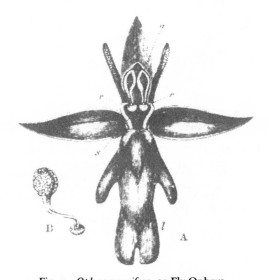

Fig. 5   *Ophrys muscifera*, or Fly Ophrys
a. anther; *r, r.* rostella, *s.* stigma, *l.* labellum
A. Flower viewed in front: the two upper petals are almost cylindrical and hairy: the two rostella stand a little in advance of the bases of the anther-cells; but this is not shown from the foreshortening of the drawing
B. One of the two pollinia removed from its anther-cell, and viewed laterally

rostellum, and this is necessary, / as the viscid matter quickly sets hard when exposed to the air. The pouch is not elastic, and does not spring up when the pollinium is removed. Such elasticity would have been useless, as there is here a separate pouch for each viscid disc; whereas in Orchis, after one pollinium has been removed, the other has to be kept covered up and ready for action. Hence it appears that nature had been so economical as to save even superfluous elasticity.

The pollinia cannot, as I have often proved, be shaken out of the anther-cells. That insects of some kind visit the flowers, though not frequently, and remove the pollinia, is certain, as we shall immediately see. Twice I have found abundant pollen on the stigmas of flowers, in which both pollinia were still in their cells; and no doubt this might have been much oftener observed. The elongated labellum affords a good landing-place for insects: at its base, just beneath the stigma, there is a rather deep depression, representing the nectary in Orchis; but I could never see a trace of nectar within it; nor have I ever observed any insects approach these inconspicuous and scentless

32

flowers, often as I have watched them. There is, however, on each side of the base of the labellum a small shining projection, having an almost metallic lustre, which appears curiously like a drop of fluid or nectar; and as these flowers are only visited occasionally by insects, Sprengel's view of the existence of sham-nectaries is far more probable in this case than in any other known to me. On several occasions I have detected minute punctures in these protuberances, but I was not able to decide whether they had been made by insects, or whether superficial cells had spontaneously burst. Similar shining protuberances are present on the labella of all the other species of Ophrys. The two rostella stand not far / apart, and project over the stigma; and if any object is gently pushed against one of them, the pouch is depressed and the viscid ball together with the pollinium adheres to it and is easily removed.

The structure of the flower leads me to believe that small insects (as we shall see in the case of Listera) crawl up the labellum to its base, and that in bending their heads downwards, so as to puncture and suck, or only to examine one of the small shining protuberances, they push against the pouch, and a pollinium is attached to their heads; they then fly to another flower, and there bending down in a similar manner, the attached and doubly-bent pollinium, after the movement of depression, strikes the sticky stigmatic surface, and leaves pollen on it. Under the next species we shall see reason for believing that the natural double curvature of the caudicle compensates for its slight power of movement, compared with that in all the species of Orchis.

| | Number of flowers | |
	Both pollinia or one removed by insects	Both pollinia in their cells
In 1858, 17 plants, bearing 57 flowers, growing near each other were examined	30	27
In 1858, 25 plants growing in another spot, and bearing 65 flowers	15	50
In 1860, 17 plants, bearing 61 flowers	28	33
In 1861, 4 plants from S. Kent, bearing 24 flowers (all the previous plants having grown in N. Kent)	15	9
Total	88	119

That insects visit the flowers of the Fly Ophrys and remove the pollinia, though not effectually or sufficiently, / the following cases show. During several years before 1858 I occasionally examined some flowers, and found that only thirteen out of 102 had one or both pollinia removed. Although at the time I recorded in my notes that most of the flowers were partly withered, I now think that I must have included many young flowers, which might perhaps have been subsequently visited; so I prefer trusting to the following observations.

We here see that, out of 207 flowers examined, not half had been visited by insects. Of the eighty-eight flowers visited, thirty-one had only one pollinium removed. As the visits of insects are indispensable for the fertilization of this orchid, it is surprising (as in the case of *Orchis fusca*) that the flowers have not been rendered more attractive to insects. The number of seed-capsules produced is proportionably even less than the number of flowers visited by insects. The year 1861 was extraordinarily favourable to this species in this part of Kent, and I never saw such numbers in flower; accordingly I marked eleven plants, which bore forty-nine flowers, but these produced only seven capsules. Two of the plants each bore two capsules, and three other plants each bore one, so that no less than six plants did not produce a single capsule! What are we to conclude from these facts? Are the conditions of life unfavourable to this species, though during the year just alluded to it was so numerous in some places as to deserve to be called quite common? Could the plant nourish more seed; and would it be of any advantage to it to produce more seed? Why does it produce so many flowers, if it already produces a sufficiency of seeds? Something seems to be out of order in its mechanism or in its conditions. We shall presently see that *Ophrys apifera* or the Bee Ophrys / presents a wonderful contrast in every flower producing a capsule.

Ophrys aranifera, or the Spider Ophrys. I am indebted to Mr Oxenden for some spikes of this rare species. Whilst the pollinia remain en-closed within their cells, the lower part of the caudicle projects up in a straight line from the viscid disc, and therefore has a very different form from the correspond-ing part of the caudicle of *O. muscifera*; but the upper part (A, fig. 6) is a little bent forward, that is, towards the labellum. The point of attachment of the caudicle to the disc is hidden within the bases of the anther-cells, and is thus kept damp; consequently, as soon as the pollinia are exposed to the air, the usual movement of depression takes

Fig. 6   *Ophrys aranifera*
A. Pollinium before the act of depression
B. Pollinium after the act of depression

place, and they sweep through an angle of about ninety degrees. By this movement they assume, supposing them to be attached to an insect's head, a position exactly adapted for striking the stigmatic surface, which is situated, relatively to the pouch-formed rostella, rather lower down in the flower than in the Fly Ophrys.

I examined fourteen flowers of the Spider Ophrys, several of which were partly withered; and in none were both pollinia, and in three alone was one pollinium removed. Hence this species, like the Fly Ophrys, is but little visited by insects in England. In parts of Italy it is even less visited, for Delpino states[2] that in Liguria hardly one flower out of 3,000 sets a / capsule, though near Florence rather more capsules are produced. The labellum does not secrete any nectar. The flowers, however, must be occasionally visited and fertilized by insects, for Dèlpino found[3] pollen-masses on the stigmas of some flowers which still retained both their own pollinia.

The anther-cells are remarkably open, so that with some plants which were sent me in a box, two pair of pollinia fell out, and stuck by their viscid discs to the petals. Here we have an instance of the first appearance of a trifling structure which is of not the least use to its possessor, but becomes when a little more developed, highly beneficial to a closely allied species; for although the open state of the anther-cells is useless to the Spider Ophrys, it is of the highest importance, as we shall presently see, to the Bee Ophrys. The flexure of the upper end of the caudicle of the pollinium is of service to the Spider and Fly Ophrys, by aiding the pollen-masses, when carried by insects to another flower, to strike the stigma; but by an increase of this bend together with increased flexibility in the Bee Ophrys, the pollinia become adapted for the widely different purpose of self-fertilization.

Ophrys arachnites. This form, of which Mr Oxenden sent me several living specimens, is considered by some botanists as only a variety of the Bee Ophrys, by others as a distinct species. The anther-cells do not stand so high above the stigma, and do not overhang it so much, as in the Bee Ophrys, and the pollen-masses are more elongated. The caudicle is only two-thirds, or even only half as long as that of the Bee / Ophrys, and is much more rigid; the

Fig. 7   Pollinium of *Ophrys arachnites*

---

[2] *Ult. Osserv. s. Dicogamia, etc.*, Parte i, 1868–9, p. 177.
[3] *Fecondazione nelle Piante Antocarpee*, 1867, p. 20.

upper part is naturally curved forward; the lower part undergoes the usual movement of depression, when the pollinia are removed from their cells. The pollen-masses never fall spontaneously out of their cells. This plant, therefore, differs in every important respect from *O. apifera*, and seems to be much more closely allied to *O. aranifera*.

Ophrys scolopax of Cavanilles. This form inhabits the north of Italy and the south of France. Mr Moggridge says[4] that at Mentone it never shows any tendency to fertilize itself, whilst at Cannes the pollen-masses naturally fall out of their cells and strike the stigma. He adds: 'This material difference between the two is accomplished by a very slight bend in the anther-cells, which are prolonged into a beak of variable length, in the case of the self-fertilizing blossoms.'

Ophrys apifera. The Bee Ophrys differs widely from the great majority of orchids in being excellently constructed for fertilizing itself. The two pouch-formed rostella, the viscid discs, and the position

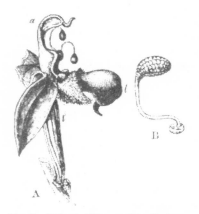

Fig. 8   *Ophrys apifera*, or Bee Ophrys
a. anther, *l.l.* labellum
A. Side view of flower, with the upper sepal and the two upper petals removed. One pollinium, with its disc still in its pouch, is represented as just falling out of the anther-cell; and the other has fallen almost to its full extent, opposite to the hidden stigmatic surface
B. Pollinium in the position in which it lies embedded

of the stigma, are nearly the same as in the other species of Ophrys; but the distance of the two pouches from each other, and the shape of

---

[4] *Journ. Linn. Soc.*, vol. viii, 1865, p. 258.

the pollen-masses are somewhat variable.[5] The caudicles of the pollinia are remarkably long, thin, and flexible, instead of being, as in all the other Ophreae seen by me, rigid enough to stand upright. They are necessarily curved forward at their upper ends, owing to the shape of the anther-cells; and the pear-shaped pollen-masses lie embedded high above and directly over the / stigma. The anther-cells naturally open soon after the flower is fully expanded, and the thick ends of the pollen-masses then fall out, the viscid discs still remaining in their pouches. Slight as is the weight of the pollen-masses, yet the caudicles are so thin and quickly become so flexible, that in the course of a few hours they sink down, until they hang freely in the air (see lower pollen-mass in fig. A) exactly opposite to and in front of the stigmatic surface. In this position a breath of air, acting on the expanded petals, sets the flexible and elastic caudicles vibrating, and they almost immediately strike the viscid stigma, and, being there secured, impregnation is effected. To make sure that no other aid was requisite, though / the experiment was superfluous, I covered up a plant under a net, so that the wind, but no insects, could pass in, and in a few days the pollinia became attached to the stigmas. But the pollinia of a spike kept in water in a still room remained free, suspended in front of the stigma, until the flowers withered.

Robert Brown first observed that the structure of the Bee Ophrys is adapted for self-fertilization.[6] When we consider the unusual and perfectly adapted length, as well as the remarkable flexibility of the caudicles; when we see that the anther-cells naturally open, and that the masses of pollen, from their weight, slowly fall down to the exact level of the stigmatic surface, and are there made to vibrate by the slightest breath of wind until the stigma is struck; it is impossible to doubt that these several points of structure and function, which occur in no other British orchid, are specially adapted for self-fertilization.

The result is what might have been anticipated. I have often noticed that the spikes of the Bee Ophrys apparently produced as many seed-capsules as flowers; and near Torquay I carefully examined many dozen plants, some time after the flowering season; and on all I found

[5] I once found a single flower on the summit of a spike, with the two rostella as completely and symmetrically confluent as in the genus Orchis, and with the two viscid discs likewise confluent, as in *Orchis pyramidalis* or *hircina*.

[6] *Transact. Linn. Soc.*, vol. xvi, p. 740. Brown erroneously believed that this peculiarity was common to the genus. As far as the four British species are concerned, it applies to this one alone.

from one to four, and occasionally five, fine capsules, that is, as many capsules as there had been flowers. In extremely few cases, with the exception of a few deformities, generally on the summit of the spike, could a flower be found which had not produced a capsule. Let it be observed what a contrast this species presents with the Fly Ophrys, which requires insect aid for its fertilization, and which from forty-nine flowers produced only seven capsules! /

From what I had then seen of other orchids, I was so much surprised at the self-fertilization of this species, that I examined during many years, and asked others to examine, the state of the pollen-masses in many hundreds of flowers, collected in various parts of England. The particulars are not worth detailing; but I may give as an instance, that Mr Farrer found in Surrey that not one flower out of 106 had lost both pollinia, and that only three had lost a single one. In the Isle of Wight, Mr More examined 136 flowers, and of these the very unusual number of ten had lost both, and fourteen had lost one; but then he found that in eleven cases the caudicles had been gnawed through apparently by snails, the discs still remaining in their pouches; so that the pollinia had not been carried away by insects. In some few cases, also, in which I found the pollinia removed, the petals were marked with the slime of snails. Nor must we forget that a blow from a passing animal, and possibly heavy storms of wind might occasionally cause the loss of one or both pollinia.

During most years the pollen-masses of the many hundred flowers which were examined, adhered with the rarest exceptions to the stigma, with their discs still enclosed within the pouches. But in the year 1868, from some cause the nature of which I cannot conjecture, out of 116 flowers gathered in two localities in Kent, seventy-five retained both pollinia in their cells; ten had one pollinium, and only thirty-one had both adhering to the stigma. Long and often as I have watched plants of the Bee Ophrys, I have never seen one visited by any insect.[7] Robert Brown imagined / that the flowers resembled bees in order to deter their visits, but this seems extremely improbable. The flowers with their pink sepals do not resemble any British bee, and it is probably true, as I have heard it said, that the plant received its name merely from the hairy labellum being somewhat like the abdomen of a

[7] Mr Gerard E. Smith, in his *Catalogue of Plants of S. Kent*, 1829, p. 25, says: 'Mr Price has frequently witnessed attacks made upon the Bee Orphrys by a bee, similar to those of the troublesome *Apis muscorum*.' What this sentence means I cannot conjecture.

humble-bee. We see how fanciful many of the names are – one species being called the Lizard and another the Frog Orchis. The resemblance of O. *muscifera* to a fly is very much closer than that of O. *apifera* to a bee; and yet the fertilization of the former absolutely depends on and is effected by the means of insects.

All the foregoing observations relate to England, but Mr Moggridge made similar ones on the Bee Ophrys in Northern Italy and Southern France, as did Treviranus[8] in Germany, and Dr Hooker in Morocco. We may therefore conclude – from the pollinia spontaneously falling on the stigma – from the co-related structure of all the parts for this purpose – and from almost all the flowers producing seed-capsules – that this plant has been specially adapted for self-fertilization. But there is another side to the case.

When an object is pushed against one of the pouches of the rostellum, the lip is depressed, and the large viscid disc adheres firmly to it; and when the object is removed, so is the pollinium, but perhaps not quite so readily as in the other species of Ophrys. Even after the pollen-masses have naturally fallen out of their cells on to the stigma, their removal can sometimes be thus effected. As soon as the disc is / drawn out of its pouch a movement of depression commences, by which the pollinium if attached to the front of an insect's head would be brought into a proper position for striking the stigma. When a pollen-mass is placed on the stigma and then withdrawn, the elastic threads by which the packets are tied together break, and leave several packets on the viscid surface. In all other orchids the meaning of these several contrivances is unmistakably clear – namely, the downward movement of the lip of the rostellum when gently pushed – the viscidity of the disc – the depression of the caudicle as soon as the disc is exposed to the air – the rupturing of the elastic threads – and the conspicuousness of the flower. Are we to believe that these adaptations for cross-fertilization in the Bee Ophrys are absolutely purposeless, as would certainly be the case if this species has always been and will always be self-fertilized? It is, however, just possible that insects, although they have never been seen to visit the flowers, may at rare intervals transport the pollinia from plant to plant, during such seasons as that of 1868, when the pollinia did not all fall out of the anther-cells so as to reach the stigmas. The whole case is perplexing in

[8] *Bot. Zeitung*, 1863, p. 241. This botanist at first doubted my observations on *Ophrys apifera* and *aranifera*, but has since fully confirmed them.

an unparalleled degree, for we have in the same flower elaborate contrivances for directly opposed objects.

That cross-fertilization is beneficial to most orchids, we may infer from the innumerable structures serving for this purpose which they present; and I have elsewhere shown in the case of many other groups of plants[9] that the benefits thus derived are of high importance. On the other hand, self-fertilization is manifestly advantageous in as far as it ensures a full / supply of seed; and we have seen with the other British species of Ophrys which cannot fertilize themselves how small a proportion of their flowers produce capsules. Judging therefore from the structure of the flowers of *O. apifera*, it seems almost certain that at some former period they were adapted for cross-fertilization, but that failing to produce a sufficiency of seed they became slightly modified so as to fertilize themselves. It is, however, remarkable on this view, that none of the parts in question show any tendency to abortion – that in the several and distant countries which the plant inhabits, the flowers are still conspicuous, the discs still viscid, and the caudicles still retain the power of movement when the discs are exposed to the air. The metallic points at the base of the labellum are, however, smaller than in the other species; and if these serve to attract insects, this difference is of some signification. As it can hardly be doubted that *O. apifera* was at first constructed so as to be regularly cross-fertilized, it may be asked will it ever revert to its former state; and it if does not so revert, will it become extinct? These questions cannot be answered, any more than in the case of those plants which are now propagated exclusively by buds, stolons, etc., but which produce flowers that rarely or never set any seed; and there is reason to believe that a sexual propagation is closely analogous to long-continued self-fertilization.

Finally Mr Moggridge has shown that in North Italy *Ophrys apifera, aranifera, arachnites*, and *scolopax* are connected by so many and such close intermediate links,[10] that all seem to form a single species in / accordance with the belief of Linnaeus, who grouped them all together under the name of *Ophrys insectifera*. Mr Moggridge further shows that in Italy *O. aranifera* flowers first, and *O. apifera* last, the intermediate forms at intermediate periods; and according to Mr Oxenden, the same fact holds good to a certain extent in Kent. The three forms

---

[9] *The Effects of Cross and Self-Fertilization in the Vegetable Kingdom*, 1876.

[10] These forms are illustrated by beautiful coloured drawings in the *Flora of Mentone*, pl. 43 to 45; and in his memoir in the *Verhandlungen der Kaiserl. Leop. Car. Akad*, (Nov. Act.), vol, xxxv, 1869.

which inhabit England do not seem to blend into one another as in Italy, and I am assured by Mr Oxenden, who has closely attended to these plants in their native homes, that *O. aranifera* and *apifera* always grow in distinct spots. The case therefore is an interesting one, as here we have forms which may be and generally have been ranked as true species, but which in North Italy have not as yet been fully differentiated. The case is all the more interesting, as the intermediate forms can hardly be due to the crossing of *O. aranifera* with *apifera*; this latter species being regularly self-fertilized and apparently never visited by insects. Whether we rank the several forms of Ophrys as closely allied species or as mere varieties of the same species, it is remarkable that they should differ in a character of such physiological importances as the flowers of some being plainly adapted for self-fertilization, whilst the flowers of others are strictly adapted for cross-fertilization, being utterly sterile if not visited by insects.

Herminium monorchis. The Musk Orchis, which is a rare British plant, is generally spoken of as having naked glands or discs, but this is not strictly correct. The disc is of unusual size, nearly equalling the mass of pollen-grains: it is subtriangular, with one side protuberant, and somewhat resembles a distorted helmet in shape: it is formed of hard tissue with the base hollowed out, and viscid; the base resting on and being covered by a narrow strip of membrane, which is / easily pushed away, and answers to the pouch in Orchis. The whole upper part of the helmet answers to the minute oval bit of membrane to which the caudicle of Orchis is attached and which in Ophrys is larger and convex. When the lower part of the helmet is moved by any pointed object, the point readily slips into its hollow base, and is there held so firmly by the viscid matter, that the whole helmet appears adapted to stick to some prominent part of an insect's body. The caudicle is short and very elastic; it is attached not to the apex of the helmet, but to the hinder end; it if had been attached to the apex, the point of attachment would have been freely exposed to the air and not kept damp; and then the pollinium when removed from its cell would not have been quickly depressed.

This movement is well marked, and serves to bring the end of the pollen-mass into a proper position for striking the stigma. The two viscid discs stand wide apart. There are two transverse stigmatic surfaces, meeting by their points in the middle; but the broad part of each lies directly beneath each disc. The labellum is remarkable from not differing much in shape from the two upper petals, and from not always occupying the same position in reference to the axis of the plant, owing to the ovarium being more or less twisted. This state of the labellum is intelligible, for as we shall see, it does not serve as a landing-place for insects. It is upturned, and together with the two other petals makes the whole flower in some degree tubular. At its base there is a hollow so deep as almost to deserve to be called a nectary; but I could not perceive any nectar, which, as I believe, remains enclosed in the intercellular spaces. The flowers are very small and inconspicuous, but emit a strong honey-like / odour. They seem highly attractive to insects; in a spike with only seven flowers recently open, four had both pollinia, and one had a single pollinium removed.

When the first edition of this book appeared I did not know how the flowers were fertilized, but my son George has made out the whole process, which is extremely curious and differs from that in any other orchid known to me. He saw various minute insects entering the flowers, and brought home no less than twenty-seven specimens with pollinia (generally with only one, but sometimes with two) attached to them. These insects consisted of minute Hymenoptera (of which *Tetrastichus diaphantus* was the commonest), of Diptera and Coleoptera, the latter being *Malthodes brevicollis*. The one indispensable point appears to be that the insect should be of very small size, the largest being only the ½₀ of an inch in length. The pollinia were always attached to the same place, namely, to the outer surface of the femur of one of the front legs, and generally to the projection formed by the articulation of the femur with the coxa. The cause of this peculiar mode of attachment is sufficiently clear: the middle part of the labellum stands so close to the anther and stigma, that insects always enter the flower at one corner, between the edge of the labellum and one of the upper petals; they also almost always crawl in with their backs turned directly or obliquely towards the labellum. My son saw several which began to crawl into the flowers in a different position; but they came out and changed their position. Standing in either corner of the flower, with their backs turned towards the labellum, they insert their heads and forelegs into the short nectary, which is seated between the two widely separated viscid discs. I ascertained that they had occupied this position by / finding three dead insects, permanently glued to the discs. Whilst sucking the nectar, which takes two or three minutes, the projecting joint of the femur stands under the large helmet-like viscid disc on either side; and when the insect retreats, the disc exactly fits on and is glued to the prominent joint, or to the surface of the femur. The movement of depression in the caudicle now takes place, and the mass of pollen-grains then projects just beyond the tibia; so that the insect, when entering another flower, can hardly fail to fertilize the stigma, which is situated directly beneath the disc on either side.

Fig. 9   *Peristylus viridis*, or Frog Orchis
Front view of flower
a. anther, *s.* stigma, *n.* orifice of central nectary, *n'n'.* lateral nectaries, *l.* labellum

Peristylus viridis. This plant, which bears the odd name of the Frog Orchis, has been placed by many botanists in the genus Habenaria or Platanthera; but as the discs are not naked, it is doubtful whether this / classification can be correct. The rostella are small and widely separated from each other. The viscid matter on the underside of the disc forms an oval ball which is enclosed within a small pouch. The upper membrane to which the caudicle is attached is of large size relatively to the whole disc, and is freely exposed to the air. Hence probably it is that the pollinia when removed from their cases do not become depressed until, as Mr T. H. Farrer has observed, twenty or thirty minutes have elapsed. Owing to this long interval, I formerly thought that they did not undergo any movement of depression. Supposing a pollinium to be attached to the head of an insect, and to have become depressed, it will stand at the proper angle, vertically, for striking the stigma. But from the lateral position of the anther-cells, notwithstanding that they converge a little towards their upper ends, it

43

is difficult at first to see how the pollinia when removed by insects are afterwards placed on the stigma; for this is of small size and is situated in the middle of the flower between the two widely separated rostella.

The explanation is, I believe, as follows. The base of the elongated labellum forms a rather deep hollow in front of the stigma, and in this hollow, but some way in advance of the stigma, a minute slit-like orifice (*n*) leads into a short bilobed nectary. Hence an insect, in order to suck the nectar with which the nectary is filled, would have to bend down its head in front of the stigma. The labellum has a medial ridge, which would probably induce an insect first to alight on either side; but, apparently to make sure of this, besides the true nectary, there are two spots (*n'n'*) which secrete drops of nectar on each side at the base of the labellum, bordered by prominent edges, directly / beneath the two pouches. Now let us suppose an insect to alight on one side of the labellum so as first to lick up the exposed drop of nectar on this side; from the position of the pouch exactly over the drop, it would almost certainly get the pollinium of this side attached to its head. If it were now to go to the mouth of the true nectary, the pollinium attached to its head from not having as yet become depressed would not touch the stigma; so that there would be no self-fertilization. The insect would then probably suck the exposed drop of nectar on the other side of the labellum, and would perhaps get another pollinium attached to its head; it would thus be considerably delayed by having to visit the three nectaries. It would then visit other flowers on the same plant, and afterwards flowers on a distinct plant; and by this time, but not before, the pollinia will have undergone the movement of depression and will be in a proper position for effecting cross-fertilization. It thus appears that the secretion of nectar at three separate points of the labellum – the wide distance apart of the two rostella – and the slow downward movement of the caudicle without any lateral movement – are all correlated for the same purpose of cross-fertilization.

To what extent this Orchis is frequented by insects, and what the kinds are, I do not know, but several of the flowers on two spikes, sent me by the Rev. B. S. Malden, had a single pollinium removed, and one flower had both removed.

We now come to two genera, namely, Gymnadenia and Habenaria or Platanthera, including four British species, which have uncovered viscid discs. The viscid matter, as before remarked, is of a somewhat different nature from that in Orchis, Ophrys, etc., and does not /

rapidly set hard. Their nectaries are stored with free nectar. With respect to the uncovered condition of the discs, the last species, or *Peristylus viridis*, is in an almost intermediate condition. The four following species compose a much broken series. In *Gymnadenia conopsea* the viscid discs are narrow and much elongated, and lie close together; in *G. albida* they are less elongated, but still approximate; in *Habenaria bifolia* they are oval and far apart; and, lastly, in *H. chlorantha* they are circular and much farther apart.

Gymnadenia conopsea. In general appearance this plant resembles pretty closely a true Orchis. The pollinia differ in having naked, narrow, strap-shaped discs, which are as long as the caudicles (fig. 10).

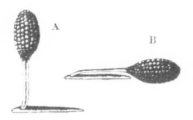

Fig. 10   *Gymnadenia conopsea*
A. Pollinium, before the act of depression
B. Pollinium, after the act of depression, but before it has closely clasped the disc

When the pollinia are exposed to the air the caudicle is depressed in from thirty to sixty seconds; and as the posterior surface of the caudicle is slightly hollowed out, it closely clasps the upper membranous surface of the disc. The mechanism of this movement will be described in the last chapter. The elastic threads by which the packets of pollen are bound together are unusually weak, as is likewise the case with / the two following species of Habenaria: this was well shown by the state of specimens which had been kept in spirits of wine. This weakness apparently stands in relation to the viscid matter of the discs not setting hard and dry as in Orchis; so that a moth with a pollinium attached to its proboscis might be enabled to visit several flowers without having the whole pollinium dragged off by the first stigma which was struck. The two strap-shaped discs lie close together, and form the arched roof of the entrance into the nectary. They are not protected, as in Orchis, by a lower lip or pouch, so that the structure of the rostellum is simpler. When we come to treat of the homologies of the rostellum we shall see that this difference is due to a small change, namely, to the lower and exterior cells of the rostellum resolving themselves into viscid matter; whereas in Orchis the exterior surface retains its early cellular or membranous condition.

As the two viscid discs form the roof of the mouth of the nectary, and are thus brought down near to the labellum, the two stigmas, instead of being confluent and standing beneath the rostellum, as in most of the species of Orchis, are lateral and separate. These stigmas consist of protuberant, almost horn-shaped, processes on each side of the nectary. That their surfaces are really stigmatic I ascertained by finding them deeply penetrated by a multitude of pollen-tubes. As in the case of *Orchis pyramidalis*, it is a pretty experiment to push a fine bristle straight into the narrow mouth of the nectary, and to observe how certainly the narrow elongated viscid discs, forming the roof, stick to the bristle. When the bristle is withdrawn, the pollinia adhering to its upper side are withdrawn; and as the discs form the sides of the arched roof, they adhere somewhat to the sides / of the bristle. They then quickly become depressed so as to lie in the same line with the bristle – one a little on one side, and the other on the other side; and if the bristle, held in the same relative position, be now inserted into the nectary of another flower, the two ends of the pollinia accurately strike the two protuberant stigmatic surfaces, situated on each side of the mouth of the nectary.

The flowers smell sweet, and the abundant nectar always contained in their nectaries seems highly attractive to Lepidoptera, for the pollinia are soon and effectually removed. For instance, in a spike with forty-five open flowers, forty-one had their pollinia removed, or had pollen left on their stigmas: in another spike with fifty-four flowers, thirty-seven had both pollinia, and fifteen had one pollinium, removed; so that only two flowers in the whole spike had neither pollinium removed.

My son George went at night to a bank where this species grows plentifully, and soon caught *Plusia chrysitis* with six pollinia, *P. gamma* with three, *Anaitis plagiata* with five, and *Triphaena pronuba* with seven pollinia attached to their proboscides. I may add that he also caught the first-named moth in my flower-garden, with the pollinia of this Orchis attached to its proboscis, but with all the pollen-grains removed, although the garden is a quarter of a mile distant from any spot where the plant grows. Many of the above moths had only a single pollinium attached, somewhat laterally to their proboscides; and this would happen in every case, unless the moth stood directly in front of the nectary and inserted its proboscis exactly between the two discs. But as the labellum is rather broad and flat, with no guiding ridges like those on the labellum of *Orchis pyramidalis*, there is nothing to / compel moths to insert their proboscides symmetrically into the nectary, and there would be no advantage in their doing so.

Gymnadenia albida. The structure of the flower of this species resembles in most respects that of the last; but, owing to the upturning of the labellum, it is rendered almost tubular. The naked elongated discs are minute and approximate. The stigmatic surfaces are partially lateral and divergent. The nectary is short, and full of nectar. Small as the flowers are, they seem highly attractive to insects: of the eighteen lower flowers on one spike, ten had both, and seven had one pollinium removed; on some older spikes all the pollinia had been removed, except from two or three of the uppermost flowers.

Gymnadenia odoratissima is an inhabitant of the Alps, and is said by Dr H. Müller[11] to resemble in all the above characters *G. conopsea*. As the flowers, which are pale coloured and highly perfumed, are not visited by butterflies, he believes that they are fertilized exclusively by moths. The North American *G. tridentata*, described by Professor Asa Gray,[12] differs in an important manner from the foregoing species. The anther opens in the bud, and the pollen-grains, which in the British species are tied together by very weak threads, are here much more incoherent, and some invariably fall on the two stigmas and on the naked cellular tip of the rostellum; and this latter part, strange to say, is penetrated by the pollen-tubes. The flowers are thus self-fertilized. Nevertheless, as Professor Gray adds, 'all the arrangements for the removal / of the pollinia by insects, including the movement of depression, are as perfect as in the species which depend upon insect aid'. Hence there can be little doubt that this species is occasionally cross-fertilized.

Habenaria or *Platanthera chlorantha*. The pollinia of the Large Butterfly Orchis differ considerably from those of any species hitherto mentioned. The two / anther-cells are separated from each other by a wide space of connective membrane, and the pollinia are enclosed in a backward sloping position (fig. 11). The viscid discs front each other,

[11] *Nature*, 31 December, 1874, p. 169.
[12] *American Journal of Science*, vol. xxxiv, 1862, p. 426, and footnote p. 260; and vol. xxxvi, 1863, p. 293. In the latter paper he adds some remarks on *G. flava* and *nivea*.

and stand in advance of the stigmatic surface. In consequence of their forward position, the caudicles and pollen-masses are much elongated. Each viscid disc is circular, and, in the early bud, consists of a mass of cells, of which the exterior layers (answering to the lip or pouch in Orchis) resolve themselves into adhesive matter. This matter has the property of remaining adhesive for at least twenty-four hours after the pollinium has been removed from its cell. The disc, externally covered

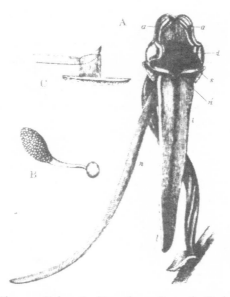

Fig. 11   *Habenaria chlorantha*, or Butterfly Orchis
a a. anther-cells, *d.* disc of pollinium, *s.* stigma, *n.* nectary, *n'.* orifice of nectary, *l.* labellum
A. Flower viewed in front, with all the sepals and petals removed except the labellum with its nectary, which is turned to one side
B. A pollinium. (This has hardly a sufficiently elongated appearance.) The drum-like pedicel is hidden behind the disc
C. Diagram, giving a section through the viscid disc, the drum-like pedicel, and the attached end of the caudicle. The viscid disc is formed of an upper membrane with a layer of viscid matter beneath

with a thick layer of adhesive matter (see fig. C, which stands so that the layer of viscid matter is below) is produced on its opposite and embedded side into a short drum-like pedicel. This pedicel is continuous with the membranous portion of the disc and is formed of the same tissue. The caudicle of the pollinium is attached in a transverse direction to the embedded end of the pedicel, and its extremity is prolonged, as a bent rudimentary tail, just beyond the drum. The caudicle is thus united to the viscid disc in a very different manner, and in a plane at right angles, to what occurs in the other British orchids. In the short drum-like pedicel, we have a small development of the long pedicel of the rostellum, which is so conspicuous in many Vandeae, and which connects the viscid disc with the true caudicles of the pollinia.

The drum-like pedicel is of the highest importance, not only by rendering the viscid disc more prominent and more likely to stick to the face of an insect whilst inserting its proboscis into the nectary beneath the stigma, but on account of its power of contraction. The pollinia lie inclined backwards in their cells (see / fig. A), above and some way on each side of the stigmatic surface; if attached in this position to the head of an insect, the insect might visit any number of flowers, and no pollen would be left on the stigma. But observe what takes place: in a few seconds after the inner end of the drum-like pedicel has been removed from its embedded position and exposed to the air, one side of the drum contracts, and this contraction draws the thick end of the pollinium inwards, so that the caudicle and the viscid surface of the disc are no longer parallel, as they were at first, and as they are represented in the section, fig. C. At the same time the drum rotates through nearly a quarter of a circle, and this moves the caudicle downwards, like the hand of a clock, depressing the thick end of the pollinium or mass of pollen-grains. Let us suppose the right-hand disc to be affixed to the right side of an insect's face, and by the time required for the insect to visit another flower on another plant, the pollen-bearing end of the pollinium will have moved downwards and inwards, and will now infallibly strike the viscid surface of the stigma, situated in the middle of the flower beneath and between the two anther-cells.

The little rudimentary tail of the caudicle projecting beyond the drum-like pedicel is an interesting point to those who believe in the modification of species; for it shows us that the disc has been carried a little inwards, and that primordially the two discs stood even still further in advance of the stigma than they do at present. We thus learn that the parent-form approached in this respect the structure of that extraordinary orchid, the *Bonatea speciosa* of the Cape of Good Hope.

The remarkable length of the nectary, containing much free nectar, the white colour of the conspicuous / flowers, and the strong sweet odour emitted by them at night all show that this plant depends for its fertilization on the larger nocturnal Lepidoptera. I have often found spikes with almost all the pollinia removed. From the lateral position and distance of the two viscid discs from each other, the same moth would generally remove only one pollinium at a time; and in a spike which had not as yet been much visited, three flowers had both pollinia, and eight flowers had only one pollinium removed. From the position of the discs it might have been anticipated that they would adhere to the side of the head or face of moths; and Mr F. Bond sent me a specimen of *Hadena dentina* with one eye covered and blinded by a disc, and a specimen of *Plusia v. aureum* with a disc attached to the edge of the eye. Mr Marshall[13] collected twenty specimens of *Cucullia umbratica* on an island in Derwentwater, separated by half-a-mile of water from any spot where *H. chorantha* grew; nevertheless, seven of these moths had the pollinia of this orchid affixed to their eyes. Although the discs are so adhesive that almost all the pollinia in a bunch of flowers which was carried in my hand and thus shaken were removed by adhering to the petals or sepals, yet it is certain that moths, probably the smaller species, often visit these flowers without removing the pollinia; for on examining the discs of a large number of pollinia whilst still in their cells I found minute lepidopterous scales glued to them.

The cause of the flowers of various kinds of orchids being constructed so that the pollinia are always affixed to the eyes or proboscides of Lepidoptera, and to the naked foreheads or proboscides of Hymenoptera, / no doubt is that the viscid discs cannot adhere to a scaly or very hairy surface; the scales themselves being easily detached. Variations in the structure of the flower of an orchid, unless they led to the viscid discs touching some part of the body of an insect where they would remain firmly attached, would be of no service, but an injury to the plant; and consequently such variations would not be preserved and perfected.

Habenaria bifolia, or *Lesser Butterfly Orchis*. I am aware that this form and the last are considered by Mr Bentham and by some other botanists as mere varieties of one another; for it is said that intermediate gradations in the position of the viscid discs occur. But we shall immediately see that the two forms differ in a large number of other characters, not to mention general aspect and the stations inhabited, with which we are not here concerned. Should these two forms be

[13] *Nature*, 12 September, 1872, p. 393.

hereafter proved to graduate into each other, independently of hybridization, it would be a remarkable case of variation; and I, for one, should be as much pleased as surprised at the fact, for these two forms certainly differ from one another more than do most species belonging to the same genus.

The viscid discs of the Lesser Butterfly Orchis are oval, and face each other. They stand far closer together than in the last species; so much so, that in the bud, when their surfaces are cellular, they almost touch. They are not placed so low down relatively to the mouth of the nectary. The viscid matter is of a somewhat different chemical nature, as shown by its much greater viscidity, if after having been long dried it is moistened, or after being kept in weak spirits of wine. The drum-like pedicel can hardly be said to be present, but is represented by a longitudinal ridge, truncated at the end where the caudicle is / attached, and there is hardly a vestige of the rudimentary tail. In fig. 12 the discs of both species, of the proper proportional sizes, are represented as seen vertically from above. The pollinia, after removal from their cells, undergo nearly the same movements as in the last species. In both forms the movement is well shown by removing a pollinium by the thick end with a pair of pincers, and holding it under the microscope, when the plane of the viscid disc will be seen to move through an angle of at least forty-five degrees. The caudicles of the Lesser Butterfly Orchis are relatively very much shorter than in the other species; the little

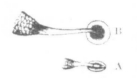

Fig. 12   B. Disc and caudicle of *H. chlorantha*, seen from above, with the drum-like pedicel foreshortened A. Disc and caudicle of *H. bifolia*, seen from above

packets of pollen are shorter, whiter, and, in a mature flower, separate much more readily from one another. Lastly, the stigmatic surface is differently shaped, being more plainly tripartite, with two lateral prominences, situated beneath the viscid discs. These prominences contract the mouth of the nectary, making it subquadrangular. Hence I cannot doubt that the Larger and Lesser Butterfly orchids are distinct species, masked by close external similarity.[14]

[14] According to Dr H. Müller, *Habenaria* or *Platanthera bifolia* of English authors is the *P. solstitialis* of Boenninghausen; and he fully agrees with me that it must be ranked as specifically distinct from *P. chlorantha*. Dr Müller states that this latter species is connected by a series of gradations with another form which in Germany is called *P. bifolia*. He gives a very full and interesting account of the variability of these

As soon as I had examined the present species, / I felt convinced, from the position of the viscid discs, that it would be fertilized in a different manner from the Larger Butterfly Orchis; and now, owing to the kindness of Mr F. Bond, I have examined two moths, namely, *Agrotis segetum* and *Anaitis plagiata*, one with three pollinia, and the other with five pollinia, attached, not to the eyes and side of the face as in the last species, but to the base of the proboscis. I may remark that the pollinia of these two species of Habenaria, when attached to moths, can be distinguished at a glance.

Professor Asa Gray has described[15] the structure of no less than ten American species of *Platanthera*. Most of them resemble in their manner of fertilization the two British species; but some of the species, in which the viscid discs do not stand far apart, have curious contrivances, such as a channelled labellum, lateral shields, etc., compelling moths to insert their proboscides directly in front. *P. hookeri*, on the other hand, differs in a very interesting manner: the two viscid discs stand widely separated from each other; consequently a moth, unless of gigantic size, would be able to suck the copious nectar without touching either disc; but this risk is avoided in the following manner: the central line of the stigma is prominent, and the labellum, instead of hanging down, as in most of the other species, is curved upwards, so that the front of the flower is made somewhat tubular and is divided into halves. Thus a moth is compelled to go to the one or other side, and its face will almost certainly be brought into contact with one of the discs. The drum of the pollinium, when removed, contracts in the same manner as I have described under *P. chlorantha*. / Professor Gray has seen a butterfly (Nisoniades) from Canada with a pollinium of this species attached to each eye. In the case of *P. flava*, moths are compelled in a different manner to enter the nectary on one side. A narrow but strong protuberance, rising from the base of the labellum, projects upwards and backwards, so as almost to touch the column; thus the moth, being forced to go to either side, is almost sure to withdraw one of the viscid discs. *P. hyperborea* and *dilatata* have been regarded by some botanists as varieties of the same species; and

---

three forms of *Platanthera*, and of their structure in relation to their manner of fertilization: *Verhandl. d. Nat. Verein. f. Pr. Rh. u. Westfal*, Jahrg. xxv, III. Folge, v. Bd. pp. 36–8.

[15] *American Journal of Science*, vol. xxxiv, 1862, pp. 143, 259, and 424, and vol. xxxvi, 1863, p. 292.

Professor Asa Gray says that he was formerly tempted to come to the same conclusion; but on closer examination he finds, besides other characters, a remarkable physiological difference, namely, that *P. dilatata*, like its congeners, requires insect aid and cannot fertilize itself; whilst in *P. hyperborea* the pollen-masses commonly fall out of the anther-cells whilst the flower is very young or in bud, and thus the stigma is self-fertilized. Nevertheless, the various structures adapted for crossing are still present.[16]

The genus Bonatea is closely allied to Habenaria, and includes plants having an extraordinary structure. *Bonatea speciosa* is an inhabitant of the Cape of Good Hope, and has been carefully described by Mr Trimen;[17] but it is impossible to explain its structure without drawings. It is remarkable from the manner in which the two stigmatic surfaces, as well as the two viscid discs, project far out in front of the flower, and from the complex nature of the labellum, which consists of seven, or probably of nine distinct parts all fused / together. As in *Platanthera flava*, there is a process at the base of the labellum which compels moths to enter the flower on either side. The nectary, according to Mr Trimen and Mr J. Mansel Weale, does not contain free nectar; but the latter author believes that the tissue of which it is composed tastes sweet, so that moths probably penetrate it for the sake of the intercellular fluid. The pollinia are of astonishing length, and when removed from their cases hang down merely from the weight of the pollen-masses, and if attached to the head of an insect would be in a proper position for adhering to the stigma. Mr Weale has likewise described some other South African species of Bonatea.[18] These differ from *B. speciosa* in having their nectaries full of nectar. He found a small butterfly, *Pyrgus elmo*, 'perfectly embarrassed by the number of pollinia of this Bonatea attached to its sternum'. But he does not specify whether the sternum was naked or covered with scales.

The South African genera Disa and Disperis are placed by Lindley in two subtribes of the Ophreae. The superb flowers of *Disa grandiflora* have been described and figured by Mr Trimen.[19] The posterior sepal,

[16] Mr J. Mansel Weale has described (*Journ. Lin. Soc. Bot.*, vol. xiii, 1871, p. 47) the method of fertilization of two South African species of Habenaria: one of these is remarkable from the pollinia not undergoing any movement or change of position when removed from their cases.

[17] *Journ. Linn. Soc. Bot.*, vol. ix, 1865, p. 156.

[18] *Journ. Linn. Soc. Bot.*, vol. x, p. 470.

[19] *Journ. Linn. Soc. Bot.*, vol. vii, 1863, p. 144.

instead of the labellum, is developed into a large nectary. In order that insects may reach the copiously stored nectar, they must insert their proboscides on either side of the column; and in accordance with this fact the viscid discs are turned outwards in an extraordinary manner. The pollinia are crooked, and when removed bend downwards from their own weight, so that no movement is necessary for placing themselves in a proper position. Considering the large supply of / nectar and that the flowers are very conspicuous, it is remarkable that they are rarely visited by insects. Mr Trimen wrote to me in 1864 that he had lately examined seventy-eight flowers, and only twelve of these had one or both pollinia removed by insects, and only five had pollen on their stigmas. He does not know what insects occasionally fertilize the flowers; but Mrs Barber has more than once seen a large fly, allied to Bombylius, with the pollinia of *Disa polygnoides* attached to the base of its proboscis. Mr Weale states[20] that *D. macrantha* differs from *D. grandiflora* and *cornuta* in producing plenty of seed, and is remarkable from often fertilizing itself. This follows from 'a very slight jerk, when the flower is fully expanded, sufficing to eject the pollinia from their widely open anther-cases, and to bring them into contact with the stigma. This in nature is not unseldom the case, as I have repeatedly found many flowers thus fertilized.' He has, however, no doubt that the flowers are likewise cross-fertilized by nocturnal insects. He adds that *D. grandiflora* in being so seldom fertilized by insects offers a case like that of *Ophrys muscifera*; whilst *D. macrantha* in being often self-fertilized closely corresponds with *Ophrys apifera*; but this latter species seems to be invariably self-fertilized.

Lastly, Mr Weale has described,[21] as far as he could make out, the manner in which a species of Disperis is fertilized by the aid of insects. It deserves notice that the labellum and two lateral sepals of this plant secrete nectar.

We have now finished with the Ophreae; but before passing on to the following tribes, I will recapitulate / the chief facts with respect to the movements of the pollinia, all due to the nicely regulated contraction of that small portion of membrane (together with the pedicel in the case of Habenaria) lying between the layer or ball of adhesive matter and the extremity of the caudicle. In a few cases, however, as with some of the species of Disa and Bonatea, the caudicles when removed

[20] *Journ. Linn. Soc. Bot.*, vol. xiii, 1871, p. 45.
[21] *Journ. Linn. Soc. Bot.*, vol. xiii, 1871, p. 42.

from their cells do not undergo any movement; the weight of the pollen-masses sufficing to depress them into a proper position. In most of the species of Orchis the stigma lies directly beneath the anther-cells, and the pollinia simply move vertically downwards. In *Orchis pyramidalis* there are two lateral and inferior stigmas, and the pollinia move downwards and outwards, diverging to the proper angle, so as to strike the two lateral stigmas. In Gymnadenia the pollinia move only downwards, but they are adapted for striking the lateral stigmas, by being attached to the upper lateral surfaces of the proboscides of Lepidoptera. In Nigritella they move upwards, but this depends merely on their being always affixed to the lower side of the proboscis. In Habenaria the stigmatic surface lies beneath and between the two widely separated anther-cells, and the pollinia here converge, instead of diverging as in *Orchis pyramidalis*, and likewise move downwards. A poet might imagine that whilst the pollinia were borne through the air from flower to flower, adhering to an insect's body, they voluntarily and eagerly placed themselves in that exact position, in which alone they could hope to gain their wish and perpetuate their race. /

CHAPTER III

ARETHUSEAE

Cephalanthera grandiflora; rostellum aborted; early penetration of the pollen-tubes; case of imperfect self-fertilization; cross-fertilization effected by insects which gnaw the labellum – *Cephalanthera ensifolia* – Pogonia – Pterostylis and other Australian orchids with the labellum sensitive to a touch – Vanilla – Sobralia.

Cephalanthera grandiflora. This orchid is remarkable from not possessing a rostellum, which is so eminently characteristic of the order. The stigma is large, and the anther stands above it. The pollen is extremely friable and readily adheres to any object. The grains are tied together by a few weak elastic threads; but they are not cemented together, so as to form compound pollen-grains, as in almost all other orchids.[1] In this latter character and in the complete abortion of the rostellum we have evidence of degradation; and Cephalanthera appears to me like a degraded Epipactis, a member of the Neotteae, to be described in the next chapter.

The anther opens whilst the flower is in bud and partly expels the pollen, which stands in two nearly free upright pillars, each nearly divided longitudinally into halves. These subdivided pillars rest against or even overhang the upper square edge of the stigma, which rises to about one-third of their height (see front / view B, and side view C, in fig. 13). Whilst the flower is still in bud, the pollen-grains which rest against the upper sharp edge of the stigma (but not those in the upper or lower parts of the mass) emit a multitude of tubes; and these deeply penetrate the stigmatic tissue. After this period the stigma bends a little forward, and the result is that the two friable pillars of pollen are drawn a little forward and stand almost completely free / from the anther-cells, being tied to the edge of the stigma and supported by the penetration of the pollen-tubes. Without this support the pillars would soon fall down.

[1] This separation of the grains was observed, and is represented, by Bauer in the plate published by Lindley in his magnificent *Illustrations of Orchidaceous Plants*.

The flower stands upright, with the lower part of the labellum turned up parallel to the column (fig. A). The tips of the lateral petals never become separated;[2] so that the pillars of pollen are protected from the wind, and as the flower stands upright they do not fall down

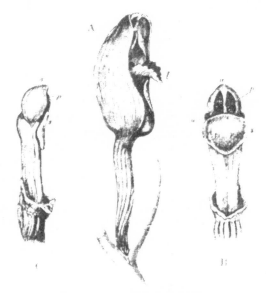

Fig. 13   *Cephalanthera grandiflora*

a. anther; in the front view, B, the two cells with the included pollen are seen, o. one of the two lateral rudimentary anthers, or auricles, p. masses of pollen, s. stigma, l. distal portion of the labellum
A. Oblique view of perfect flower, when fully expanded
B. Front view of column, with all the petals and sepals removed
C. Side view of column, with all the sepals and petals removed; the narrow pillars of pollen (p) between the anther and stigma can just be seen

from their own weight. These are points of much importance to the plant, as otherwise the pollen would have been blown or fallen down and been wasted. The labellum is formed of two portions; when the flower is mature, the small triangular distal portion turns down at right angles to the basal portion; and thus offers a small landing-place for insects in front of the triangular entrance, situated halfway up the almost tubular flower. After a short time, as soon as the flower is fully

[2] Bauer figures the flowers much more widely expanded than is here represented: all that I can say is that I have not seen them in this condition.

fertilized, the small distal portion of the labellum rises up, shuts the triangular door, and again perfectly encloses the organs of fructification.

Although I have often searched for nectar within the cup of the labellum, I have never found even a trace. The terminal portion of the labellum is frosted with globular papillae of an orange colour, and within the cup there are several transversely wrinkled, longitudinal ridges of a darker orange tint. These ridges are often gnawed by some animal, and I have found minute, bitten-off fragments lying within the base of the cup. In the summer of 1862 the flowers were visited less frequently by insects than is usual, as shown by the unbroken state of the pollen-masses; nevertheless, / out of seventeen flowers which were examined one day, five had their ridges gnawed, and on the next day, seven out of nine other flowers were in this state. As there was no appearance of slime, I do not believe that they had been attacked by slugs; but whether they had been gnawed by winged insects, which alone would be effectual for cross-fertilization, I know not. The ridges had a taste like that of the labellum of certain Vandeae, in which tribe (as we shall hereafter see) this part of the flower is often gnawed by insects. Cephalanthera is the only British orchid, as far as I have observed, which attracts insects, by thus offering to them solid food.

The early penetration of the stigma by a multitude of pollen-tubes, which were traced far down the stigmatic tissue, apparently gives us another case, like that of the Bee Ophrys, of perpetual self-fertilization. I was much surprised at this fact, and asked myself: Why does the distal portion of the labellum open for a short period? What is the use of the great mass of pollen above and below that layer of grains, the tubes of which alone penetrate the upper edge of the stigma? The stigma has a large flat viscid surface; and during several years I have almost invariably found masses of pollen adhering to its surface, and the friable pillars by some means broken down. It occurred to me that, although the flowers stand upright, and the pillars are well protected from the wind, yet that the pollen-masses might ultimately topple over from their own weight, and so fall on the stigma, thus completing the act of self-fertilization. Accordingly, I covered with a net a plant having four buds, and examined the flowers as soon as they had withered; the broad stigmas of three of them were perfectly free from pollen, but a little had fallen on one corner of the fourth. With the exception of / the summit of one pillar in this latter flower, all the other pillars still stood upright and unbroken. I looked at the flowers of some surrounding plants, and everywhere found, as I had so often done before, broken-down pillars and masses of pollen on the stigmas.

From the usual state of the pillars of pollen, as well as from the gnawed condition of the ridges on the labellum, it may be safely inferred that insects of some kind visit the flowers, disturb the pollen, and leave masses of it on the stigmas. We thus see that the turning down of the distal portion of the labellum, by which a temporary landing-place and an open door are afforded – the upturned labellum, by which the flower is made tubular so that insects are compelled to crawl close by the stigmatic surface – the pollen readily cohering to any object, and standing in friable pillars protected from the wind – and, lastly, the large masses of pollen above and below that layer of grains, the tubes of which alone penetrate the edge of the stigma – are all co-ordinated structures, far from useless; and they would be quite useless if these flowers were always self-fertilized.

To ascertain how far the early penetration of the upper edge of the stigma by the tubes of those grains which rest on it, is effectual for fertilization, I covered up a plant, just before the flowers opened, and removed the thin net as soon as they had begun to wither. From long experience I am sure that this temporary covering could not have injured their fertility. The four covered flowers produced seed-capsules as fine in appearance as those on any of the surrounding plants. When ripe, I gathered them, and likewise capsules from several of the surrounding plants, growing under similar conditions, and weighed the seed in a chemical balance. The seeds from the four capsules on the / uncovered plants weighed 1·5 grain; whilst those from an equal number of capsules on the covered plant weighed under 1 grain; but this does not give a fair idea of the relative difference of their fertility, for I observed that a great number of the seeds from the covered plant consisted of minute and shrivelled husks. Accordingly I mixed the seeds well together, and took four little lots from one heap and four little lots from the other heap, and, having soaked them in water, compared them under the microscope: out of forty seeds from the uncovered plants there were only four bad ones, whereas out of forty seeds from the covered-up plants there were at least twenty-seven bad; so that there were nearly seven times as many bad seeds from the covered plants, as from those left free to the access of insects.

We may therefore conclude that this orchid is constantly self-fertilized, although in a very imperfect manner; but this would be

59

highly useful to the plant, if insects failed to visit the flowers. The penetration of the pollen-tubes, however, is apparently even more serviceable by retaining the pillars of pollen in their proper places, so that insects, in crawling into the flowers, may get dusted with pollen. Self-fertilization also may, perhaps, be aided by insects, carrying pollen from the same flower on to the stigma; but an insect thus smeared with pollen could hardly fail likewise to cross the flowers on other plants. From the relative position of the parts, it seems indeed probable (but I omitted to prove this by the early removal of the anthers, so as to observe whether pollen was brought to the stigma from other flowers) that an insect would more frequently get dusted by crawling out of a flower than by crawling into one; and this would of course facilitate a cross between distinct individuals. Hence / Cephalanthera offers only a partial exception to the rule that the flowers of orchids are generally fertilized by pollen from another plant.

Cephalanthera ensifolia. According to Delpino,[3] the flowers of this species are visited by insects, as shown by the removal of the pollen-masses. He believes that this is effected by their bodies being first rendered sticky by means of the stigmatic secretion. It is not clear whether the flowers also fertilize themselves. Each pollen-mass is divided into two, instead of being merely subdivided, so that there are four distinct pollen-masses.

Pogonia ophioglossoides. The flowers of this plant, an inhabitant of the United States, resemble, as described by Mr Scudder,[4] those of Cephalanthera in not having a rostellum, and in the pollen-masses not being furnished with caudicles. The pollen consists of powdery grains not united by threads. Self-fertilization seems to be effectually prevented; and the flowers on distinct plants must intercross, for each plant generally bears only a single flower.

Pterostylis trullifolia and *longifolia.* I may here briefly mention some orchids, inhabitants of Australia and New Zealand, which are included by Lindley in the same family of the Arethuseae with Cephalanthera and Pogonia, and are remarkable from their labella being extremely sensitive or irritable. Two of the petals and one of the sepals form a hood which encloses the column, as may be seen at A in the accompanying figure of *Pterostylis longifolia.*

The distal portion of the labellum affords a landing-place for

---

[3] *Ult. Osservaz. sulla Dicogamia*, part ii, 1875, p. 149.
[4] *Proc. Boston Soc. Nat. Hist.*, vol. ix, 1863, p. 182.

insects, in nearly the same manner as with Cephalanthera; but when this organ is touched it rapidly springs up, carrying with it the touching insect, / which is thus temporarily imprisoned within the otherwise almost completely closed flower. The labellum remains shut

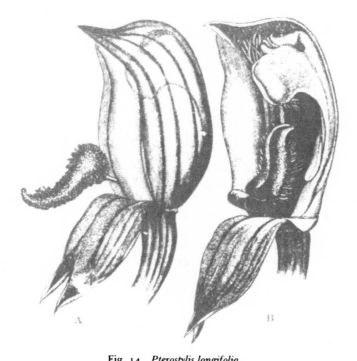

Fig. 14   *Pterostylis longifolia*
(Copied from Mr R. D. Fitzgerald's *Australian Orchids*)
A. Flower in its natural state: the outline of the column is dimly seen within
B. Flower with the near lateral petal removed, showing the column with its two
   shields, and the labellum in the position which it occupies after having been
   touched

from half an hour to one hour and a half, and on reopening is again sensitive to a touch. Two membranous shields project on each side of the / upper part of the column, with their edges meeting in front, as may be seen in fig. B. In this drawing the petal on the near side has been cut away, and the labellum is represented in the position which it assumes after having been touched. As soon as the labellum has thus risen, an imprisoned insect cannot escape except by crawling through the narrow passage formed by the two projecting shields. In thus escaping it can hardly fail to remove the pollinia, as, before coming into contact with them, its body will have been smeared with the viscid matter of the rostellum. On being imprisoned in another flower, and on again escaping by the same passage, it will almost certainly leave at least one of the four pollen-masses on the adhesive stigma, and thus fertilize the flower.

All that I have here said is taken from the admirable description given by Mr Cheeseman[5] of *Pterostylis trullifolia*; but I have copied the figure of *P. longifolia* from Mr Fitzgerald's great work on the Australian orchids, as it shows plainly the relation of all the parts.

Mr Cheeseman placed insects within several flowers of *P. trullifolia*, and saw them afterwards crawl out, generally with pollinia attached to their backs. He also proved the importance of the irritable labellum by removing it from twelve flowers whilst young, and in this case insects which entered the flowers would not have been compelled to crawl out through the passage; and not one of these flowers produced a capsule. The flowers seem to be frequented exclusively by Diptera; but what attraction they present is not known, as they do not secrete nectar. Mr Cheeseman believes that hardly a quarter of the flowers produce capsules; notwithstanding that on one occasion he examined 110 / flowers in a withered condition, and seventy-one of these had pollen on their stigmas, and only twenty-eight had all four pollinia still within their anthers. All the New Zealand species bear solitary flowers, so that distinct plants cannot fail to be intercrossed. I may add that Mr Fitzgerald also placed a small beetle on the labellum of *P. longifolia*, which was instantly carried into the flower and imprisoned; afterwards he saw it crawl out with two pollinia attached to its back. Nevertheless he doubts, from reasons which seem to me quite insufficient, whether the sensitiveness of the labellum is not as great a disadvantage as an advantage to the plant.

Mr Fitzgerald has described another orchid belonging to the same subtribe, *Caladenia dimorpha*, which has an irritable labellum. He kept a plant in his room, and says: 'A house-fly lighting on the lip was carried by its spring against the column, and becoming entangled in the gluten of the stigma, and struggling to escape, removed the pollen from the anther and smeared it on the stigma.' He adds, 'Without some such aid the species of this genus never produce seed.' But from

[5] *Transact. New Zealand Institute*, vol. v, 1873, p. 352; and vol. vii, p. 351.

the analogy of other orchids we may feel sure that insects usually behave very differently from the fly which he saw caught on the stigma, and no doubt they carry the pollen-masses from plant to plant. The labellum of another Australian genus, Calaena, one of the Arethuseae, is said by Dr Hooker[6] to be irritable; so that when touched by an insect it shuts up suddenly against the column, and temporarily encloses its prey as it were within a box. The labellum is covered by curious papillae, which, as far as Mr Fiztgerald has seen, are not gnawed by insects. /

Mr Fitzgerald describes and figures several other genera, and states with respect to *Acianthus fornicatus* and *exsertus* that neither species produce seeds if protected from insects, but are easily fertilized by pollen placed on their stigmas. Mr Cheeseman[7] has witnessed the fertilization of *Acianthus sinclairii* in New Zealand, the flowers of which are incessantly visited by Diptera, without whose aid the pollinia are never removed. Out of eighty-seven flowers borne by fourteen plants, no less than seventy-one matured capsules. This plant according to the same observer exhibits one remarkable peculiarity, namely, that the pollen-masses are attached to the rostellum by means of the exserted pollen-tubes, which serve as a caudicle; and the pollen-masses are thus removed together with the rostellum, which is viscid, when the flowers are visited by insects. The flowers of the allied Cyrtostylis are also much frequented by insects, but the pollinia are not so regularly removed as those of the Acianthus; and with Corysanthes, only five out of 200 flowers produced capsules.

The *Vanillidae* according to Lindley form a subtribe of the Arethuseae. The large tubular flowers of *Vanilla aromatica* are manifestly adapted to be fertilized by insects; and it is known that when this plant is cultivated in foreign countries, for instance in Bourbon, Tahiti, and the East Indies, it fails to produce its aromatic pods unless artificially fertilized. This fact shows that some insect in its American home is specially adapted for the work; and that the insects of the above-named tropical regions, where the Vanilla flourishes, either do not visit the flowers, though they secrete an abundance of nectar, or do not visit them / in the proper manner.[8] I will mention

---

[6] *Flora of Tasmania*, vol. ii, p. 17.

[7] *Transact. New Zealand Insitute*, vol. vii, 1875, p. 349.

[8] For Bourbon see *Bul. Soc. Bot. de France*, vol. i, 1854, p. 290. For Tahiti see H. A. Tilley, *Japan, the Amour, etc.*, 1861, p. 375. For the East Indies see Morren in *Annals and Mag. of Nat. Hist.*, 1839, vol. iii, p. 6. I may give an analogous but more striking

only two peculiarities in the structure of the flowers: the anterior part of the pollen-masses is semi-waxy and the posterior part somewhat friable; the grains are not cemented together into compound grains, and the single grains are not united by fine elastic threads but by viscid matter; this matter would aid in causing the pollen to adhere to an insect, but I should have thought that such aid was superfluous, as the viscid rostellum is well developed. The other peculiarity is that the labellum, in front of the stigma, and some way beneath it, is furnished with a stiff hinged brush, formed of a series of combs one over the other, which point downwards. This structure would allow an insect to crawl easily into a flower, but would compel it whilst retreating to press close against the column; and in doing so it would remove the pollen-masses, leaving them on the stigma of the next flower which was visited.

The genus Sobralia is allied to Vanilla, and Mr Cavendish Browne informs me that he saw a large humble-bee enter a flower of S. *macrantha* in his hothouse, and when it crawled out it had the two large pollen-masses firmly fixed to its back, nearer to the tail than to the head. The bee then looked about, and seeing no other flower re-entered the same one of / the Sobralia, but quickly retreated, leaving the pollen-masses on the stigma, with the viscid discs alone adhering to its back. The nectar of this Guatemala orchid seemed too powerful for our British bee, for it stretched out its legs and lay for a time as if dead on the labellum, but afterwards recovered. /

---

case from Mr Fitzgerald, who says 'that *Sarcochilus parviflorus* (one of the Vandeae) produces capsules not unfrequently in the Blue Mountains of New South Wales; removed from thence to Sydney, a number of plants, though flowering well, have not borne any seed if left to themselves, though invariably fertile when the pollen-masses were removed and placed on the stigma'. Yet the Blue Mountains are less than one hundred miles distant from Sydney.

CHAPTER IV

NEOTTEAE

Epipactis palustris; curious shape of the labellum and its importance in the fructification of the flower – Other species of Epipactis – Epipogium – *Goodyera repens* – *Spiranthes autumnalis*; perfect adaptation by which the pollen of a younger flower is carried to the stigma of an older flower on another plant – *Listera ovata*; sensitiveness of the rostellum; explosion of viscid matter; action of insects; perfect adaptation of the several organs – *Listera cordata* – *Neottia nidus-avis*; its fertilization effected in the same manner as in Listera – Thelymitra, self-fertile.

We have now arrived at a third tribe, the Neotteae of Lindley, which includes several British genera. These present many interesting points with respect to their structure and manner of fertilization.

The Neotteae have a free anther standing behind the stigma. Their pollen-grains are tied together by fine elastic threads, which partially cohere and project at the *upper* end of the pollen-mass, being there attached (with some exceptions) to the back of the rostellum. Consequently the pollen-masses have no true and distinct caudicles. In one genus alone (Goodyera) the pollen-grains are collected into packets as in Orchis. Epipactis and Goodyera agree pretty closely in their manner of fertilization with the Ophreae, but are more simply organized. Spiranthes comes under the same category, but has been differently modified in some respects.

Epipactis palustris.[1] The lower part of the large / stigma is bilobed and projects in front of the column (see *s* in the side and front views, C, D, fig. 15). On its square summit a single, nearly globular rostellum is seated. The anterior face of the rostellum (*r*, C, D) projects a little beyond the surface of the upper part of the stigma, and this is of importance. In the early bud the rostellum consists of a friable mass of cells, with the exterior surface rough: these superficial cells undergo a great change during development, and become converted into a soft,

---

[1] I am much indebted to Mr A. G. More, of Bembridge, in the Isle of Wight, for repeatedly sending me fresh specimens of this beautiful Orchis.

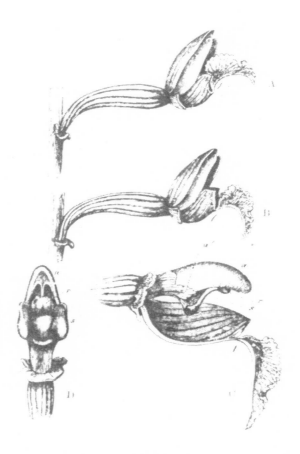

Fig. 15   *Epipactis palustris*

a. anther, with the two open cells seen in the front view D, *a'*. rudimentary anther, or auricle, referred to in a future chapter, *r*. rostellum, *s*. stigma, *l*. labellum

A. Side view of flower, with the lower sepals removed, in its natural position

B. Side view of flower, with the distal portion of the labellum depressed, as if by the weight of an insect

C. Side view of flower, somewhat enlarged, with all the sepals and petals removed, excepting the labellum, of which the near side has been cut away; the massive anther is seen to be of large size

D. Front view of column, somewhat enlarged, with all the sepals and petals removed: the rostellum has sunk down a little in the specimen figured, and ought to have stood higher, so as to hide more of the anther-cells

smooth, highly elastic membrane or tissue, so excessively tender that it can be penetrated by a human hair; when thus penetrated, or when slightly rubbed, the surface becomes milky and in some degree viscid, so that the pollen-grains adhere to it. In some cases, though I observed this more plainly in *Epipactis latifolia*, the surface of the rostellum apparently becomes milky and viscid without having been touched. This exterior soft elastic membrane forms a cap to the rostellum, and is internally lined with a layer of much more adhesive matter, which, when exposed to the air, dries in from five to ten minutes. By a slight upward and backward push with any object, the whole cap, with its viscid lining, is removed with the greatest ease; a minute square stump, the basis of the rostellum, being alone left on the summit of the stigma.

In the bud-state the anther stands quite free behind the rostellum and stigma; it opens longitudinally whilst the flower is still unexpanded, and exposes the two oval pollen-masses, which now lie loose in their cells. The pollen consists of spherical granules, cohering in fours, but not affecting each other's shapes: and these compound grains are tied together by fine elastic threads. The threads are collected into bundles extending longitudinally along the middle line of the / front of each pollinium, where it comes into contact with the back of the uppermost part of the rostellum. From the number of these threads this middle line looks brown, and each pollen-mass here shows a tendency to divide longitudinally into halves. In all these respects there is a close general resemblance to the pollinia of the Ophreae.

The line where the parallel threads are the most numerous is the line of greatest strength; elsewhere the pollen-masses are extremely friable, so that large portions can easily be broken off. In the bud-state the rostellum is curved a little backwards, and is pressed against the recently-opened anther; and the above-mentioned slightly projecting bundles of threads become firmly attached to the posterior flap of the membranous cap of the rostellum. The point of attachment lies a little beneath the summit of the pollen-masses; but the exact point is somewhat variable, for I have met with specimens in which the attachment was one-fifth of the length of the pollen-masses from their summits. This variability is so far interesting, as it is a step leading to the structure of the Ophreae, in which the confluent threads, or caudicles, always spring from the lower ends of the pollen-masses. After the pollinia are firmly attached by their threads to the back of the rostellum, the rostellum bends a little forwards, and this partly draws the pollinia out of the anther-cells. The upper end of the anther

67

consists of a blunt, solid point, not including pollen; this blunt point projects slightly beyond the face of the rostellum, which circumstance, as we shall see, is important.

The flowers stand out (fig. A) almost horizontally from the stem. The labellum is curiously shaped, as may be seen in the drawings: the distal half, which projects beyond the other petals and forms an excellent / landing-place for insects, is joined to the basal half by a narrow hinge, and naturally (fig. A) is turned a little upwards, so that its edges pass within the edges of the basal portion. So flexible and elastic is the hinge that the weight of even a fly, as Mr More informs me, depresses the distal portion; it is represented in fig. B in this state; but when the weight is removed it instantly springs up to its former position (fig. A), and with its curious medial ridges partly closes the entrance into the flower. The basal portion of the labellum forms a cup, which at the proper time is filled with nectar.

Now let us see how all the parts, which I have been obliged to describe in detail, act. When I first examined these flowers I was much perplexed: trying in the same manner as I should have done with a true Orchis, I slightly pushed the protuberant rostellum downwards, and it was easily ruptured; some of the viscid matter was withdrawn, but the pollinia remained in their cells. Reflecting on the structure of the flower, it occurred to me that an insect in entering one in order to suck the nectar, would depress the distal portion of the labellum, and consequently would not touch the rostellum; but that, when within the flower, it would be almost compelled, from the springing up of this distal half of the labellum, to rise a little upwards and back out parallel to the stigma. I then brushed the rostellum lightly upwards and backwards with the end of a feather and other such objects; and it was pretty to see how easily the membranous cap of the rostellum came off, and how well from its elasticity it fitted any object, whatever its shape might be, and how firmly it clung to the object owing to the viscidity of its under surface. Large masses of pollen, adhering by the elastic threads to the cap of the rostellum were at the same time withdrawn. /

Nevertheless the pollen-masses were not removed nearly so cleanly as those which had been naturally removed by insects. I tried dozens of flowers, always with the same imperfect result. It then occurred to me, that an insect in backing out of the flower would naturally push with some part of its body against the blunt and projecting upper end of the anther, which overhangs the stigmatic surface. Accordingly I so held a brush that, whilst brushing upwards against the rostellum, I pushed against the blunt solid end of the anther (see fig. C); this at once eased the pollinia, and they were withdrawn in an entire state. At last I understood the mechanism of the flower.

The large anther stands above and behind the stigma, forming an angle with it (fig. C), so that the pollinia when withdrawn by an insect would adhere to its head or body in a position fitted to strike the sloping stigmatic surface as soon as another flower was visited. Hence we have not here, or in any of the Neotteae, that movement of depression so common with the pollinia of the Ophreae. When an insect with the pollinia attached to its back or head enters another flower, the easy depression of the distal portion of the labellum probably plays an important part; for the pollen-masses are extremely friable, and if they were struck against the tips of the petals much of the pollen would be lost; but as it is, an open gangway is offered, and the viscid stigma, with its lower protuberant part lying in front, is the first object against which the pollen-masses projecting forwards from the insect's head or back would naturally strike. I may add that in one large lot of flower-spikes, a great majority of the pollinia had been naturally and cleanly removed.

In order to ascertain whether I was right in believing / that the distal hinged portion of the labellum was of importance in the fertilization of the flowers, I asked Mr More to remove this part from some young flowers, and to mark them. He tried the experiment on eleven flowers, three of which did not produce seed-capsules; but this may have been accidental. Of the eight capsules which were produced, two contained about as many seeds as those from unmutilated flowers on the same plant; but six capsules contained much fewer seeds. Most of the seeds were well-formed. These experiments, as far as they go, support the view that the distal part of the labellum is of importance in causing insects to enter and leave the flowers in the best manner for their fertilization.

Since the appearance of the first edition of this book, my son William has observed for me this Epipactis in the Isle of Wight. Hive-bees seem to be the chief agents in fertilization; for he saw them visit about a score of flowers, and many had pollen-masses attached to their foreheads, just above the mandibles. I had supposed that insects always crawled into the flowers; but hive-bees are too large to do this; they always clung, whilst sucking the nectar, to the distal and hinged half of the labellum, which was thus pressed downwards. Owing to this part being elastic and tending to spring up, the bees, as they left the flowers, seemed to fly rather upwards; and this favoured, in the manner previously explained, the complete withdrawal of the pollen-masses, quite as well as if the insects had crawled, in an upward direction, out of the flower. Perhaps the upward movement may not be so necessary in all cases as I had supposed; for, judging from the manner in which the pollen-masses were attached to the hive-bees, the back part of their heads could hardly fail to press against and lift up the / blunt, solid, upper end of the anther, thus freeing the pollen-masses. Various other insects besides hive-bees visit the flowers. My son saw several large flies (*Sarcophaga carnosa*) haunting them; but they did not enter in so neat and regular a manner as the hive-bees; nevertheless two had pollen-masses attached to their foreheads. Several smaller flies (*Coelopa frigida*) were also seen entering and leaving the flowers, with pollen-masses adhering rather irregularly to the dorsal surface of the thorax. Three or four distinct kinds of Hymenoptera (one of small size being *Crabro brevis*) likewise visited the flowers; and three of these Hymenoptera had pollen-masses attached to their backs. Other still more minute Diptera, Coleoptera, and ants were seen sucking the nectar; but these insects appeared to be too small to transport the pollen-masses. It is remarkable that some of the foregoing insects should visit the flowers; for Mr F. Walker informs me that the Sarcophaga frequents decaying animal matter, and the Coelopa haunts seaweed, occasionally settling on flowers. The Crabro also, as I hear from Mr F. Smith, collects small beetles (Halticae) for provisioning its nest. It is equally remarkable, seeing how many kinds of insects visit this Epipactis, that although my son watched hundreds of plants for some hours on three occasions, not a single humble-bee alighted on a flower, though many were flying about.

Epipactis latifolia. This species agrees with the last in most respects. The rostellum, however, projects considerably further beyond the face of the stigma, and the blunt upper end of the anther less so. The viscid matter lining the elastic cap of the rostellum takes a longer time to get dry. The upper petals and sepals are more widely expanded than in *E. palustris*: the distal portion of the labellum is smaller, and is / firmly united to the basal portion (fig. 16), so that it is not flexible and elastic; it apparently serves only as a landing-place for insects. The fertilization of this species depends simply on an insect striking in an upward and backward direction the highly protuberant rostellum, which it would be apt to do when retreating from the flower after having sucked the copious nectar in the cup of the labellum. Apparently it is not at all necessary that the insect should push upwards the blunt upper end of the anther; at least I found that the pollinia could be removed easily by simply dragging off the cap of the rostellum in an upward or backward direction.

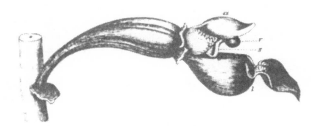

Fig. 16   *Epipactis latifolia*
Flower viewed sideways, with all the sepals and petals removed, except the labellum
a. anther, *r.* rostellum, *s.* stigma, *l.* labellum

As some plants grew close to my house, I have been able to observe here and elsewhere their manner of fertilization during several years. Although hive-bees and humble-bees of many kinds were constantly flying over the plants, I never saw a bee or any dipterous insect visit the flowers; but in Germany Sprengel caught a fly with the pollinia of this plant attached to its back. On the other hand I have repeatedly / observed the common wasp (*Vespa sylvestris*) sucking the nectar out of the open cup-shaped labellum. I thus saw the act of fertilization effected by the pollen-masses being removed by the wasps, and afterwards carried attached to their foreheads to other flowers. Mr Oxenden also informs me that a large bed of *E. purpurata* (which is considered by some botanists to be a distinct species, and by others a variety) was frequented by 'swarms of wasps'. It is very remarkable that the sweet nectar of this Epipactis should not be attractive to any kind of bee. If wasps were to become extinct in any district, so probably would the *Epipactis latifolia*.

To show how effectually the flowers are fertilized, I may add that during the wet and cold season of 1860 a friend in Sussex examined five spikes bearing eighty-five expanded flowers; of these, fifty-three had the pollinia removed, and thirty-two had them in place: but as many of the latter were immediately beneath the buds, a larger

71

number would almost certainly have been afterwards removed. In Devonshire I found a spike with nine open flowers, and the pollinia in all were removed with one exception, and in this case a fly, too small to remove the pollinia, had become glued to the rostellum, and had there miserably perished.

Dr H. Müller has published[2] some interesting observations on the difference in structure and manner of fertilization, as well as on the intermediate forms between *Epipactis rubiginosa, microphylla,* and *viridiflora.* The latter species is remarkable for the absence of a rostellum, and for being regularly self-fertilized. Self-fertilization here follows from the incoherent pollen-grains in the lower part of the pollen-masses / emitting, whilst still within the anther-cells, their tubes, which penetrate the stigma; and this occurs even in the bud. This species, however, is probably visited by insects, and occasionally crossed; for the labellum contains nectar. *E. microphylla* is intermediate in structure between *E. latifolia,* which is always fertilized by the aid of insects, and *E. viridiflora,* which does not necessarily require any such aid. The whole of this memoir by Dr H. Müller deserves to be attentively studied.

Epipogium gmelini. This plant, which has only once been found in Great Britain, has been fully described by Dr Rohrbach in a special memoir.[3] The structure and manner of fertilization is in many respects like that of Epipactis, to which genus the author believes the present one to be allied, though placed by Lindley among the Arethuseae. Rohrbach saw the flowers visited by *Bombus lucorum,* but it appears that only a few produce capsules.

Goodyera repens.[4] This genus is rather closely related to Epipactis, in most of the characters with which we are concerned. The shield-like rostellum is almost square, and projects beyond the stigma; it is supported on each side by sloping sides rising from the upper edge of the stigma, in nearly the same manner as we shall presently see in Spiranthes. The surface of the protuberant part of the rostellum is rough, and when dry can be seen to be formed of cells; it is delicate, and, when slightly pricked, a little milky viscid fluid exudes; it is lined by a layer of very adhesive matter, which quickly sets hard when

---

[2] *Verhandl. d. Nat. Ver. f. Westfal.,* Jahrg, xxv, III. Folge, v. Bd. pp. 7–36.

[3] *Ueber den Blüthenbau von Epipogium,* 1866; see also Irmisch, *Beiträge zur Biologie der Orchideen,* 1853, p. 55.

[4] Specimens of this rare Highland orchid were kindly sent me by the Rev. G. Gordon of Elgin.

exposed / to the air. The protuberant surface of the rostellum, when gently rubbed upwards, is easily removed, and carries with it a strip of membrane, to the hinder part of which the pollinia are attached. The sloping sides which support the rostellum are not removed at the same time, but remain projecting up like a fork and soon wither. The anther is borne on a broad elongated filament; and a membrane on both sides unites this filament to the edges of the stigma, forming an imperfect cup or clinandrum. The anther-cells open in the bud, and the pollen-masses become attached by their anterior faces, just beneath their summits, to the back of the rostellum. Ultimately the anther opens widely, leaving the pollinia almost naked, but partially protected within the membranous cup or clinandrum. Each pollinium is partially divided lengthways; the pollen-grains cohere in subtriangular packets, including a multitude of compound grains, each consisting of four grains; and these packets are tied together by strong elastic threads, which at their upper ends run together and form a single flattened brown elastic ribbon, of which the truncated extremity adheres to the back of the rostellum.

The surface of the orbicular stigma is remarkably viscid, which is necessary in order that the unusually strong threads connecting the packets of pollen should be ruptured. The labellum is partially divided into two portions; the terminal portion is reflexed, and the basal portion is cup-formed and filled with nectar. The passage between the rostellum and labellum is contracted whilst the flower is young; but when mature the column moves further back from the labellum, so as to allow of insects with the pollinia adhering to their proboscides, to enter the flowers more freely. In many of the specimens received, the pollinia had been / removed, and the fork-shaped supporting sides of the rostellum were partially withered. Mr R. B. Thompson informs me that in the north of Scotland he saw many humble-bees (*Bombus pratorum*) visiting the flowers with pollen-masses attached to their proboscides. This species grows also in the United States; and Professor Asa Gray[5] confirms my account of its structure and manner of fertilization, which is likewise applicable to another and very distinct species, namely, *Goodyera pubescens*.

Goodyera is an interesting connecting link between several very

[5] *Amer. Journal of Science*, vol. xxxiv, 1862, p. 427. I formerly thought that with this plant and Spiranthes, it was the labellum which moved from the column to allow of the more free entrance of insects; but Professor Gray is convinced that it is the column which moves.

distinct forms. In no other member of the Neotteae observed by me is there so near an approach to the formation of a true caudicle;[6] and it is curious that in this genus alone the pollen-grains cohere in large packets, as in the Ophreae. If the nascent caudicles had been attached to the lower ends of the pollinia, and they are attached a little beneath their summits, the pollinia would have been almost identical with those of a true Orchis. In the rostellum being supported by sloping sides, which wither when the viscid disc is removed – in the existence of a membranous cup or clinandrum between the stigma / and anther – and in some other respects, we have a clear affinity with Spiranthes. In the anther having a broad filament we see a relation to Cephalanthera. In the structure of the rostellum, with the exception of the sloping sides, and in the shape of the labellum, Goodyera resembles Epipactis. Goodyera probably shows us the state of the organs in a group of orchids, now mostly extinct, but the parents of many living descendants.

Spiranthes autumnalis. This orchid with its pretty name of Ladies'-tresses, presents some interesting peculiarities.[7] The rostellum is a long, thin, flat projection, joined by sloping shoulders to the summit of the stigma. In the middle of the rostellum a narrow vertical brown object (fig. 17, C) may be seen, bordered and covered by transparent membrane. This brown object I will call 'the boat-formed disc'. It forms the middle portion of the posterior surface of the rostellum, and consists of a narrow strip of the exterior membrane in a modified condition. When removed from its attachment, its summit (fig. E) is seen to be pointed, with the lower end rounded; it is slightly bowed, so as altogether to resemble a boat or canoe. It is rather more than $4/100$ of an inch in length, and less than $1/100$ in breadth. It is nearly rigid, and appears fibrous, but is really formed of elongated and thickened cells, partially confluent.

---

[6] In a foreign species, *Goodyera discolor*, sent me by Mr Bateman, the pollinia approach in structure still more closely those of the Ophreae; for the pollinia extend into long caudicles, resembling in form those of an Orchis. The caudicle is here formed of a bundle of elastic threads, with very small and thin packets of pollen-grains attached to them and arranged like tiles one over the other. The two caudicles are united together near their bases, where they are attached to a disc of membrane lined with viscid matter. From the small size and extreme thinness of the basal packets of pollen, and from the strength of their attachment to the threads, I believe that they are in a functionless condition; if so, these prolongations of the pollinia are true caudicles.

[7] I am indebted to Dr Battersby of Torquay, and to Mr A. G. More of Bembridge, for sending me specimens. I subsequently examined many growing plants.

This boat, standing vertically up on its stern, is filled with thick, milky, extremely adhesive fluid, which, when exposed to the air, rapidly turns brown, and in about one minute sets quite hard. An object is well glued to the boat in four or five seconds, and when the / cement is dry the attachment is wonderfully strong. The transparent sides of the rostellum consist of membrane, attached behind to the edges of the boat, and folded over in front, so as to form the anterior face of the rostellum. This folded membrane, therefore, covers, almost like a deck, the cargo of viscid matter within the boat.

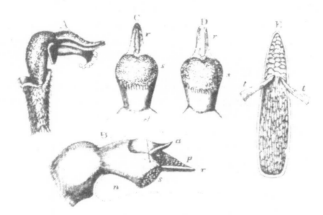

Fig. 17 *Spiranthes autumnalis*, or Ladies'-tresses

a. anther, *p.* pollen-masses, *t.* threads of the pollen-masses, *cl.* margin of clinandrum, *r.* rostellum, *s.* stigma, *n.* nectar receptacle

A. Side view of flower in its natural position, with the two lower sepals alone removed. The labellum can be recognized by its fringed and reflexed lip

B. Side view enlarged of a mature flower, with all the sepals and petals removed. The positions of the labellum and of the upper sepal are shown by the dotted lines

C. Front view of the stigma, and of the rostellum with its embedded, central, boat-formed disc

D. Front view of the stigma and of the rostellum after the disc has been removed

E. Disc, removed from the rostellum, greatly enlarged, viewed posteriorly, with the attached elastic threads of the pollen-masses; the pollen-grains have been removed from the threads

The anterior face of the rostellum is slightly furrowed in a longitudinal line over the middle of the boat, and / is endowed with a remarkable kind of irritability; for, if the furrow be touched very gently by a needle, or if a bristle be laid along the furrow, it instantly splits along its whole length, and a little milky adhesive fluid exudes. This action is not mechanical, or due to simple violence. The fissure runs up the whole length of the rostellum, from the stigma beneath to the summit: at the summit the fissure bifurcates, and runs down the back of the rostellum on each side and round the stern of the boat-formed disc. Hence after this splitting action the boat-formed disc lies quite free, but embedded in a fork in the rostellum. The act of splitting apparently never takes place spontaneously. I covered a plant with a net, and after five of the flowers had fully expanded they were kept protected for a week: I then examined their rostella, and not one had split; whereas almost every flower on the surrounding and uncovered spikes, which would almost certainly have been visited and touched by insects, had their rostella fissured, though they had been open for only twenty-four hours. Exposure for two minutes to the vapour of a little chloroform causes the rostellum to split; and this we shall hereafter see is likewise the case with some other orchids.

When a bristle is laid for two or three seconds in the furrow of the rostellum, and the membrane has consequently become fissured, the viscid matter within the boat-formed disc, which lies close to the surface and indeed slightly exudes, is almost sure to glue the disc longitudinally to the bristle, and both are withdrawn together. When the disc, with the pollinia attached to it, is withdrawn, the two sides of the rostellum (fig. D), which have been described by some botanists as two distinct foliaceous projections, are left sticking up like a fork. This is the common condition / of the flowers after they have been open for a day or two, and have been visited by insects. The fork soon withers.

Whilst the flower is in bud, the back of the boat-formed disc is covered with a layer of large rounded cells, so that the disc does not strictly form the exterior surface of the back of the rostellum. These cells contain slightly viscid matter: they remain unaltered (as may be seen at fig. E) towards the upper end of the disc, but at the point where the pollinia are attached they disappear. Therefore I at one time concluded that the viscid matter contained in these cells, when they burst, serve to fasten the threads of the pollinia to the disc; but, as in several other genera, in which a similar attachment has to be effected, I could see no trace of such cells, this view may be erroneous.

The stigma lies beneath the rostellum, and projects with a sloping surface, as may be seen at B in the side-view: its lower margin is rounded and fringed with hairs. On each side a membrane (cl, B) extends from the edges of the stigma to the filament of the anther, thus forming a membranous cup or clinandrum, in which the lower ends of the pollen-masses lie safely protected.

Each pollinium consists of two leaves of pollen, quite disconnected at their lower and upper ends, but united for about half their length in the middle by elastic threads. A very slight modification would convert the two pollinia into four distinct masses, as occurs in the genus Malaxis and in many foreign orchids. Each leaf consists of a double layer of pollen-grains, joined by fours together, and these united by elastic threads, which are more numerous along the edges of the leaves, and converge at the / summit of the pollinium. The leaves are very brittle, and, when placed on the adhesive stigma, large pieces are easily broken off.

Long before the flower expands, the anther-cells, which are pressed against the back of the rostellum, open in their upper part, so that the included pollinia come into contact with the back of the boat-formed disc. The projecting threads then become firmly attached to rather above the middle part of the back of the disc. The anther-cells afterwards open lower down, and their membranous walls contract and become brown; so that by the time the flower is fully expanded the upper part of the pollinia lie quite naked, with their bases resting in a little cup formed by the withered anther-cell, and laterally protected by the clinandrum. As the pollinia thus lie loose, they are easily removed.

The tubular flowers are elegantly arranged in a spire round the spike, and project from it horizontally (fig. A). The labellum is channelled down the middle, and is furnished with a reflexed and fringed lip, on which bees alight; its basal internal angles are produced into two globular processes, which secrete an abundance of nectar. The nectar is collected (n, fig. B) in a small receptacle in the lower part of the labellum. Owing to the protuberance of the inferior margin of the stigma and of the two lateral inflexed nectaries, the orifice into the nectar-receptacle is much contracted. When the flower first opens the receptacle contains nectar, and at this period the front of the rostellum, which is slightly furrowed, lies close to the channelled labellum; consequently a passage is left, but so narrow that only a fine bristle can be passed down it. In a day or two the column moves a little farther from the labellum, and a wider / passage is left for insects to deposit pollen on the stigmatic surface. On this slight movement of the column the fertilization of the flower absolutely depends.[8]

[8] Professor Asa Gray was so kind as to examine for me *Spiranthes gracilis* and *cernua* in the United States. He found the same general structure as in our *S. autumnalis*, and was struck with the narrowness of the passage into the flower. He

With most orchids the flowers remain open for some time before they are visited by insects; but with Spiranthes I have generally found the boat-formed discs removed very soon after their expansion. For example, in the two last spikes which I happened to examine there were numerous buds on the summit of one, with only the seven lowest flowers expanded, of which six had their discs and pollinia removed; the other spike had eight expanded flowers, and the pollinia of all were removed. We have seen that when the flowers first open they would be attractive to insects, for the receptacle already contains nectar; and at this period the rostellum lies so close to the channelled labellum that a bee could not pass down its proboscis without touching the medial furrow of the rostellum. This I know to be the case by repeated trials with a bristle.

We thus see how beautifully everything is contrived that the pollinia should be withdrawn by insects visiting the flowers. They are already attached to the disc by their threads, and, from the early withering of the anther-cells, they hang loosely suspended but protected within the clinandrum. The touch of the / proboscis causes the rostellum to split in front and behind, and frees the long, narrow, boat-formed disc, which is filled with extremely viscid matter, and is sure to adhere longitudinally to the proboscis. When the bee flies away, so surely will it carry away the pollinia. As the pollinia are attached parallel to the disc, they adhere parallel to the proboscis. When the flower first opens and is best adapted for the removal of the pollinia, the labellum lies so close to the rostellum, that the pollinia attached to the proboscis of an insect cannot possibly be forced into the passage so as to reach the stigma; they would be either upturned or broken off: but we have seen that after two or three days the column becomes more reflexed and moves from the labellum – a wider passage being thus left. When I inserted the pollinia attached to a fine bristle into the nectar-receptacle of a flower in this condition (n, fig. B), it was pretty to see how surely the sheets of pollen were left adhering to the viscid stigma. It may be observed in the diagram, B, that owing to the projection of the stigma, the orifice into the nectar-receptacle (n) lies close to the lower side of

---

has since confirmed (*Amer. Journ. of Science*, vol. xxxiv, p. 427) my account of the structure and action of all the parts in Spiranthes, with the exception that it is the column and not the labellum, as I formerly thought, which moves as the flowers become mature. He adds that the widening of the passage, which plays so important a part in the fertilization of the flower, 'is so striking that we wonder how we overlooked it'.

the flower; insects would therefore insert their proboscides along this lower side, and an open space above is thus left for the attached pollinia to be carried down to the stigma, without being brushed off. The stigma evidently projects so that the ends of the pollinia may strike against it.

Hence, in Spiranthes, a recently expanded flower, which has its pollinia in the best state for removal, cannot be fertilized; and mature flowers will be fertilized by pollen from younger flowers, borne, as we shall presently see, on a separate plant. In conformity with this fact the stigmatic surfaces of the older flowers are far more viscid than those of the / younger flowers. Nevertheless, a flower which in its early state had not been visited by insects would not necessarily, in its later and more expanded condition, have its pollen wasted; for insects, in inserting and withdrawing their proboscides, bow them forwards or upwards, and would thus often strike the furrow in the rostellum. I imitated this action with a bristle, and often succeeded in withdrawing the pollinia from old flowers. I was led to make this trial from having at first chosen old flowers for examination; and on passing a bristle, or fine culm of grass, straight down into the nectary, the pollinia were never withdrawn; but when it was bowed forward, I succeeded. Flowers which have not had their pollinia removed can be fertilized as easily as those which have lost them; and I have seen not a few cases of flowers with their pollinia still in place, with sheets of pollen on their stigmas.

At Torquay I watched for about half an hour a number of these flowers growing together, and saw three humble-bees of two kinds visit them. I caught one and examined its proboscis: on the superior lamina, some little way from the tip, two perfect pollinia were attached, and three other boat-formed discs without pollen; so that this bee had removed the pollinia from five flowers, and had probably left the pollen of three on the stigmas of other flowers. The next day I watched the same flowers for a quarter of an hour, and caught another humble-bee at work; one perfect pollinium and four boat-formed discs adhered to its proboscis, one on the top of the other, showing how exactly the same part of the rostellum had each time been touched.

The bees always alighted at the bottom of the spike, and, crawling spirally up it, sucked one flower / after the other. I believe humble-bees generally act in this manner when visiting a dense spike of flowers, as it is the most convenient method; on the same principle that a woodpecker always climbs up a tree in search of insects. This seems an

79

insignificant observation; but see the result. In the early morning, when the bee starts on her rounds, let us suppose that she alighted on the summit of a spike; she would certainly extract the pollinia from the uppermost and last opened flowers; but when visiting the next succeeding flower, of which the column in all probability would not as yet have moved from the labellum (for this is slowly and very gradually effected), the pollen-masses would be brushed off her proboscis and wasted. But nature suffers no such waste. The bee goes first to the lowest flower, and, crawling spirally up the spike, effects nothing on the first spike which she visits till she reaches the upper flowers, and then she withdraws the pollinia. She soon flies to another plant, and, alighting on the lowest and oldest flower, into which a wide passage will have been formed from the greater reflexion of the column, the pollinia strike the protuberant stigma. If the stigma of the lowest flower has already been fully fertilized, little or no pollen will be left on its dried surface; but on the next succeeding flower, of which the stigma is adhesive, large sheets of pollen will be left. Then as soon as the bee arrives near the summit of the spike she will withdraw fresh pollinia, will fly to the lower flowers on another plant, and fertilize them; and thus, as she goes her rounds and adds to her store of honey, she continually fertilizes fresh flowers and perpetuates the race of our autumnal Spiranthes, which will yield honey to future generations of bees.

Spiranthes australis. This species, an inhabitant / of Australia, has been described and figured by Mr Fitzgerald.[9] The flowers are arranged on the spike in the same manner as in *S. autumnalis*; and the labellum with two glands at its base closely resembles that of our species. It is therefore an extraordinary fact that Mr Fitzgerald could not detect even in the bud any trace of a rostellum or of viscid matter. He states that the pollinia touch the upper edge of the stigma, and fertilize it at an early age. Protecting a plant from the access of insects by a bell-glass made no difference in its fertility; and Mr Fitzgerald, though he examined many flowers, never noticed the slightest derangement of the pollinia, or any pollen on the surfaces of the stigmas. Here then we have a species which fertilizes itself as regularly as does *Ophrys apifera*. It would, however, be desirable to ascertain whether insects ever visit the flowers, which it may be presumed secrete nectar, as glands are present; and any such insects should be

[9] *Australian Orchids*, part ii, 1876.

examined, so as to make certain that pollen does not adhere to some part of their bodies.

Listera ovata, or Tway-blade. This orchid is one of the most remarkable in the whole order. The structure and action of the rostellum has been the subject of a valuable paper in the *Philosophical Transactions*, by Dr Hooker,[10] who has described minutely and of course correctly its

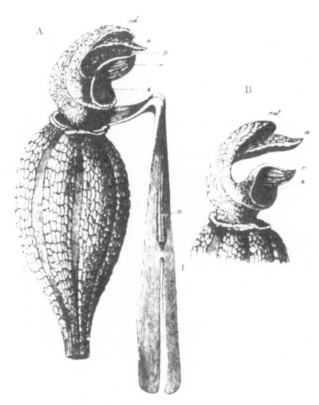

Fig. 18   *Listera ovata*, or Tway-blade
(Partly copied from Hooker)

col. summit of column, *a.* anther, *p.* pollen, *r.* rostellum, *s.* stigma, *l.* labellum, *n.* nectar-secreting furrow
A. Flower viewed laterally, with all the sepals and petals, except the labellum, removed
B. Ditto, with the pollinia removed, and with the rostellum bent down after the ejection of the viscid matter

[10] *Philosophical Transactions*, 1854, p. 259.

curious structure; he did not, however, attend to the part which insects play in the fertilization of the flowers. C. K. Sprengel well knew the importance of insect-agency, but he misunderstood both the structure and the action of the rostellum.

The rostellum is of large size, thin, or foliaceous, / convex in front and concave behind, with its sharp summit slightly hollowed out on each side; it arches over the stigmatic surface (fig. 18, A, *r*, *s*). Internally, / it is divided by longitudinal septa into a series of loculi, which contain viscid matter and have the power of violently expelling it. These loculi show traces of their original cellular structure. I have met with this structure in no other genus except in the closely allied Neottia. The anther, situated behind the rostellum and protected by a broad expansion of the top of the column, opens in the bud. When the flower is fully expanded, the pollinia are left quite free, supported behind by the anther-cells, and lying in front against the concave back of the rostellum, with their upper pointed ends resting on its crest. Each pollinium is almost divided into two masses. The pollen-grains are attached together in the usual manner by a few elastic threads; but the threads are weak, and large masses of pollen can be broken off easily. After the flower has long remained open, the pollen becomes more friable. The labellum is much elongated, contracted at its base, and bent downwards, as represented in the drawing; the upper half above the bifurcation is furrowed along the middle; and the borders of this furrow secrete much nectar.

As soon as the flower opens, if the crest of the rostellum be touched ever so lightly, a large drop of viscid fluid is instantaneously expelled; and this, as Dr Hooker has shown, is formed by the coalescence of two drops proceeding from two depressed spaces on each side of the centre. A good proof of this fact was afforded by some specimens kept in weak spirits of wine, which apparently had expelled the viscid matter slowly, and here two separate little spherical balls of hardened matter had been formed, attached to the two pollinia. The fluid is at first slightly opaque and milky; but on exposure to the air for less than a second, a film forms over it, and in two or three / seconds the whole drop sets hard, soon assuming a purplish-brown tint. So exquisitely sensitive is the rostellum, that a touch from the thinnest human hair suffices to cause the explosion. It will take place under water. Exposure to the vapour of chloroform for about one minute also caused an explosion; but the vapour of sulphuric ether did not thus act, though one flower was exposed for five, and another for twenty minutes to a strong dose. The rostellum of these two flowers when afterwards touched exploded in the usual manner, so that sensitiveness had not been lost in either case. The viscid fluid when pressed between two plates of glass before it has set hard is seen to be structureless; but it has a reticulated appearance, perhaps caused by the presence of globules of a denser immersed in a thinner fluid. As the pointed tips of the pollinia lie on the crest of the rostellum, they are always caught by the exploded drop: I have never seen this once to fail. So rapid is the explosion and so viscid the fluid, that it is difficult to touch the rostellum with a needle, however quickly this may be done, without removing the pollinia. Hence, if a bunch of flowers be carried home in the hand, some of the sepals or petals will almost certainly touch the rostellum and withdraw the pollinia; and this gives the false appearance of their having been ejected to a distance.

After the anther-cells have opened and the naked pollinia have been left resting on the concave back of the rostellum, this latter organ curves a little forwards, and perhaps the anther also moves a little backwards. This movement is of much importance; if it did not occur, the tip of the anther, within which the pollinia are lodged, would be caught by the exploded viscid matter, and the pollinia would be for ever locked up / and rendered useless. I once found an injured flower which had been pressed and had exploded before fully expanding, and the anther with the enclosed pollen-masses was permanently glued to the crest of the rostellum. The rostellum, which is naturally somewhat arched over the stigma, quickly bends forwards and downwards at the moment of the explosion, so as then to stand (fig. B) at right angles to the surface of the stigma. The pollinia, if not removed by the touching object which causes the explosion, become fixed to the rostellum, and by its movement are likewise drawn a little forward. If their lower ends are now freed by a needle from the anther-cells, they spring up; but they are not by this movement placed on the stigma. In the course of some hours, or of a day, the rostellum not only slowly recovers its original slightly-arched position, but becomes quite straight and parallel to the stigmatic surface. This backward movement of the rostellum is of service; for if after the explosion it had remained permanently projecting at right angles over the stigma, pollen could not readily have been deposited by insects on the viscid surface of the stigma. When the rostellum is touched so quickly that the pollinia are not removed, they are, as I have just said, drawn a little forward; but by the subsequent backward movement of the rostellum they are pushed back again into their original position.

From the account now given we may safely infer how the fertilization of this orchid is effected. Small insects alight on the labellum for the sake of the nectar copiously secreted by it; as they lick this they slowly crawl up its narrowed surface until their heads stand directly beneath the overarching crest of the rostellum; when they raise their heads they touch the crest; this then explodes, and the pollinia are instantly / and firmly cemented to their heads. As soon as the insect flies away, it withdraws the pollinia, carries them to another flower, and there leaves masses of the friable pollen on the adhesive stigma.

In order to witness what I felt sure would take place, I watched for an hour a group of plants on three occasions; each time I saw numerous specimens of two small hymenopterous insects, namely, a Haemiteles and a Cryptus, flying about the plants and licking up the nectar; most of the flowers, which were visited over and over again, already had their pollinia removed, but at last I saw both these species crawl into younger flowers, and suddenly retreat with a pair of bright yellow pollinia sticking to their foreheads; I caught them, and found the point of attachment was to the inner edge of the eye; on the other eye of one specimen there was a ball of the hardened viscid matter, showing that it had previously removed another pair of pollinia, and in all probability had subsequently left them on the stigma of a flower. As these insects were captured, I did not witness the act of fertilization; but Sprengel saw a hymenopterous insect leave its pollen-mass on the stigma. My son watched another bed of this orchid at some miles' distance, and brought me home the same hymenopterous insects with attached pollinia, and he saw Diptera also visiting the flowers. He was struck with the number of spider-webs spread over these plants, as if the spiders were aware how attractive the Listera was to insects.

To show how delicate a touch suffices to cause the rostellum to explode, I may mention that I found an extremely minite hymenopterous insect vainly struggling to escape, with its head cemented by the hardened viscid matter, to the crest of the rostellum / and to the tips of the pollinia. The insect was not so large as one of the pollinia, and after causing the explosion had not strength enough to remove them; it was thus punished for attempting a work beyond its strength, and perished miserably.

In Spiranthes the young flowers, which have their pollinia in the best state for removal, cannot possibly be fertilized; they must remain in a virgin condition until they are a little older and the column has moved away from the labellum. Here the same end is gained by widely different means. The stigmas of the older flowers are more adhesive than those of the younger flowers. These latter have their pollinia ready for removal; but immediately after the rostellum has exploded, it curls forwards and downwards, thus protecting the stigma for a time; but it slowly becomes straight again, and now the mature stigma is left freely exposed, ready to be fertilized.

I wished to know whether the rostellum would explode, if never touched; but I have found it difficult to ascertain this point, as the flowers are highly attractive to insects, and it is scarcely possible to exclude very minute ones, the touch of which suffices to cause the explosion. Several plants were covered by a net and left till the surrounding plants had set their capsules; and the rostella in most of the covered-up flowers were found not to have exploded, though their stigmas were withered, and the pollen mouldy and incapable of removal. Some few of the very old flowers, however, when roughly touched, were still capable of a feeble explosion. Other flowers under the nets had exploded, and they had the tips of their pollinia fixed to the crest of the rostellum; but whether these had been touched by some minute insect, or had exploded spontaneously, it was impossible to determine. / It should be observed, that although I looked carefully, not a grain of pollen could be found on the stigmas of any of these flowers, and their ovaria had not swollen. During a subsequent year, several plants were again covered by a net, and I found that the rostellum lost its power of explosion in about four days; the viscid matter having turned brown within the loculi of the rostellum. The weather at the time was unusually hot, and this probably hastened the process. After the four days the pollen had become very incoherent, and some had fallen on the two corners, and even over the whole surface of the stigma, which was penetrated by the pollen-tubes. But the scattering of the pollen was largely aided by, and perhaps wholly depended on, the presence of thrips – insects so minute that they could not be excluded by any net, and which abounded on the flowers. This plant, therefore, is capable of occasional self-fertilization, if the access of winged insects be prevented; but I have every reason to believe that this occurs very rarely in a state of nature.

That insects do their work of cross-fertilization effectually is shown by the following cases. The seven upper flowers on a young spike with

85

many unexpanded buds, still retained their pollinia, but these had been removed from the ten lower flowers; and there was pollen on the stigmas of six of them. In two spikes taken together, the twenty-seven lower flowers all had their pollinia removed, and had pollen on their stigmas; these were succeeded by five open flowers with the pollinia not removed and without any pollen on the stigmas; and these were succeeded by eighteen buds. Lastly, in an older spike with forty-four fully expanded flowers, the pollinia had been removed from every single one; and there was pollen, / generally in large quantity, on all the stigmas which I examined.

I will recapitulate the several special adaptations for the fertilization of this plant. The anther-cells open early, leaving the pollen-masses free, protected by the summit of the column, and with their tips resting on the concave crest of the rostellum. The rostellum then slowly curves over the stigmatic surface, so that its explosive crest stands at a little distance from the summit of the anther; and this is very necessary, otherwise the summit would be caught by the viscid matter, and the pollen for ever locked up. The curvature of the rostellum over the stigma and over the base of the labellum is excellently adapted to favour an insect striking the crest when it raises its head, after having crawled up the labellum and licked the last drop of nectar. The labellum, as C. K. Sprengel has remarked, becomes narrower where it joins the column beneath the rostellum, so that there is no risk of an insect going too much to either side. The crest of the rostellum is so exquisitely sensitive, that a touch from a very minute insect causes it to rupture at two points, and instantly two drops of viscid fluid are expelled, which coalesce. This viscid fluid sets hard in so wonderfully rapid a manner that it rarely fails to cement the tips of the pollinia, nicely laid on the crest of the rostellum, to the forehead of the touching insect. As soon as the rostellum has exploded it suddenly curves downwards so as to project at right angles over the stigma, protecting it from impregnation at an early age, in the same manner as the stigmas of the young flowers of Spiranthes are protected by the labellum clasping the column. But as the column of Spiranthes after a time moves from the labellum, leaving a free passage for the introduction / of the pollinia, so here the rostellum moves backwards, and not only recovers its former arched position, but stands upright, leaving the stigmatic surface, now rendered more adhesive, perfectly free for pollen to be left on it. The pollen-masses, when once cemented to an insect's forehead, will remain attached to it, until they are brought into contact with the stigma of a mature flower; and then these encumbrances will be removed, by the rupturing of the weak elastic threads which tie the grains together; the flower being at the same time fertilized.

Listera cordata. Professor Dickie of Aberdeen was so kind as to send me, but rather too late in the season, two sets of specimens. The flowers have essentially the same structure as in the last species. The loculi of the rostellum are very distinct. Two or three little hairy points project from the middle of the crest of the rostellum; but I do not know whether these have any functional importance. The labellum has two basal lobes (of which vestiges may be seen in *L. ovata*) which curve up on each side; and these would compel an insect to approach the rostellum straight in front. In two of the flowers the pollinia were firmly cemented to the crest of the rostellum; but in almost all the others the pollinia had been previously removed by insects.

In the following year Professor Dickie observed the flowers on living plants, and he informs me that, when the pollen is mature, the crest of the rostellum is directed towards the labellum, and that, as soon as touched, the viscid matter explodes, the pollinia becoming attached to the touching object; after the explosion, the rostellum bends downwards, thus protecting the virgin stigmatic surface; subsequently it rises up and exposes the stigma; so that here everything goes on / as I have described under *Listera ovata.* The flowers are frequented by minute Diptera and Hymenoptera.

Neottia nidus-avis. I made numerous observations on this plant, the Bird's-nest Orchis,[11] but they are not worth giving, as the action and structure of every part is almost identically the same as in *Listera ovata* and *cordata.* On the crest of the rostellum there are about six minute rough points, which seem particularly sensitive to a touch, causing the expulsion of the viscid matter. The exposure of the rostellum to the vapour of sulphuric ether for twenty minutes did not prevent this action, when it was touched. The labellum secretes plenty of nectar, which I mention merely as a caution, because during one cold and wet season I looked several times and could not see a drop, and was perplexed at the apparent absence of any attraction for insects; nevertheless, had I looked more perseveringly, perhaps I should have found some.

---

[11] This unnatural sickly looking plant has generally been supposed to be parasitic on the roots of the trees under the shade of which it lives; but, according to Irmisch (*Beiträge zur Biologie und Morphologie der Orchideen,* 1853, p. 25), this certainly is not the case.

The flowers must be freely visited by insects, for all in one large spike had their pollinia removed. Another unusually fine spike, sent me by Mr Oxenden from South Kent, had borne forty-one flowers, and it produced twenty-seven large seed-capsules, besides some smaller ones. Dr H. Müller of Lippstadt informs me that he has seen Diptera sucking the nectar and removing the pollinia.

The pollen-masses resemble those of Listera, in consisting of compound grains tied together by a few weak threads; they differ in being much more incoherent; after a few days they swell and overhang the sides and summit of the rostellum; so that if the rostellum of a rather old flower be touched and an explosion / caused, the pollen-masses are not so neatly caught by their tips as those of Listera. Thus a good deal of the friable pollen is often left behind in the anther-cells and is apparently wasted. Several plants were protected from the access of winged insects by a net, and after four days the rostella had almost lost their sensitiveness and power to explode. The pollen had become extremely incoherent, and in all the flowers much had fallen on the stigmas which were penetrated by the pollen-tubes. The spreading of the pollen seems to be in part caused by the presence of thrips, many of which minute insects were crawling about the flowers, dusted all over with pollen. The covered-up plants produced plenty of capsules, but many of these were much smaller and contained fewer seeds than those produced by the adjoining uncovered plants.

If insects had been forced by the labellum being more upturned to brush against the anther and stigma, they would always have been smeared with the pollen as soon as it became friable; and they would thus have fertilized the flowers effectually without the aid of the explosive rostellum. This conclusion interested me, because, when previously examining Cephalanthera, with its aborted rostellum, its upturned labellum and friable pollen, I had speculated how a transition, with each gradation useful to the plant, could have been effected from the state of the pollen in the similarly constructed flowers of Epipactis, with their pollinia attached to a well-developed rostellum, to the present condition of Cephalanthera. *Neottia nidusavis* shows us how such a transition might have been effected. This orchid is at present mainly fertilized by means of the explosive rostellum, which acts effectually only as long as the pollen remains in mass; but we have seen that as the flower grows old the pollen swells and becomes friable, and is then apt to / fall or be transported by minute crawling insects on to the stigma. By this means self-fertilization is assured, should larger insects fail to visit the flowers. Moreover, the pollen in this state readily adheres to any object; so that by a slight change in the shape of the flower, which is already less open or more tubular than that of Listera, and by the pollen becoming friable at a still earlier age, its fertilization would be rendered more and more easy without the aid of the explosive rostellum. Ultimately it would become a superfluity; and then, on the principle that every part which is not brought into action tends to disappear, from causes which I have elsewhere endeavoured to explain,[12] this would happen with the rostellum. We should then see a new species, in the condition of Cephalanthera as far as its means of fertilization were concerned, but in general structure closely allied to Neottia and Listera.

Mr Fitzgerald, in the Introduction to his *Australian Orchids*, says that *Thelymitra carnea*, one of the Neotteae, invariably fertilizes itself by means of the incoherent pollen falling on the stigma. Nevertheless a viscid rostellum, and other structures adapted for cross-fertilization are present. The flowers seldom expand, and never until they have fertilized themselves; so that they seem tending towards a cleistogene condition. *Thelymitra longifolia* is likewise fertilized in the bud, according to Mr Fitzgerald, but the flowers open for about an hour on fine days, and thus cross-fertilization is at least possible. On the other hand, the species of the allied genus Diuris are said to be wholly dependent on insects for their fertilization. /

[12] *Variation of Animals and Plants under Domestication*, 2nd edit. vol. ii, p. 309.

CHAPTER V

MALAXEAE AND EPIDENDREAE

Malaxis paludosa – Masdevallia, curious closed flowers – Bolbophyllum, labellum kept in constant movement by every breath of air – Dendrobium, contrivance for self-fertilization – Cattleya, simple manner of fertilization – Epidendrum – Self-fertile Epidendreae.

I have now described the manner of fertilization of fifteen genera, found in Britain, which belong, according to Lindley's classification, to the Ophreae, Arethuseae, and Neotteae. A brief account of several foreign genera belonging to these same tribes has been added, from observations published since the appearance of the first edition of this book. We will now turn to the great exotic tribes of the Malaxeae, Epidendreae, and Vandeae, which ornament in so wonderful a manner the tropical forests. My chief object in examining these latter forms has been to ascertain whether their flowers were as a general rule fertilized by pollen brought by insects from another plant. I also wished to learn whether the pollinia underwent those curious movements of depression by which, as I had discovered, they are placed, after being removed by insects, in the proper position for striking the stigmatic surface.

By the kindness of many friends and strangers I have been enabled to examine fresh flowers of several species, belonging to at least fifty exotic genera, in the several subtribes of the above three great tribes.[1] / It is

[1] I am particularly indebted to Dr Hooker, who on every occasion has given me his invaluable advice, and has never become weary of sending me specimens from the Royal Gardens at Kew.

Mr James Veitch, jun., has generously given me many beautiful orchids, some of which were of especial service. Mr R. Parker also sent me an extremely valuable series of forms. Lady Dorothy Nevill most kindly placed her magnificent collection of orchids at my disposal: Mr Rucker of West Hill, Wandsworth, sent me repeatedly large spikes of Catasetum, a Mormodes of extreme value, and some Dendrobiums. Mr Rodgers of Sevenoaks has given me interesting information. Mr Bateman, so well known for his magnificent work on orchids, sent me a number of interesting forms, including the wonderful *Angraecum sesquipedale*. I am greatly indebted to Mr Turnbull of Down for allowing me the free use of his hothouses, and for giving me some

not my intention to describe the means of fertilization in all these genera, but merely to select a few curious cases which illustrate the foregoing descriptions. The diversity of the contrivances adapted to favour the intercrossing of flowers, seems to be exhaustless.

MALAXEAE

Malaxis paludosa. This rare orchid[2] is the sole representative of the tribe in this country, and it is the smallest of all the British species. The labellum is turned upwards,[3] instead of downwards, so that it does not afford a landing-place for insects as in most other orchids. Its lower margin clasps the column, making the entrance into the flower tubular. From / its position it partially protects the organs of fructification (fig. 19). In most of the Orchideae, the upper sepal and the two upper petals afford protection; but here these two petals and all the sepals are reflexed (as may be seen in the drawing, fig. A), apparently to allow insects freely to visit the flower. The position of the labellum is the more remarkable, because it has been purposely acquired, as shown by the ovarium being spirally twisted. In all orchids the labellum is properly directed upwards, but assumes its usual position on the lower side of the flower by the twisting of the ovarium; but in Malaxis the twisting has been carried so far that the flower occupies the position which it would have held if the ovarium had not been at all twisted, and which the ripe ovarium afterwards assumes, by a process of gradual untwisting.

When the minute flower is dissected, the column is seen to be longitudinally tripartite; the middle portion of the upper half (see fig.

---

interesting orchids; and to his gardener, Mr Horwood, for his aid in some of my observations.

Professor Oliver has kindly assisted me with his large stores of knowledge, and has called my attention to several papers. Lastly, Dr Lindley has sent me fresh and dried specimens, and has in the kindest manner helped me in various ways.

To these gentlemen I can only express my cordial thanks for their unwearied and generous kindness.

[2] I am greatly indebted to Mr Wallis, of Hartfield, in Sussex, for numerous living specimens of this orchid.

[3] Sir James Smith, I believe, first noticed this fact in the *English Flora*, vol. iv, p. 47, 1828. Towards the summit of the spike the lower sepal does not depend, as represented in the woodcut (fig. 19, A), but projects nearly at right angles. Nor are the flowers always so completely twisted round as here represented.

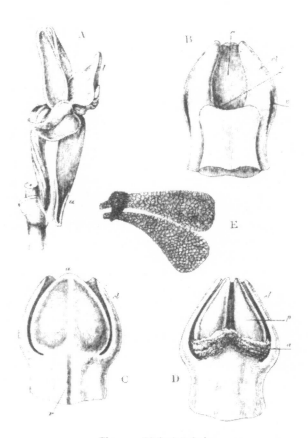

Fig. 19   *Malaxis paludosa*
(Partly copied from Bauer, but modified from living specimens)

a. anther, *v.* spiral vessels, *p.* pollen, *r.* rostellum, *cl.* clinandrum, *s.* stigma, *l.* labellum, *u.* the sepal which in most orchids stands on the upper side of the flower

A. Perfect flower viewed laterally, with the labellum in its natural position, upwards
B. Column viewed in front, showing the rostellum, the pocket-like stigma, and the anterior lateral portions of the clinandrum
C. Back view of the column in a flower-bud, showing the anther with the included pear-shaped pollinia dimly seen, and the posterior edges of the clinandrum
D. Back view of an expanded flower, with the anther now contracted and shrivelled, exposing the pollinia
E. The two pollinia attached to a little transverse mass of viscid matter, hardened by spirits of wine

B) is the rostellum. The upper edge of the lower part of the column projects where united to the base of the rostellum, and forms a rather deep fold. This fold is the stigmatic cavity, and may be compared to a waistcoat pocket. I found pollen-masses which had their broad ends pushed by insects into this pocket; and a bundle of pollen-tubes had here penetrated the stigmatic tissue.

The rostellum, which stands immediately above the stigmatic cavity, is a tall-membranous projection of a whitish colour, formed of square cells, and is covered with a thin layer of viscid matter: it is slightly concave posteriorly, and its crest is surmounted by a minute tongue-shaped mass of viscid matter. The column, with its narrow pocket-like stigma and the / rostellum above, is united on each side behind to a green membranous expansion, convex exteriorly and concave interiorly, of which the summits on each side are pointed and stand a little above the crest of the rostellum. These two membranes sweep round (see back views, figs C and D), and are united to the filament or base of the anther; they thus form a cup-like clinandrum behind the rostellum. The use of this cup is to protect laterally the pollen-masses. When I have to treat of the homologies of the different parts, it will be shown by the course of the spiral vessels that these two membranes consist of the two upper anthers of the inner whorl, in a rudimentary condition, but utilized for this special purpose.

In a flower before it expands, a little mass or drop of viscid fluid may be seen on the crest of the rostellum, rather overhanging its front surface. After the flower has remained open for a little time, this drop shrinks and becomes more viscid. Its chemical nature is different from that of the viscid matter in most orchids, for it remains fluid for many days, though fully exposed to the air. From these facts I concluded that the viscid fluid exuded from the crest of the rostellum; but fortunately I examined a closely allied Indian form, namely, the *Microstylis rhedii* (sent me from Kew by Dr Hooker), and in this, before the flower opened, there was a similar drop of viscid matter; but on opening a still younger bud, I found a minute, regular, tongue-shaped projection on the crest of the rostellum, formed of cells, which when slightly disturbed resolved themselves into a drop of viscid matter. At this age, also, the front surface of the whole rostellum, between its crest and the pocket-like stigma, was coated with cells filled with similar brown viscid matter; so that there can / be little doubt, had I examined a young enough bud of Malaxis, I should have found a similar minute tongue-shaped cellular projection on the crest of the rostellum.

The anther opens widely whilst the flower is in bud, and then shrivels and contracts downwards, so that, when the flower is fully expanded, the pollinia are quite naked, with the exception of their broad lower ends, which rest in two little cups formed by the shrivelled anther-cells. This contraction of the anther is represented in fig. D in comparison with fig. C, which shows the state of the anther in a bud. The upper and much pointed ends of the pollinia rest on, but project beyond, the crest of the rostellum; in the bud they are unattached, but by the time the flower opens they are always caught by the posterior surface of the drop of viscid matter, of which the anterior surface projects slightly beyond the face of the rostellum. That they are caught without any mechanical aid I ascertained by allowing some buds to open in my room. In fig. E the pollinia are shown exactly as they appeared (but not quite in their natural position) when removed by a needle from a specimen kept in spirits of wine, in which the irregular little mass of viscid matter had become hardened and adhered firmly to their tips.

The pollinia consist of two pairs of very thin leaves of waxy pollen; and the four leaves are formed of angular compound grains which never separate. As the pollinia are almost loose, being retained merely by the adhesion of their tips to the viscid fluid, and by their bases resting in the shrivelled anther-cells, and as the petals and sepals are much reflexed, the pollinia, when the flower is fully expanded, would have been liable to be blown away or out of their proper position, / had it not been for the membranous expansions on each side of the column forming the clinandrum, within which they lie safely.

When an insect inserts its proboscis or head into the narrow space between the upright labellum and the rostellum, it will infallibly touch the little projecting viscid mass, and as soon as it flies away it will withdraw the pollinia. I easily imitated this action by inserting any small object into the tubular flower between the labellum and rostellum. When the insect visits another flower, the very thin pollen-leaves attached parallel to the proboscis, or head, will be forced into the pocket-like stigma with their broad ends foremost. I found pollinia in this position glued to the upper membranous expansion of the rostellum, and with a large number of pollen-tubes penetrating the stigmatic tissue. The use of the thin layer of viscid matter, which coats the surface of the rostellum in this genus and in Microstylis, and which is of no use for the transportal of the pollen from flower to flower, seems to be to keep the leaves of pollen fixed in the narrow stigmatic cavity when their lower ends have been inserted by insects. This fact is rather interesting under a homological point of view, for, as we shall hereafter see, the primordial nature of the viscid matter of the rostellum is that which is common to the stigmatic secretion of most flowers, namely, the retention of the pollen, when placed by any means on its stigma.

The flowers of the Malaxis, though so small and inconspicuous, are highly attractive to insects. This was shown by the pollinia having been removed from all the flowers on the spikes which I examined, excepting from one or two close under the buds. In some old flower-spikes every single pollinium had / been carried away. Insects sometimes remove only one of the two pairs. I noticed a flower with all four pollen-leaves still in place, with a single one in the stigmatic cavity; and this must clearly have been brought by some insect. Within the stigmas of many other flowers pollen-leaves were observed. The plant produces plenty of seed; and thirteen of the twenty-one lower flowers on one spike had formed large capsules.

We will now turn to some exotic genera. The pollinia of *Pleurothallis prolifera* and *ligulata* (?) have a minute caudicle, and mechanical aid is requisite to force the viscid matter from the underside of the rostellum into the anther, thus to catch the caudicles and remove the pollinia. On the other hand, in our British Malaxis and in *Microstylis rhedii* from India, the upper surface of the minute tongue-shaped rostellum becomes viscid and adheres to the pollinia without any mechanical aid. This appears likewise to be the case with *Stelis racemiflora*, but the flowers were not in a good state for examination. I mention this latter flower partly because some insect in the hothouse at Kew had removed most of the pollinia, and had left some of them adhering to the lateral stigmas. These curious little flowers are widely expanded and much exposed; but after a time the three sepals close together with perfect exactness, so that it is scarcely possible to distinguish an old flower from a bud: yet, to my surprise, the closed flowers opened when immersed in water.

The allied *Masdevallia fenestrata* bears an extraordinary flower. The three sepals instead of closing, as in the case of Stelis after the flower has remained for a time expanded, cohere together and never open. Two minute, lateral, oval windows (hence the name *fenestrata*), are seated high up the flower opposite each / other, and afford the only entrance; but the presence of these two minute windows (fig. 20) shows how necessary it is that insects should visit the flower in this case as in that of most other orchids. How insects perform the act of fertilization I have failed to understand. At the bottom of the roomy and dark chamber formed by the closed sepals, the minute column stands, and in front of it is the furrowed labellum, with a highly flexible hinge, and on each side the two upper petals; a little tube being thus formed. When therefore a minute insect enters, or which is less probable, a larger insect inserts its proboscis through either window, it has to find by the sense of touch the inner tube in order to reach the nectary at the base of the flower. Within the little tube, formed by the column, labellum, and lateral petals, a broad and hinged rostellum projects at right angles, which can easily be upturned. Its under surface is viscid, and this viscid matter soon sets hard and dry. The minute caudicles of the pollinia, projecting out of the anther-case, rest on the base of the upper membranous surface of the rostellum. The stigmatic cavity when mature is not very deep. After cutting away the sepals I vainly endeavoured, by pushing a bristle into the tubular flower, to remove the pollinia, but by the aid of a bent needle, this was effected without much difficulty. The whole structure of the flower seems as if intended to prevent the flower from being easily fertilized; and this proves that we do not understand its structure. Some small insect had entered one of / the flowers in the hothouse at Kew, for many eggs were deposited within it, near the base.

Fig. 20   *Masdevallia fenestrata*
The window on the near side is shown darkly shaded
n. nectary

Of Bolbophyllum I examined the curious little flowers of four species, which I will not attempt fully to describe. In *B. cupreum* and *cocoinum*, the upper and lower surfaces of the rostellum resolve themselves into viscid matter, which has to be forced upwards by insects into the anther, so as to secure the pollinia. I effected this easily by passing a needle down the flower, which is rendered tubular by the position of the labellum, and then withdrawing it. In *B. rhizophorae* the anther-case moves backwards, when the flower is mature, leaving the two pollen-masses fully exposed, adhering to the upper surface of the rostellum. They are held together by viscid matter, and, judging from the action of a bristle, are always removed together. The stigmatic chamber is very deep with an oval orifice, which exactly fits one of the two pollen-masses. After the flower has remained open for some time, the sides of the oval orifice close in and shut the stigmatic chamber completely – a fact which I have observed in no other orchid, and which, I presume, is here related to the much exposed condition of the whole flower. When the two pollinia were attached to a needle or bristle, and were forced against the stigmatic chamber, one of the two glided into the small orifice more readily than could have been anticipated. Nevertheless, it is evident that insects must place themselves on successive visits to the flowers in precisely the same position, so as first to remove the two pollinia, and then force one of them into the stigmatic orifice. The two upper filiform petals would serve as guides to the insect; but the labellum, instead of making the flower tubular, hangs down just like a tongue out of a widely open mouth. /

The labellum in all the species which I have seen, more especially in *B. rhizophorae*, is remarkable by being joined to the base of the column by a very narrow, thin, white strap, which is highly elastic and flexible; it is even highly elastic when stretched, like an india-rubber band. When the flowers of this species were blown by a breath of wind the tongue-like labella all oscillated to and fro in a very odd manner. In some species not seen by me, as in *B. barbigerum*, the labellum is furnished with a beard of fine hairs, and these are said to cause the labellum to be in almost constant motion from the slightest breath of air. What the use can be of this extreme flexibility and liability to movement in the labellum, I cannot conjecture, unless it be to attract the notice of insects, as the flowers of these species are dull-coloured, small, and inconspicuous, instead of being large, brightly-coloured, and conspicuous or odoriferous, as in so many other orchids. The labella of some of the species are said to be irritable, but I could not detect a trace of this quality in those examined by me. According to Lindley, the labellum of the allied *Megaclinium falcatum* spontaneously oscillates up and down.

The last genus of the Malaxeae which I will mention is Dendrobium, of which one at least of the species, namely *D. chrysanthum*, is interesting, from being apparently contrived to effect its own fertilization, if an insect, when visiting the flower, should fail to remove the pollen-masses. The rostellum has an upper and a small lower surface composed of membrane; and between these is a thick mass of milky-white matter which can be easily forced out. This white matter is less viscid than is usual; but when exposed to the air a film forms over it in less than half a minute, and it soon sets into a waxy or cheesy / substance. The large concave but shallow stigmatic surface is seated

97

beneath the rostellum. The produced anterior lip of the anther (see A) almost entirely covers the upper surface of the rostellum. The filament of the anther is of considerable length, but is hidden in the side view, A, behind the middle of the anther; in the section, B, it is seen, after it has sprung forward: it is elastic, and presses the anther firmly down on the inclined surface of the clinandrum / (see fig. B) which lies behind the rostellum. When the flower is expanded the two pollinia, united

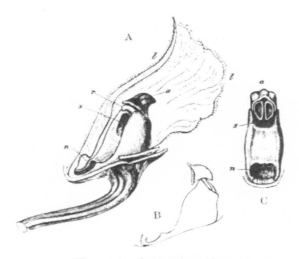

Fig. 21   *Dendrobium chrysanthum*
a. anther, *s.* stigma, *r.* rostellum, *l.* labellum, *n.* nectary
A. Lateral view of flower, with the anther in its proper position, before the ejection of the pollinia. All the sepals and petals are removed except the labellum, which is longitudinally bisected
B. Outline of column, viewed laterally, after the anther has ejected the pollinia
C. Front view of column, showing the empty cells of the anther, after it has ejected its pollinia. The anther is represented hanging too low down, and covering more of the stigma than it really does

into a single mass, lie quite loose on the clinandrum and under the anther-case. The labellum embraces the column, leaving a passage in front. The middle portion of the labellum (as may be seen in fig. A) is thickened, and extends up as far as the top of the stigma. The lowest part of the column is developed into a saucer-like nectary, which secretes honey.

As an insect forces its way into one of these flowers, the labellum, which is elastic, will yield, and the projecting lip of the anther will protect the rostellum from being disturbed; but as soon as the insect retreats, the lip of the anther will be lifted up, and the viscid matter from the rostellum forced into the anther, gluing the pollen-mass to the insect, which will thus be transported to another flower. I easily imitated this action; but as the pollen-masses have no caudicle and lie rather far back within the clinandrum beneath the anther, and as the matter from the rostellum is not highly viscid, they were sometimes left behind.

Owing to the inclination of the base of the clinandrum, and owing to the length and elasticity of the filament, as soon as the anther is lifted up it always springs forward, over the rostellum, and remains hanging there with its lower empty surface (fig. C) suspended over the summit of the stigma. The filament now stretches across the space (see fig. B) which was originally covered by the anther. Several times, having cut off all the petals and labellum, and laid the flower under the microscope, I raised the lip of the anther with a needle, without disturbing the rostellum, and saw the anther assume, with a spring, the position / represented sideways in fig. B, and frontways in fig. C. By this springing action the anther scoops the pollinium out of the concave clinandrum, and pitches it up in the air, with exactly the right force so as to fall down on the middle of the viscid stigma, where it adheres.

Under nature, however, the action cannot be as thus described, for the labellum hangs downwards; and to understand what follows, the drawing should be placed in an almost reversed position. If an insect failed to remove the pollinium by means of the viscid matter from the rostellum, the pollinium would first be jerked downwards on to the protuberant surface of the labellum, placed immediately beneath the stigma. But it must be remembered that the labellum is elastic, and that at the same instant that the insect, in the act of leaving the flower, lifts up the lip of the anther, and so causes the pollinium to be shot out, the labellum will rebound back, and striking the pollinium will pitch it upwards, so as to hit the adhesive stigma. Twice I succeeded in effecting this by imitating the retreat of an insect, with the flower held in its natural position; and on opening it, found the pollinium glued to the stigma.

This view of the use of the elastic filament, seeing how complicated the action must be, may appear fanciful; but we have seen so many and such curious adaptations, that I cannot believe the strong elasticity of the filament and the thickening of the middle part of the labellum to be useless points of structure. If the action be as I have described, we can perceive their meaning, for it would be an advantage to the plant that its single large pollen-mass should not be wasted, supposing that it failed to adhere to an insect by means of the viscid matter from the rostellum. / This contrivance is not common to all the species of the genus; for in neither *D. bigibbum* nor *D. formosum* was the filament of the anther elastic, nor was the middle line of the labellum thickened. In *D. tortile* the filament is elastic; but as I examined only a single flower, and before I had made out the structure of *D. chrysanthum*, I cannot say how it acts.

Mr Anderson states[4] that on one occasion the flowers of his *Dendrobium cretaceum* did not expand, and yet they produced capsules, one of which he sent me. Almost all the numerous seeds in this capsule contained embryos, thus differing greatly from the cases presently to be given of the self-fertilized seeds from the non-expanded flowers of a Cattleya. Mr Anderson remarks that Dendrobiums are the sole representatives of the Malaxeae which, as far as he has seen, spontaneously form capsules. He likewise states that in the immense group of the Vandeae, hereafter to be described, none of the species under his care, with the exception of some belonging to the sub-division of the Brassidae and of *Sarcanthus parishii*, has ever spontaneously produced a capsule.

EPIDENDREAE

The Epidendreae and Malaxeae are characterized by the pollen-grains cohering into large waxy masses. In the latter of these groups the pollinia are said not to be furnished with caudicles, but this is not universally the case, for they exist in *Masdevallia fenestrata* and some other species in an efficient condition, although unattached and of minute size. In the Epidendreae, on the other hand, free or unattached caudicles are always present. For my purpose these / two great tribes might have been run together; as the distinction drawn from the presence of caudicles does not always hold good. But difficulties of this nature are frequently encountered in the classification of largely developed or so-called natural groups, in which there has been comparatively little extinction.

[4] *Journal of Horticulture*, 1863, pp. 206, 287.

I will begin with the genus Cattleya, of which I have examined several species. These are fertilized in a very simple manner, different from that in any British orchid. The rostellum (*r*, fig. 22, A, B) is a broad, tongue-shaped projection, which arches slightly over the

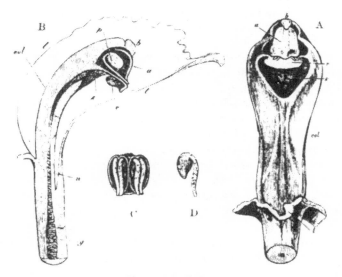

Fig. 22 *Cattleya*

a. anther, *b*. spring at the top of the column, *p*. pollen-masses, *r*. rostellum, *s*. stigma, *col*. column, *l*. labellum, *n*. nectary, *g*. ovarium, or germen

A. Front view of column, with all the sepals and petals removed
B. Section and lateral view of the flower, with all the sepals and petals removed, except the bisected labellum shown only in outline
C. Anther viewed on the underside, showing the four caudicles with the four pollen-masses beneath
D. A single pollinium, viewed laterally, showing the pollen-mass and caudicle

stigma; the upper surface is formed of smooth membrane; the lower surface together with the central portion (originally a mass of cells) consists of a very thick layer of viscid matter. This viscid mass is hardly separated from the viscid matter thickly coating the stigmatic surface which lies close beneath the rostellum. The projecting upper lip of the anther rests on, and opens close over the base of the upper membranous surface of the tongue-shaped rostellum. The anther is kept closed by a spring, at its point of attachment on the top of the column. The pollinia consist of four (or eight in *Cattleya crispa*) waxy

101

masses, each furnished (see figs C and D) with a ribbon-like tail, formed of a bundle of highly elastic threads, to which numerous separate pollen-grains are attached. The pollen therefore consists of two kinds, namely, waxy masses and separate though compound grains (each, as usual, consisting of four) united by elastic threads. This latter kind of pollen is identical with that of Epipactis and other Neotteae.[5] These tails, with their appended pollen-grains, act as caudicles, / and are thus designated, for they serve as the means for the removal of the larger waxy masses from the anther-cells. The tips of the caudicles are generally reflexed, and in the mature flower protrude a little way out of the anther-case (see fig. A) lying on the base of the upper membranous lip of the rostellum. The labellum enfolds the column, making the flower / tubular, and its lower part is produced into a nectary which penetrates the ovarium.

Now for the action of these parts. If any body of size proportional to that of the tubular flower be forced into it – a dead humble-bee acts very well – the tongue-shaped rostellum is depressed, and the object often gets slightly smeared with viscid matter; but in withdrawing it, the rostellum is upturned, and a surprising quantity of viscid matter is forced over the edges and sides, and at the same time into the lip of the anther, which is also slightly raised by the upturning of the rostellum. Thus the protruding tips of the caudicles are instantly glued to the retreating object, and the pollinia are withdrawn. This hardly ever failed to occur in my repeated trials. A living bee or other large insect alighting on the fringed edge of the labellum, and scrambling into the flower, would depress the labellum and would be less likely to disturb the rostellum, until it had sucked the nectar and began to retreat. When a dead bee, with the four waxy balls of pollen dangling by their caudicles from its back, is forced into another flower, some or all of them are caught with certainty by the broad, shallow, and highly viscid stigmatic surface, which likewise tears off the grains of pollen from the threads of the caudicles.

That living humble-bees can thus remove the pollinia is certain. Sir W. C. Trevelyan sent to Mr Smith of the British Museum a *Bombus hortorum*, which was forwarded to me – caught in his hothouse, where a *Cattleya* was in flower – with its whole back, between the wings, smeared with dried viscid matter, and with the four pollinia attached

---

[5] The pollen-masses of Bletia are admirably represented on a large scale in Bauer's drawings, published by Lindley in his *Illustrations*.

to it by their caudicles, ready to be caught by the stigma of any other flower if the bee had entered one. /

Those species which I have examined of Laelia, Leptotes, Sophronitis, Barkeria, Phaius, Evelyna, Bletia, Chysis, and Coelogyne, resemble Cattleya in the caudicles of the pollinia being free, and in the viscid matter from the rostellum not coming into contact with them without mechanical aid, as well as in their general manner of fertilization. In *Coelogyne cristata* the upper lip of the rostellum is much elongated. In *Evelyna carivata* and Chysis eight balls of waxy pollen are all united to a single caudicle. In Barkeria the labellum, instead of enfolding the column, is pressed against it, and this would effectually compel insects to brush against the rostellum. In Epidendrum we have a slight difference; for the upper surface of the rostellum, instead of permanently remaining membranous, as in the above-named genera, is so tender that by a touch it breaks up, together with the whole lower surface, into a mass of viscid matter. In this case the whole of the rostellum, together with the adherent pollinia, must be removed by insects as they retreat from the flower. I observed in *E. glaucum* that viscid matter exuded from the upper surface of the rostellum when touched, as happens with Epipactis. In fact it is difficult to say, in these cases, whether the upper surface of the rostellum should be called membrane or viscid matter. With Chysis this matter sets nearly hard and dry in twenty minutes, and quite so in thirty minutes after its removal from the rostellum.

In *Epidendrum floribundum* there is a rather greater difference: the anterior horns of the clinandrum (i.e. the cup on the summit of the column in which the pollinia lie) approach each other so closely as to adhere to the two sides of the rostellum, which consequently lies in a nick, with the pollinia seated over / it; and as, in this species, the upper surface of the rostellum resolves itself into viscid matter, the caudicles of the pollinia become glued to it without any mechanical aid. The pollinia, though thus attached, cannot, of course, be removed from their anther-cells without the aid of insects. In this species it seems possible (though, from the position of parts, not probable) that an insect might drag the pollinia out and leave them on the stigma of the same flower. In all the other species of Epidendrum which I examined, and in all the above-mentioned genera, it is evident that the viscid matter has to be forced upwards into the lip of the anther by a retreating insect, which would thus necessarily carry the pollinia from one flower to the stigma of another.

Nevertheless, self-fertilization takes place in some Epidendreae. Dr Crüger says[6] that 'we have in Trinidad three plants belonging to this family (a Schomburgkia, Cattleya, and Epidendron) which rarely open their flowers, and they are invariably found to be impregnated when they do open them. In these cases it is easily seen that the pollen masses have been acted on by the stigmatic fluid, and that the pollen-tubes descend from the pollen-masses *in situ* down into the ovarian canal.' Mr Anderson, a skilful cultivator of orchids in Scotland, also states that several of his Epidendreae fertilize themselves spontaneously.[7] In the case of *Cattleya crispa*, the flowers sometimes do not expand properly; nevertheless they produce capsules, one of which he sent to me. It contained an abundance of seeds, but on examination I found that / only about one per cent contained an embryo. Similar seeds were more carefully examined by Mr Gosse, who found that two per cent contained an embryo. About twenty-five per cent of the seeds from a self-fertilized capsule of *Laelia cinnabarina*, also sent to me by Mr Anderson, were found to be good. It is therefore doubtful whether the capsules spontaneously self-fertilized in the West Indies, as described by Dr Crüger, were fully and properly fertilized. Fritz Müller informs me that he has discovered in South Brazil an Epidendrum which bears three pollen-producing anthers, and this is a great anomaly in the order. This species is very imperfectly fertilized by insects; but by means of the two lateral anthers the flowers are regularly self-fertilized. Fritz Müller assigns good reasons for his belief that the appearance of the two additional anthers in this Epidendrum, is a case of reversion to the primitive condition of the whole group.[8] /

---

[6] *Journ. Linn. Soc. Bot.*, vol. viii, 1864, p. 131.

[7] *Journal of Horticulture*, 1863, p. 206 and 287: in the latter paper Mr Gosse gives an account of his microscopical examination of the self-fertilized seeds.

[8] See also *Bot. Zeitung*, 1869, p. 226, and 1870, p. 152.

CHAPTER VI

VANDEAE

Structure of the column and pollinia – Importance of the elasticity of the pedicel; its power of movement – Elasticity and strength of the caudicles – Calanthe with lateral stigmas, manner of fertilization – *Angraecum sesquipedale*, wonderful length of nectary – Species with the entrance into the stigmatic chamber much contracted, so that the pollen-masses can hardly be inserted – Coryanthes, extraordinary manner of fertilization.

We now come to the immense tribe of the Vandeae, which includes many of the most magnificent productions of our hothouses, but like the Epidendreae has no British representative. I have examined twenty-nine genera. The pollen consists of waxy masses, as in the two last tribes, and each ball of pollen is furnished with a caudicle, which becomes, at an early period of growth, united to the rostellum. The caudicle is seldom attached directly to the viscid disc, as in most of the Ophreae, but to the upper and posterior surface of the rostellum; and this part is removed by insects, together with the disc and pollen-masses. The sectional diagram (fig. 23), with the parts separated, will best explain the type-structure of the Vandeae. As in the rest of the Orchideae there are three confluent pistils; of these the dorsal one (2) forms the rostellum arching over the two others (3) which unite to form a single stigma. On the left hand we have the filament (1) bearing the anther. The anther opens at an early period, and the tips of the two caudicles (but only one caudicle and one pollen-mass are represented / in the diagram) protrude in a not fully-hardened condition through a small slit, and adhere to the back of the rostellum. The upper surface of the rostellum is generally hollowed out for the reception of the pollen-masses; it is represented as smooth in the diagram, but is really often furnished with crests or knobs for the attachment of the two caudicles. The anther afterwards opens more widely along its under surface, and leaves the two pollen-masses unattached, excepting by their caudicles to the rostellum.

During an early period of growth, a remarkable change has been

105

going on in the rostellum: either its extremity or its lower surface become excessively viscid (forming the viscid disc), and a line of separation, / at first appearing as a zone of hyaline tissue, is gradually formed, which sets free the disc, as well as the whole upper surface of the rostellum, as far back as the point of attachment of the caudicles. If any object now touches the viscid disc, it, together with the whole back of the rostellum, the caudicles and pollen-masses, can all be readily removed together. In botanical works the whole structure between the

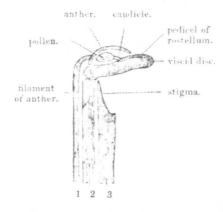

Fig. 23   Imaginary section, illustrative of the structure of the column in the Vandeae

1. The filament, bearing the anther with its pollen-masses; the anther is represented after it has opened along its whole under surface, so that the section shows only the dorsal surface
2. The upper pistil, with the upper part modified into the rostellum
3. The two lower confluent pistils, bearing the two confluent stigmas

disc or viscid surface (generally called the gland) and the balls of pollen is designated as the caudicle; but as these parts play an essential part in the fertilization of the flower, and as they are fundamentally different in their origin and in their minute structure, I shall call the two elastic ropes, which are developed strictly within the anther-cells, the caudicles; and the portion of the rostellum to which the caudicles are attached (see diagram), and which is not viscid, the pedicel. The viscid portion of the rostellum I shall call, as heretofore, the viscid surface or disc. The whole may be conveniently spoken of as the pollinium.

In the Ophreae we have (except in *O. pyramidalis* and a few other species) two separate viscid discs. In the Vandeae, with the exception of Angraecum, we have only one disc. The disc is naked, or is not enclosed in a pouch. In Habenaria the discs, as we have seen, are separated from the two caudicles by short drum-like pedicels, answering to the single and generally much more largely developed pedicel in the Vandeae. In the Ophreae the caudicles of the pollinia, though elastic, are rigid, and serve to place the packets of pollen at the right distance from the insect's head or proboscis, so as to reach the stigma. In the Vandeae this end is gained by the pedicel of the rostellum. The two caudicles in the Vandeae are embedded and attached within a deep cleft in the pollen-masses, / and until stretched are rarely visible, for the pollen-masses lie close to the pedicel of the rostellum. These caudicles answer both in position and function to the elastic threads, by which the packets of pollen are tied together in the Ophreae, at the point where they become confluent; for the function of the true caudicle in the Vandeae is to break when the masses of pollen, transported by insects, adhere to the stigmatic surface.

In many Vandeae the caudicles are easily ruptured, and the fertilization of the flower, as far as this point is concerned, is a simple affair; but in other cases their strength, and the length to which they can be stretched before they break, are surprising. I was at first perplexed to understand what purpose these qualities could serve. The explanation probably is that the pollen-masses in this tribe are very precious objects; in most of the genera a flower produces only two, and judging from the size of the stigma both are generally left adhering to it. In other genera, however, the orifice leading into the stigma is so small that probably only one pollen-mass is left on it, and in this case the pollen from one flower would suffice to fertilize two flowers, but never a greater number. From the large size of the flowers of many of the Vandeae, they no doubt are fertilized by large insects, and these whilst flying about would be likely to brush away and lose the pollinia attached to them, unless the caudicles were very strong and highly elastic. So again, when an insect thus provided visited a flower either too young, with its stigma not yet sufficiently adhesive, or one already impregnated, with its stigma beginning to dry, the strength of the caudicle would prevent the pollen-masses from being uselessly removed and lost.

Although the stigmatic surface is astonishingly adhesive at the proper period in many of these orchids, / for instance, in Phalaenopsis and Saccolabium, yet when I inserted their pollinia attached to a rough object into the stigmatic chamber, they did not adhere with sufficient force to prevent their removal from the object. I even left them for some little time in contact with the adhesive surface, as an insect would do whilst feeding; but when I pulled the pollinia straight out of the stigmatic chamber, the caudicles, though they were stretched to a great length, did not rupture, nor did their attachment to the object yield so that the balls of pollen were withdrawn. It then occurred to me that an insect in flying away would not pull the pollinia straight out of the chamber, but would pull at nearly right angles to its orifice. Accordingly I imitated the action of a retreating insect, and dragged the pollinia out of the stigmatic chamber at right angles to its orifice; and now the friction on the caudicles thus caused, together with the adhesiveness of the stigmatic surface, generally sufficed to rupture them; the pollen-masses being left on the stigma. Thus, it seems that the great strength and extensibility of the caudicles, which, until stretched, lie embedded within the pollen-masses, serve to protect the pollen-masses from being accidentally lost by an insect whilst flying about, and yet, by friction being brought into play, allow them at the proper time, to be left adhering to the stigmatic surface; the fertilization of the flower being thus safely effected.

The discs and pedicels of the pollinia present great diversities in shape, and an apparently exhaustless number of adaptations. Even in species of the same genus, as in Oncidium, these parts differ greatly. I here give a few figures (fig. 24), taken almost at hazard. The pedicel

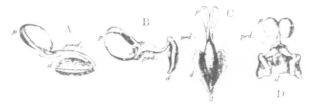

Fig. 24   *Pollinia of Vandeae*
d. viscid disc, *ped.* pedicel, *p.* pollen-masses. The caudicles, being embedded within the pollen-masses, are not shown
A. Pollinium of *Oncidium grande* after partial depression
B. Pollinium of *Brassia maculata* (copied from Bauer)
C. Pollinium of *Stanhopea saccata* after depression
D. Pollinium of *Sarcanthus teretifolius* after depression

generally consists, as far as I have seen, of a thin ribbon-shaped membrane (fig. A); sometimes / it is almost cylindrical (fig. C) but often of the most diversified shapes. The pedicel is generally nearly straight, but in *Miltonia clowesii* it is naturally curved; and in some cases, as we shall immediately see, it assumes, after removal, various shapes. The extensible and elastic caudicles, by which the pollen-masses are attached to the pedicel, are barely or not at all visible, being embedded in a cleft or hollow within each pollen-mass. The disc, which is viscid on the underside, consists of a piece of thin or thick membrane of varied forms. In Acropera it is like a pointed cap; in some cases it is tongue-shaped, or heart-shaped (fig. C), or saddle-shaped, as in some Maxillarias, or like a thick cushion (fig. A), as in many species of Oncidium, with the pedicel attached at one end, instead of, as is more usual, nearly to the centre. In *Angraecum distichum* and *sesquipedale* the rostellum is notched, and two separate, thin, membranous discs can be removed, each carrying by a short pedicel a pollen-mass. In *Sarcanthus teretifolius* the disc (fig. D) is / very oddly shaped; and as the stigmatic chamber is deep and likewise curiously shaped, we are led to believe that the disc is fastened with great precision to the square projecting head of some insect.[1]

In most cases there is a plain relation between the length of the pedicel and the depth of the stigmatic chamber, into which the pollen-masses have to be inserted. In some few cases, however, in which a long pedicel and a shallow stigma co-exist, we shall presently meet with curious compensating actions. After the disc and pedicel have been removed, the shape of the remaining part of the rostellum is of course altered, being now slightly shorter and thinner, and sometimes notched. In Stanhopea, the entire circumference of the extremity of the rostellum is removed, and a thin, pointed, needle-like process alone is left, which originally ran up the centre of the disc.

If we now turn to the diagram (fig. 23, p. 150), and suppose the rectangularly bent rostellum to be thinner and the stigma to lie closer beneath it than is there represented, we shall see that, if an insect with a pollinium attached to its head were to fly to another flower and occupy exactly the same position which it held whilst the attachment was effected, the pollen-masses would be in the right position for striking the stigma, especially if, from their weight, they were to become in the least degree depressed. This is all that takes place in *Lycaste skinnerii, Cymbidium giganteum, Zygopetalum mackai, Angraecum eburneum, Miltonia clowesii*, in a Warrea, and, I believe, in *Galeandra*

---

[1] I may here remark that Delpino (*Fecondazione nelle Piante*, Firenze, 1867, p. 19) says he has examined flowers of Vanda, Oncidium, Epidendrum, Phaius, and Dendrobium, and is able to confirm in general my statements.

funkii. But if in our diagram we suppose, for instance, / the stigma to be seated at the bottom of a deep cavity, low down in the column, or the anther to be seated higher up, or the pedicel of the rostellum to slope more upwards, etc. − all of which contingencies occur in various species − in such cases, an insect with a pollinium attached to its head, if it flew to another flower, would not place the pollen-masses on the stigma, unless their position had become greatly changed after attachment.

This change is effected in many Vandeae in the same manner as is so general with the Ophreae, namely, by a movement of depression in the pollinium in the course of about half a minute after its removal from the rostellum. I have seen this movement conspicuously displayed, generally causing the pollinium to rotate through about a quarter of a circle, in several species of Oncidium, Odontoglossum, Brassia, Vanda, Aerides, Sarcanthus, Saccolabium, Acropera, and Maxillaria. In *Rodriguezia suaveolens* the movement of depression is remarkable from its extreme slowness; in *Eulophia viridis* from its small extent. Mr Charles Wright, in a letter to Professor Asa Gray, says that he observed in Cuba a pollinium of an Oncidium attached to a humble-bee, and he concluded at first that I was completely mistaken about the movement of depression; but after several hours it moved into the proper position for fertilizing the flower. In some of the cases above specified in which the pollinia apparently undergo no movement of depression, I am not sure that there was not a very slight one after a time. In the various Ophreae the anther-cells are sometimes seated exteriorly and sometimes interiorly with respect to the stigma; and there are corresponding outward and inward movements in the pollinia: but in the Vandeae the anther-cells always lie, as far as I have seen, / directly over the stigma, and the movement of the pollinium is always directly downwards. In Calanthe, however, the two stigmas are placed exteriorly to the anther-cells, and the pollinia, as we shall see, are made to strike them by a peculiar mechanical arrangement of the parts.

In the Ophreae the seat of contraction, which causes the act of depression, is in the upper surface of the viscid disc, close to the point of attachment of the caudicles: in most of the Vandeae the seat is likewise in the upper surface of the disc, but at the point where the pedicel is united to it, and therefore at a considerable distance from the point of attachment of the true caudicles. The contraction is hygrometric, but to this subject I shall return in the ninth chapter; therefore the movement does not take place until the pollinium has been removed from the rostellum, and the point of union between the disc and pedicel has been exposed for a few seconds or minutes to the air. If, after the contraction and consequent movement of the pedicel, the whole body be placed into water, the pedicel slowly moves back and resumes its former position with respect to the viscid disc. When taken out of water, it again undergoes the movement of depression. It is of importance to notice these facts, as we thus get a test by which this movement can be distinguished from certain other movements.

In *Maxillaria ornithorhyncha*, we have a unique case. The pedicel of the rostellum is much elongated, and is entirely covered by the produced front lip of the anther, and is thus kept damp. When removed it bends quickly backwards on itself, at about its central point, and thus becomes only half as long as it was before. When placed in water it resumes its original straight form. If the pedicel had not been in some / manner shortened, it is hardly possible that the flower could have been fertilized. After this movement, the pollinium attached to any small object can be inserted into the flower, and the balls of pollen readily adhere to the stigmatic surface. Here we have an instance of one of those compensating actions in the pollinia, before alluded to, in relation to the shallowness of the stigma.

In some cases besides hygrometric movements, elasticity comes into play. In *Aerides odorata* and *virens*, and in an *Oncidium* (*roseum?*), the pedicel of the rostellum is fastened down in a straight line, at one extremity by the disc, and at the other by the anther; it has, however, a strong elastic tendency to spring up at right angles to the disc. Consequently if the pollinium, attached by its viscid disc to some object, is removed from the anther, the pedicel instantly springs up and stands at nearly right angles to its former position, with the pollen-masses carried aloft. This has been noticed by other observers; and I agree with them that the object gained is to free the pollen-masses from the anther-cells. After this upward elastic spring, the downward hygrometric movement immediately commences, which, oddly enough carries the pedicel back again into almost exactly the same position, relatively to the disc, which it held whilst forming part of the rostellum. In Aerides the end of the pedicel, to which the pollen-masses are attached by short dangling caudicles, after springing up, remains a little curved upwards; and this curvature seems well adapted to drop the pollen-masses into the deep stigmatic cavity over the ledge in front. The difference between the first elastic and the second or reversed hygrometric movement, was well shown by placing the pollinium of the above Oncidium into / water, after both movements had taken place; and the pedicel then moved into the same position which it had at first assumed through its elasticity; this movement not being in any way affected by the water. When taken out of water the hygrometric movement of depression soon commenced for the second time.

In *Rodriguezia secunda* there was no hygrometric movement of depression in the pedicel as in the before-mentioned *R. suaveolens*, but there was a rapid downward movement, due to elasticity, and of this I have seen no other instance; for when the pedicel was put into water it showed no tendency to recover its original position, as occurred in many other cases.

In *Phalaenopsis grandiflora* and *amabilis* the stigma is shallow and the pedicel of the rostellum long. Some compensating action is therefore

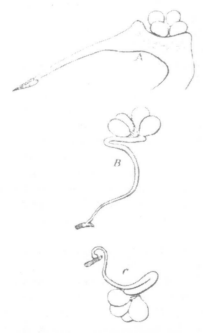

Fig. 25   *Pollinium of Ornithocephalus*
(From a sketch by Fritz Müller)

A. Pollinium still attached to the rostellum with the pollen-mass still lying in the clinandrum on the summit of the column
B. Pollinium in the position which it first assumes from the elasticity of the pedicel
C. Pollinium in the position ultimately assumed from the hygrometric movement

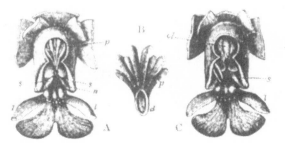

Fig. 26   *Calanthe masuca*

p. pollen-masses, *s s*. the two stigmas, *ln*. mouth of nectary, *l*. labellum, *d*. viscid disc, *cl*. in fig. C, clinandrum the pollen-masses being removed

A. Flower viewed from above, with the anther-case removed, showing the eight pollen-masses in their proper position within the clinandrum. All the sepals and petals have been cut away except the labellum

B. Pollen-masses attached to the viscid disc, seen from the underside

C. Flower in same position as in A, but with the disc and pollen-masses removed, and now showing the deeply notched rostellum and the empty clinandrum in which the pollen-masses lay. Within the left-hand stigma two pollen-masses may be seen adhering to its viscid surface

requisite, which, differently from that in *Maxillaria ornithorhyncha* is effected by elasticity. There is no movement of depression; but, when the pollinium is removed, the straight pedicel suddenly curls up in the middle, thus ⸻ : the full-stop on the left hand may represent the balls of pollen, and the thick hyphen to the right may be supposed to represent the triangularly shaped disc. The pedicel does not straighten itself when placed in water. The end carrying the balls of pollen is a little raised up after this elastic movement, and the pedicel, with one end raised, and with the middle part upwardly bowed, is well adapted to drop the pollen-masses into the deep stigmatic cavity, over a ledge in front. Fritz Müller informs me of a case in which the shortening of a very long pedicel is effected partly by elasticity and partly by a hygrometric movement. A small Ornithocephalus, growing in South Brazil, has a very long pedicel, / which is shown closely attached to the rostellum in the accompanying figure A.

The pedicel when freed suddenly bends into the form represented at B, and soon afterwards owing to the hygrometric contraction curls up into the odd figure shown at C. When placed in water it resumes the form represented at B. /

In *Calanthe masuca* and the hybrid *C. dominii* the structure is very different to what it is in most other Vandeae. We here have two oval, pit-like stigmas on each side of the rostellum (fig. 26). The viscid disc is oval (fig. B), and has no pedicel, but eight masses of pollen are attached to it by very short and easily ruptured caudicles. These pollen-masses radiate from the disc like the leaves of a fan. The rostellum is broad, and its sides slope on each side towards the lateral pit-like stigmas. When the disc is removed the rostellum is seen (fig. C) to be deeply notched in the middle. The labellum is united to the column almost up to its summit, leaving a passage (n, A) to / the long nectary close beneath the rostellum. The labellum is studded with singular, wartlike, globular excrescences.

If a thick needle be inserted into the mouth of the nectary (fig. A), and then withdrawn, the viscid disc is removed, bearing with it the elegant fan of radiating pollen-masses. These undergo no change in position. But if the needle be now inserted into the nectary of another flower, the ends of the pollen-masses necessarily hit the upper and laterally sloping sides of the rostellum, and, glancing off both ways, strike down into the two lateral pit-like stigmas. The thin caudicles being easily ruptured, the pollen-masses are left adhering like little darts to the viscid surface of both stigmas (see left-hand stigma in fig. C), and the fertilization of the flower is completed in a simple manner pleasing to behold.

I should have stated that a narrow transverse rim of stigmatic tissue, beneath the rostellum, connects the two lateral stigmas; and it is probable that some of the middle pollen-masses may be inserted through the notch in the rostellum, so as to adhere to this rim. I am the more inclined to this opinion from having found in the elegant *Calanthe vestita* the rostellum extending so widely over the two lateral stigmas, that apparently all the pollen-masses must be inserted beneath its surface.

The *Angraecum sesquipedale*, of which the large six-rayed flowers, like stars formed of snow-white wax, have excited the admiration of travellers in Madagascar, must not be passed over. A green, whip-like nectary of astonishing length hangs down beneath the labellum. In several flowers sent me by Mr Bateman I found the nectaries eleven and a half inches long, with only the lower inch and a half filled with nectar. / What can be the use, if may be asked, of a nectary of such disproportionate length? We shall, I think, see that the fertilization of the plant depends on this length, and on nectar being contained only within the lower and attenuated extremity. It is, however, surprising that any insect should be able to reach the nectar. Our English sphinxes have proboscides as long as their bodies; but in Madagascar there must be moths with proboscides capable of extension to a length of between ten and eleven inches! This belief of mine has been ridiculed by some entomologists, but we now know from Fritz Müller[2] that there is a sphinx-moth in South Brazil which has a proboscis of nearly sufficient length, for when dried it was between ten and eleven inches long. When not protruded it is coiled up into a spiral of at least twenty windings.

The rostellum is broad and foliaceous, and arches rectangularly over the stigma and over the orifice of the nectary: it is deeply notched by a cleft enlarged or widened at the inner end. Hence the rostellum nearly resembles that of Calanthe after the disc has been removed (see fig. 26, C). The under surfaces of both margins of the cleft, near their ends, are bordered by narrow strips of viscid membrane, easily removed; so that there are two distinct viscid discs. A short membranous pedicel is attached to the middle of the upper surface of each disc; and the pedicel carries a pollen-mass at its other end. Beneath the rostellum a narrow, ledge-like, adhesive stigma is seated.

I could not for some time understand how the pollinia of this orchid were removed, or how the stigma was fertilized. I passed bristles and needles / down the open entrance into the nectary and through the cleft in the rostellum with no result. It then occurred to me that, from the length of the nectary, the flower must be visited by large moths, with a proboscis thick at the base; and that to drain the last drop of nectar, even the largest moth would have to force its proboscis as far down as possible. Whether or not the moth first inserted its proboscis by the open entrance into the nectary, as is most probable from the shape of the flower, or through the cleft in the rostellum, it would ultimately be forced in order to drain the nectary to push its proboscis through the cleft, for this is the straightest course; and by slight pressure the whole foliaceous rostellum is depressed. The distance from the outside of the flower to the extremity of the nectary can be thus shortened by about a quarter of an inch. I therefore took a cylindrical rod one-tenth of an inch in diameter, and pushed it down through the cleft in the rostellum. The margins readily separated, and were pushed downwards together with the whole rostellum. When I slowly withdrew the cylinder the rostellum rose from its elasticity, and the margins of the cleft were upturned so as to clasp the cylinder. Thus the viscid strips of membrane on each underside of the cleft rostellum

[2] See letter with a drawing by Hermann Müller, *Nature*, 1873, p. 223.

came into contact with the cylinder, and firmly adhered to it; and the pollen-masses were withdrawn. By this means I succeeded every time in withdrawing the pollinia; and it cannot, I think, be doubted that a large moth would thus act; that is, it would drive its proboscis up to the very base through the cleft of the rostellum, so as to reach the extremity of the nectary; and then the pollinia attached to the base of its proboscis would be safely withdrawn.

I did not succeed in leaving the pollen-masses on / the stigma so well as I did in withdrawing them. As the margins of the cleft rostellum must be upturned before the discs adhere to a cylindrical body, during its withdrawal, the pollen-masses become affixed some little way from its base. The two discs did not always adhere at exactly opposite points. Now, when a moth with the pollinia adhering to the base of its proboscis, inserts it for a second time into the nectary, and exerts all its force so as to push down the rostellum as far as possible, the pollen-masses will generally rest on and adhere to the narrow, ledge-like stigma which projects beneath the rostellum. By acting in this manner with the pollinia attached to a cylindrical object, the pollen-masses were twice torn off and left glued to the stigmatic surface.

If the Angraecum in its native forests secretes more nectar than did the vigorous plants sent me by Mr Bateman, so that the nectary ever becomes filled, small moths might obtain their share, but they would not benefit the plant. The pollinia would not be withdrawn until some huge moth, with a wonderfully long proboscis, tried to drain the last drop.[3] If such great moths were to become extinct in Madagascar, assuredly the Angraecum would become extinct. On the other hand, as the nectar, at least in the lower part of the nectary, is stored safe from the depredation of other insects, the extinction of the Angraecum would probably be a serious loss to these moths. We can thus understand how the astonishing length of the / nectary had been acquired by successive modifications. As certain moths of Madagascar became larger through Natural Selection in relation to their general conditions of life, either in the larval or mature state, or as the proboscis alone was lengthened to obtain honey from the Angraecum

[3] Mr Belt suggests (*The Naturalist in Nicaragua*, 1874, p. 133) that the great length of the nectary of this plant serves to prevent other moths which are not well-adapted for the fertilization of the flowers from sucking the nectar, and that its development can thus be accounted for. I have no doubt of the truth of this principle, but it is hardly applicable here, as the moth has to be compelled to drive its proboscis as deeply down as possible into the flower.

and other deep tubular flowers, those individual plants of the Angraecum which had the longest nectaries (and the nectary varies much in length in some orchids), and which, consequently, compelled the moths to insert their proboscides up to the very base, would be best fertilized. These plants would yield most seed, and the seedlings would generally inherit long nectaries; and so it would be in successive generations of the plant and of the moth. Thus it would appear that there has been a race in gaining length between the nectary of the Angraecum and the proboscis of certain moths; but the Angraecum has triumphed, for it flourishes and abounds in the forests of Madagascar, and still troubles each moth to insert its proboscis as deeply as possible in order to drain the last drop of nectar.

I could add descriptions of many other curious structures in the Vandeae, more especially from the letters of Fritz Müller with respect to those of Brazil; but the reader would be wearied. I must, however, make a few remarks on certain genera, the fertilization of which remains a mystery, chiefly on account of the narrowness of the mouth of the stigma, as this renders the insertion of the pollen-masses extremely difficult. Two closely allied species or varieties of Acropera, viz., A. luteola and loddigesii have been observed by me during several seasons, and every detail of their structure seems as if specially adapted to render their fertilization almost impossible. I have met with hardly / any other such case, not that I fully understand the contrivances in any orchid, for new and admirable ones become apparent, the longer I study even one of our commonest British species.

The thin and elongated rostellum of Acropera projects at right angles to the column (see diagram, fig. 23, p. 150); and the pedicel of the pollinium is of course equally long and much thinner. The disc consists of an extremely small cap, viscid within, which fits on the extremity of the rostellum. The viscid matter sets hard but slowly. The upper sepal forms a hood enclosing and protecting the column. The labellum is an extraordinary organ, baffling all description: it is articulated to the column by a thin strap, so elastic and flexible that a breath of wind sets it vibrating. It hangs downwards; and the retention of this position seems to be of importance, for the footstalk (ovarium) of each flower is curved into a semicircle, so as to compensate for the pendulous habit of the plant. The two upper petals and the lateral lobes of the labellum serve as guides leading into the hood-like upper sepal.

The pollinium, when adhering by its disc to an object, undergoes the common movement of depression; and this seems superfluous, for the stigmatic cavity lies (see diagram, fig. 23) high up at the base of the rectangularly projecting rostellum. But this is a comparatively trifling difficulty; the real difficulty lies in the orifice of the stigmatic chamber being so narrow that the pollen-masses, though consisting of thin sheets, can hardly be forced in. I repeatedly tried, and succeeded only three or four times. Even after leaving them to dry for four hours before a fire, and thus to shrink a little, I rarely succeeded in forcing them into the stigma. I examined quite young flowers and / almost withered ones, for I imagined that the mouth of the chamber might be of larger size at some period of growth; but the difficulty of insertion remained the same. Now when we observe that the viscid disc is extraordinarily small, and consequently its power of attachment not so firm as with orchids having a large disc, and that the pedicel is very long and thin, it would seem almost indispensable that the stigmatic chamber should be unusually large for the easy insertion of the pollinium, instead of being much contracted. Moreover, the stigmatic surface, as Dr Hooker has likewise observed, is singularly little adhesive!

The flowers when ready for fertilization do not secrete nectar;[4] but this is no difficulty, for as Dr Crüger has seen humble-bees gnawing the projections on the labellum of the closely allied *Gongora maculata*, there can be little doubt that the distal cup-shaped part of the labellum of Acropera offers a similar attraction to insects. After numberless trials in many ways, I have found that the pollinia can be removed with certainty only by pushing the rostellum a little upwards with a camel-hair brush, held in such a position that the tip slides along the underside of the rostellum, so as to brush off the little viscid cap on its extremity, into which the hairs enter and are glued fast. I further find that if the brush with a pollinium thus attached to its tip is pushed into and then withdrawn from the stigmatic cavity, the mouth of which is furnished with a sharp ridge, the end of the pedicel / which bears the viscid cap is often left sticking within the chamber, with the pollen-masses close outside. Many flowers were thus treated, and three of

[4] Mr Scott has observed that after the flowers of Acropera and of two species in the allied genus of Gongora have been fertilized, an abundance of nectar exudes from the front of the column; but at no other time could he find a trace of nectar. This exudation can, therefore, be of no use to the plant with respect to its fertilization, and must be viewed as an excretion.

them produced fine capsules. Mr Scott also succeeded in fertilizing two flowers in the same apparently unnatural manner, as he likewise did on one occasion by placing a pollen-mass, moistened with the viscid matter from a distinct kind of Orchis, at the mouth of the stigmatic chamber. These facts lead me to suspect that an insect with the extremity of its abdomen produced into a sharp point alights on the flower, and then turns round to gnaw the distal portion of the labellum. In doing so it removes the pollinium, the viscid cap of which adheres to the extremity of its abdomen. The insect then visits another flower, by which time the movement of depression will have caused the pedicel to lie flat on its back; and from occupying the same position as before, the insect will be apt to insert the end of its abdomen into the stigmatic chamber, and the viscid cap will then be scraped off by the ledge in front, and the pollen-masses will be left close outside, as in the above experiments. The whole operation would probably be aided by the oscillatory movement of the labellum whilst gnawed by an insect. This whole view is very improbable, but it is the only one, as far as I can see, which explains the fertilization of the flower.

The allied genera Gongora, Acineta, and Stanhopea present nearly the same difficulty from the narrowness of the entrance into the stigmatic chamber. Mr Scott tried repeatedly but in vain to force the pollen-masses into the stigma of *Gongora atro-purpurea* and *truncata*; but he readily fertilized them by cutting off the clinandrum and placing pollen-masses on the now exposed stigma; as he likewise did in the case of / Acropera. Dr Crüger says[5] that *Gongora maculata* 'often bears fruit in Trinidad. It is visited, exclusively during the day, as far as I can see, by a splendid bee, probably a Euglossa, but with the tongue nearly twice as long as the body. The tongue passes out behind the abdomen, and is there curved upwards. As these bees only come for biting and gnawing the anterior side of the labellum, the protruding tongue touches or approaches the gland (i.e., viscid disc) at every retrograde movement of the insect. By this it can hardly fail to be loaded sooner or later with the pollen-masses, which are then easily inserted into the stigmatic cleft. I have, however, not as yet observed this fact.' I am surprised that Dr Crüger should speak of the pollen-masses being easily inserted, and I suppose that he must have experimented with dried and shrunken ones. The doubled-up, immensely elongated proboscis, projecting beyond the abdomen,

---

[5] *Journ. Linn. Soc. Bot.*, vol. viii, 1864, p. 131.

would answer as well as a pointed extremity to the abdomen, which in the case of Acropera I imagine is the instrument for removing the pollen-masses; but I presume that with Gongora it is not the viscid disc, but the broad and free ends of the pollen-masses which are inserted into the stigmatic cavity. As in the case of Acropera, I found it scarcely possible to insert the pollen-masses of Gongora into the stigma; but some which were removed from the anther and left exposed to the sun for nearly five hours, became much shrunk and formed thin sheets; and these could be inserted without much difficulty into the cleft-like entrance of the stigma. The pollinia attached to an insect flying about in the torrid zone would shrink after a time; and the delay thus caused would ensure the / flowers being fertilized with pollen from a distinct plant.

With respect to Stanhopea, Dr Crüger says[6] that in the West Indies a bee (Euglossa) often visits the flowers for the sake of gnawing the labellum, and he caught one with a pollinium attached to its back; but he adds that he cannot understand how the pollen-masses are inserted into the narrow mouth of the stigma. With *Stanhopea oculata* I found that the pollinia could almost always be attached to my naked or gloved finger, by gently sliding it down the concave surface of the arched column; but this occurred only within a short time after the expansion of the flowers, whilst they are highly odoriferous. By again sliding my finger down the column, the pollinia were almost always rubbed off by the sharp edge of the stigmatic chamber, and were left adhering close to its entrance. Flowers thus treated occasionally, though rarely, yielded capsules. The removal of the pollinia from my finger seemed to depend on the existence of a point projecting beyond the viscid disc, and which I suspect is specially adapted for this purpose. If this be so, the pollen-masses must emit their tubes without being inserted into the stigmatic chamber. I may add that the pollen-masses shrink very little by being thoroughly dried, and could not in this state be easily inserted.

The entrance into the stigma is in like manner, as I hear from Fritz Müller,[7] so much contracted in Cirrhaea and Notylia, which belong to another subdivision of the Vandeae, that the pollinia can be inserted / into it only with extreme difficulty. In the case of Cirrhaea he found that this could be effected more easily, after they had shrunk a little

---

[6] *Journ. Linn. Soc. Bot.*, vol. viii, 1864, p. 130. Bronn has described the structure of *Stanhopea devoniensis*, in his German translation of the first edition of this work.

[7] *Bot. Zeitung*, 1868, p. 630.

from being left to dry for half an hour or an hour. He observed two flowers with pollen-masses naturally inserted by some means into their stigmas. On several occasions after forcing the end of a pollen-mass into the mouth of the stigma, he witnessed a most curious process of deglutition. The extremity of the pollen-mass swells from imbibing moisture, and as the chamber gradually widens downwards, the swelling part is forced downwards; so that the whole is at last drawn inwards and disappears. In the case of Notylia, Fritz Müller observed that the entrance into the stigma became a little larger after the flower had remained expanded for about a week. In whatever manner this latter plant is fertilized, it is certain that it must be impregnated with pollen from a distinct plant; as it offers one of those extraordinary cases in which its own pollen acts like poison on the stigma.

In the last edition of this work it was shown that the ovaria of mature flowers of Acropera do not contain any ovules. But I erred greatly in the interpretation of this fact, for I concluded that the sexes were separate. I was however soon convinced of my error by Mr Scott, who succeeded in artificially fertilizing the flowers with their own pollen. A remarkable discovery by Hildebrand,[8] namely, that in many orchids the ovules are not developed unless the stigma is penetrated by the pollen-tubes, and that their development occurs only after an interval of several weeks or even months, explains the state of the ovarium in Acropera, as observed by me. According also to / Fritz Müller,[9] the ovules of many endemic Epidendreae and Vandeae in Brazil remain in a very imperfect state of development for some months, and even in one case for half a year, after the flowers had been fertilized. He suggests that a plant which produces hundreds of thousands of ovules, would waste much power if these were formed and did not happen to be fertilized, and we know that fertilization is a doubtful and difficult operation with many orchids. It would therefore be an advantage to such plants, if the ovules were not at all developed until their fertilization was assured by the pollen-tubes having already penetrated the stigma.

Coryanthes. I will conclude this chapter by giving an account of the fertilization of the flowers of Coryanthes, which is effected in a manner that might perhaps have been inferred from their structure, but would have appeared utterly incredible had it not been repeatedly

[8] *Bot. Zeitung*, 1863, 30 October, et seq., and 4 August, 1865.
[9] *Bot. Zeitung*, 1868, p. 164.

witnessed by a careful observer, namely, the late Dr Crüger, Director of the Botanical Gardens at Trinidad. The flowers are very large and hang downwards. The distal portion of the labellum (L) in the following woodcut, fig. 27, is converted into a large bucket (B). Two appendages (H), arising from the narrowed base of the labellum, stand directly over the bucket and secrete so much fluid that drops may be seen falling into it. This fluid is limpid and so slightly sweet that it does not deserve to be called nectar, though evidently of the same nature; nor does it serve to attract insects. M. Ménière estimates that the total quantity secreted by a single flower is about an English ounce.[10] When the bucket is full the fluid overflows by the spout (P). / This spout is closely over-arched by the end of the column, which bears the stigma and pollen-masses in such a position, that an insect forcing its way out of the bucket through this passage would first brush with its back against the stigma and afterwards against the viscid discs of the pollinia, and thus remove them. We are now prepared to hear what Dr Crüger says about the fertilization of an allied species, the *C. macrantha*, the labellum of which is provided with crests.[11] I may premise that he sent me specimens of the bees which he saw gnawing these crests, and they belong, as I am informed by Mr F. Smith, to the genus Euglossa. Dr Crüger states that these bees may be 'seen in great numbers disputing with each other for a place on the edge of the hypochil (i.e. the basal part of the labellum). Partly by this contest, partly perhaps intoxicated by the matter they are indulging in, they tumble down into the "bucket", half-full of a fluid secreted by organs situated at the base of the column. They then crawl along in the water towards the anterior side of the bucket, where there is a passage for them between the opening of this and the column. If one is early on the look-out, as these Hymenopterae are early risers, one can see in every flower how fecundation is performed. The humble-bee, in forcing its way out of its involuntary bath, has to exert itself considerably, as the mouth of the epichil (i.e. the distal part of the labellum) and the face of the column fit together exactly, and are very stiff and elastic. The first bee, then, which is immersed will have the gland / of the pollen-mass glued to its back. The insect then generally

---

[10] *Bulletin de la Soc. Bot. de France*, vol. ii, 1855, p. 351.

[11] *Journal of Linn. Soc. Bot.*, vol. viii, 1864, p. 130. There is a drawing of this species in Paxton's *Mag. of Botany*, vol. v, p. 31, but it is too complicated to be reproduced. There is also a drawing of *C. feildingii* in *Journal of Hort. Soc.*, vol. iii, p. 16. I am indebted to Mr Thiselton Dyer for informing me of these figures.

gets through the passage, and comes out with this peculiar appendage, to return nearly immediately to its feast, when it is generally precipitated a second time into the bucket, passing out through the same opening, and so inserting the pollen-masses into the stigma while it forces its way out, and thereby impregnating either the same or some other flower. I have often seen this; and sometimes there are so many of these humble-bees assembled that there is a continual procession of them through the passage specified.'

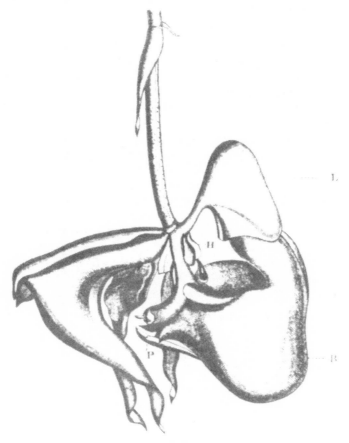

Fig. 27   *Coryanthes speciosa*
(Copied from Lindley's *Vegetable Kingdom*)
L. labellum, B. bucket of the labellum, H. fluid-secreting appendages, P. spout of bucket, over-arched by the end of the column, bearing the anther and stigma

There cannot be the least doubt that the fertilization of the flower absolutely depends on insects crawling out through the passage formed by the extremity of the labellum and the over-arching column. If the large distal portion of the labellum or bucket had been dry, the bees could easily have escaped by flying away. Therefore we must believe that the fluid is secreted by the appendages in such extraordinary quantity and is collected in the bucket, not as a palatable attraction for the bees, as they are known to gnaw the labellum, but for the sake of wetting their wings, and thus compelling them to crawl out through the passage.

I have now described, perhaps in too much detail, a few of the many contrivances by which the Vandeae are fertilized. The relative position and shape of the parts – friction, viscidity, elastic and hygrometric movements, all nicely related to one another – come into play. But all these appliances are subordinate to the aid of insects. Without their aid, not a plant belonging to this tribe, in the species of the twenty-nine genera examined by me, would set a seed. It is also certain in a majority of the cases, that insects withdraw the pollinia only when retreating from the flower, and / by carrying them away, effect a union between two flowers, generally on distinct plants. This can hardly fail to occur in all the many cases in which the pollinia slowly change their position, when removed from the rostellum, in order to assume a proper direction for striking the stigma; for the insects during this interval will have had time to fly from the flowers on one plant which will serve as the male, to those on another plant which will serve as the female. /

CHAPTER VII

VANDEAE *continued* – CATASETIDAE

Catasetidae, the most remarkable of all orchids – The mechanism by which the pollinia of Catasetum are ejected to a distance and are transported by insects – Sensitiveness of the horns of the rostellum – Extraordinary difference in the male, female, and hermaphrodite forms of *Catasetum tridentatum* – *Mormodes ignea*, curious structure of the flowers; ejection of the pollinia – *Mormodes luxata* – *Cycnoches ventricosum*, manner of fertilization.

I have reserved for separate description one subfamily of the Vandeae, namely, the Catasetidae, which must, I think, be considered as the most remarkable of all orchids.

I will begin with Catasetum. A brief inspection of the flower shows that here, as with most other orchids, some mechanical aid is requisite to remove the pollen-masses from their cells, and to carry them to the stigmatic surface. We shall, moreover, presently see that Catasetum is exclusively a male form; so that the pollen-masses must be transported to the female plant, in order that seed should be produced. The pollinium is furnished with a viscid disc of huge size; but this, instead of being placed in a position likely to touch and adhere to an insect visiting the flower, is turned inwards and lies close to the upper and back surface of a chamber, which must be called the stigmatic chamber, though functionless as a stigma. There is nothing in this chamber to attract insects; and even if they did enter it, the viscid surface of the disc could not possibly come into contact with them. /

How then does Nature act? She has endowed these plants with, what must be called for want of a better term, sensitiveness, and with the remarkable power of forcibly ejecting their pollinia even to a considerable distance. Hence, when certain definite points of the flower are touched by an insect, the pollinia are shot forth like an arrow, not barbed however, but having a blunt and excessively adhesive point. The insect, disturbed by so sharp a blow, or after having eaten its fill, flies sooner or later away to a female plant, and, whilst standing in the same position as before, the pollen-bearing end of the arrow is inserted into the stigmatic cavity, and a mass of pollen is left on its viscid surface. Thus, and thus alone, can the five species of Catasetum which I have examined be fertilized.

In many Orchideae, as in Listera, Spiranthes, and Orchis, the surface of the rostellum is so far sensitive, that, when touched or when exposed to the vapour of chloroform, it ruptures in certain defined lines. So it is in the tribe of the Catasetidae, but with this remarkable difference, that in Catasetum the rostellum is prolonged into two curved tapering horns, or, as I shall call them, antennae, which stand over the labellum where insects alight. If these are touched even very lightly, they convey some stimulus to the membrane which surrounds and connects the disc of the pollinium with the adjoining surface, causing it instantly to rupture; and as soon as this happens the disc is suddenly set free. We have also seen in several Vandeae that the pedicels of the pollinia are fastened flat down in a state of tension, and are highly elastic, so that, when freed, they immediately spring up, apparently for the sake of detaching the pollen-masses from the anther-cells. In the genus Catasetum, on the / other hand, the pedicels are fastened down in a curved position; and when freed by the rupture of the attached edges of the disc, they straighten themselves with such force, that not only do they drag the balls of pollen together with the anther-cells from their places of attachment, but the whole pollinium is jerked forward, over and beyond the tips of the so-called antennae, to the distance sometimes of two or three feet. Thus, as throughout nature, pre-existing structures and capacities are utilized for new purposes.

Catasetum saccatum.[1] I will first describe the male forms, belonging to five species, which are included under the generic name of Catasetum. The general appearance of the present species is represented in the following woodcut, fig. 28. A side view of the flower, with all the petals and sepals excepting the labellum cut off, is shown by B; and A gives a front view of the column. The upper sepal and two upper petals surround and protect the column; the two lower sepals project out at right angles. The flower stands more or less inclined to either side, but with the labellum downwards, as represented in the drawing. The dull

[1] I am much indebted to Mr James Veitch of Chelsea for the first specimen which I saw of this orchid; subsequently Mr S. Rucker, so well known for his magnificent collection of orchids, generously sent me two fine spikes, and has aided me in the kindest manner with other specimens.

coppery and orange-spotted tints – the yawning cavity in the great fringed labellum – the one antenna projecting with the other hanging down – give to these flowers a strange, lurid, and almost reptilian appearance.

In front of the column, in the middle, the deep stigmatic chamber (fig. 28, A, *s*), may be seen; but this is best shown in the section (fig. 29, C, *s*), in which all / the parts are a little separated from each other, in order that the mechanism may be intelligible. In the middle of the roof of the stigmatic chamber, far back (*d*, in A, fig. 28), the upturned anterior edge of the viscid disc can just be seen. The upper membranous surface of the disc, before it is ruptured, is continuous with the fringed bases of the two antennae between which it lies. The rostellum projects over the disc and stigmatic chamber (see section C, fig. 29), and is prolonged on each side so as to form the two antennae; the middle part is covered by the ribbon-like pedicel (*ped.*) of the pollinium. The lower end of the pedicel is attached to the disc, and the upper end to the two pollen-masses (*p*) within the anther-cell. The pedicel in its natural position is held much bowed round the protuberant rostellum; when freed it forcibly straightens itself, and at the same time its lateral edges curl inwards. At an early period of growth, it is continuous with the rostellum, but subsequently becomes separated from it by the solution of a layer of cells.

The pollinium when set free and after it has straightened itself, is represented at D, fig. 29. Its under surface, which lies in contact with the rostellum, is shown at E, with the lateral edges of the pedicel now curled inwards. In this latter view, the clefts in the undersides of the two pollen-masses are shown. Within these clefts, near their bases, a layer of strong extensible tissue is attached, forming the caudicles, by which the pollen-masses are united to the pedicel. The lower end of the pedicel is joined to the disc by a flexible hinge, which occurs in no other genus, so that the pedicel can play backwards and forwards, as far as the upturned end (fig. D) of the disc permits. The disc is large and thick; it consists of a strong upper / membrane, to which the pedicel is united, with an inferior cushion of great thickness, of pulpy, flocculent, and viscid matter. The posterior margin is much the most viscid part, and this necessarily first strikes any object when the pollinium is ejected. The viscid matter soon sets hard. The whole surface of the disc is kept damp before ejection, by resting close against the roof of the stigmatic chamber; but in the section (fig. C) it is represented, like the other parts, a little separated from the roof.

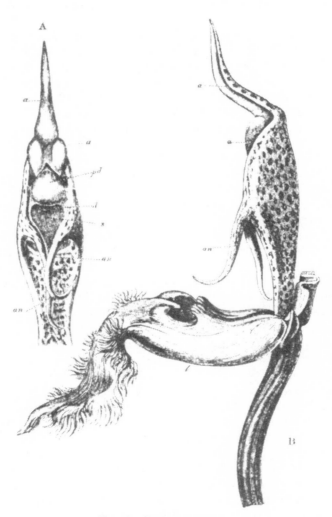

Fig. 28   *Catasetum saccatum*

a. anther, *an.* antennae of the rostellum, *d.* disc of pollinium, *f.* filament of anther, *g.* germen or ovarium, *l.* labellum, *p.* pollen-masses, *pd.* or *ped.* pedicel of pollinium, *s.* stigmatic chamber

A. Front view of column
B. Side view of flower, with all the sepals and petals removed except the labellum *l*

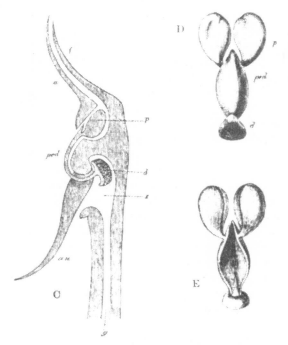

Fig. 29 *Catasetum saccatum*

a. anther, *an.* antennae of the rostellum, *d.* disc of pollinium, *f.* filament of anther, *g.* germen or ovarium, *p.* pollen-masses, *pd.* or *ped.* pedicel of pollinium, *s.* stigmatic chamber

C. Diagrammatic section through the column, with all the parts a little separated
D. Pollinium, upper surface
E. Pollinium, lower surface, which before removal lies in close contact with the rostellum *l*

The connective membrane of the anther (*a* in all the figures) is produced into a spike, which adheres loosely to the pointed end of the column; this pointed end (*f*, fig. C) is homologically the filament of the anther.

The anther has this peculiar shape apparently for the sake of leverage, so that it may be easily torn off by a pull at its lower end, when the pollinium is jerked out by the elasticity of the pedicel.

The labellum stands at right angles to the column, or hangs a little downwards; its lateral and basal lobes are turned under the middle portion, so that an insect can stand only in front of the column. In the middle of the labellum there is a deep cavity, bordered by crests. This cavity does not secrete nectar, but its walls are thick and fleshy, with a slightly sweet nutritious taste; and it will presently be shown that they are gnawed by insects. The extremity of the left-hand antenna stands immediately over the cavity, and would infallibly be touched by an insect visiting this part of the labellum for any purpose.

The antennae are the most singular organs of the flower, and occur in no other genus. They form rigid, curved horns, tapering to a point. They consist of a narrow ribbon of membrane, with the edges curled inwards so as to touch; each horn therefore is tubular, / with a slit down one side, like an adder's fang. They are composed of numerous, much elongated, generally hexagonal cells, pointed at both ends; and these cells (like those in most of the other tissues of the flower) have nuclei with nucleoli. The antennae are prolongations of the sides of the anterior face of the rostellum. As the viscid disc is continuous with a little fringe of membrane on each side, and as this fringe is continuous with the bases of the antennae, these latter organs are put into direct connection with the disc. The pedicel of the pollinium passes, as already stated, between the bases of the two antennae. The antennae are not free for their whole length; but their exterior edges are firmly united to and blend for a considerable space with the margins of the stigmatic chamber.

In all the flowers which I examined, taken from three plants, the two antennae which are alike in structure occupied the same relative position. The extreme part of the left-hand antenna bends upwards (see B, fig. 28, in which the position is shown plainer than in A), and at the same time a little inwards, so that its tip is medial and guards the entrance into the cavity of the labellum. The right-hand antenna hangs down, with its tip turned a little outwards; and as we shall immediately see, is almost paralysed, so as to be functionless.

Now for the action of the parts. When the left-hand antenna of this species (or either of the antennae in three of the following species) is touched, the edges of the upper membrane of the disc, which are continuously united with the surrounding surface, instantly rupture, and the disc is set free. The highly elastic pedicel then instantly flicks[a] the heavy disc out of the stigmatic chamber with such force, that the whole pollinium is ejected, bringing away with it the two / balls of pollen, and tearing the loosely attached spike-like anther from the top of the column. The pollinium is always ejected with its viscid disc foremost. I imitated the action with a minute strip of whalebone, slightly weighted at one end to

---

[a] Original reads 'flirts'.

represent the disc; this was then bent half round a cylindrical object, the upper end being at the same time gently held by the smooth head of a pin, to represent the retarding action of the anther, the lower end was then suddenly set free, and the whalebone was pitched forward, like the pollinium of the Catasetum, with the weighted end foremost.

That the disc is first jerked out of the stigmatic chamber, I ascertained by pressing the middle of the pedicel; and when I touched the antenna the disc instantly sprung forth, but, owing to the pressure on the pedicel, the pollinium was not dragged out of the anther-cell. Besides the spring from the straightening of the pedicel, elasticity in a transverse direction comes into play: if a quill be split lengthways, and the half be forced longitudinally on a too thick pencil, immediately the pressure is removed the quill jumps off; and an analogous action takes place with the pedicel of the pollinium, owing to the sudden inward curling of its edges, when set free. These combined forces suffice to eject the pollinium with considerable force to the distance of two or three feet. Several persons have told me that, when touching the flowers of this genus in their hothouses, the pollinia have struck their faces. I touched the antennae of *C. callosum* whilst holding the flower at about a yard's distance from a window, and the pollinium hit the pane of glass, and stuck by its adhesive disc, to the smooth vertical surface.

The following observations on the nature of the / excitement which causes the disc to separate from the surrounding parts, include some made on the following species. Several flowers were sent me by post and by the railroad, and must have been much jarred, but they had not exploded. I let two flowers fall from a height of two or three inches on the table, but the pollinia were not ejected. I cut off with a crash with a pair of scissors the thick labellum and ovarium close beneath the flower; but this violence produced no effect. Nor did deep pricks in various parts of the column, even within the stigmatic chamber. A blow, sufficiently hard to knock off the anther, causes the ejection of the pollinium, as occurred to me once by accident. Twice I pressed rather hard on the pedicel, and consequently on the underlying rostellum, without any effect. Whilst pressing on the pedicel, I gently removed the anther, and then the pollen-bearing end of the pollinium sprang up from its elasticity, and this movement caused the disc to separate. M. Ménière,[2] however, states that the anther-case sometimes detaches itself, or can be gently detached, without the disc separating;

[2] *Bull. de la Soc. Bot. de France*, vol. i, 1854, p. 367.

and that then the upper end of the pedicel, bearing the pollen-masses, swings downwards in front of the stigmatic chamber.

After trials made on fifteen flowers of three species, I find that no moderate degree of violence on any part of the flower, except on the antennae, produces any effect. But when the left-hand antenna of *C. saccatum*, or either antenna of the three following species, is touched, the pollinium is instantly ejected. The extreme tip and the whole length of the antennae are sensitive. In one specimen of *C. tridentatum* a touch from a bristle sufficed; in five specimens of / *C. saccatum* a gentle touch from a fine needle was necessary; but in four other specimens a slight blow was requisite. In *C. tridentatum* a stream of air and of cold water from a small pipe did not suffice; nor in any case did a touch from a human hair; so that the antennae are less sensitive than the rostellum of Listera. Such extreme sensitiveness would indeed have been useless to the plant, for, as is now known, the flowers are visited by powerful insects.

That the disc does not separate owing to the simple mechanical movement of the antennae is certain; for they adhere firmly for a considerable space to the sides of the stigmatic chamber, and are thus immovably fixed near their bases. If a vibration is conveyed along them, it must be of some special nature, for ordinary jars of manifold greater strength do not excite the act of rupture. The flowers in some cases, when they first arrived, were not sensitive, but after the cut-off spikes had stood for a day or two in water they became sensitive. Whether this was owing to fuller maturity or to the absorption of water, I know not. Two flowers of *C. callosum*, which were completely torpid, were immersed in tepid water for an hour; and then the antennae became highly sensitive; this indicates either that the cellular tissue of the antennae must be turgid in order to receive and convey the effects of a touch, or, as is more probable, heat increases their sensitiveness. Two other flowers placed in hot water, but not so hot as to scald my fingers, spontaneously ejected their pollinia. A plant of *C. tridentatum* had been kept for some days in a rather cool house, and the antennae were consequently in a torpid condition; a flower was cut off and placed in water at a temperature of 100 °F (37.7 °C), and no effect was immediately produced; but when it was / looked at after an interval of 1h. 30m. the pollinium was found ejected. Another flower was placed in water at 90 °F (32·2 °C), and after 25m. the pollinium was found ejected: two other flowers left for 20m. in water at 87 °F (30·5 °C) did not explode, though they were afterwards proved to be sensitive to a slight touch. Lastly, four flowers were placed in water at 83°F (28·3°C); two of these did not eject their pollinia in 45m., and were then found to be sensitive; whereas the other two, when looked at after 1h. 15m., had spontaneously ejected their pollinia. These cases show that immersion in water raised to a temperature only a little higher than that to which the plant had been exposed, causes the membrane by which the discs are attached to rupture. A thin stream of almost boiling water was allowed to fall through a fine pipe on the antennae of some flowers on the above plant; these were softened and killed but the pollinia were not ejected. Nor did sulphuric acid, dropped on the tips of the antennae, cause any action; though their upper parts which had not been injured by the acid were afterwards found to be sensitive to a touch. In these two latter cases, I presume that the shock was so sudden and violent that the tissue was instantly killed. Considering the above several facts, we may infer that it must be some molecular change which is conveyed along the antennae, causing the membrane round the discs to rupture. In *C. tridentatum* the antennae were one inch and a tenth in length, and a gentle touch from a bristle on the extreme tip was conveyed, as far as I could perceive, instantaneously throughout this length. I measured several cells in the tissue composing the antennae of this species, and on a rough average it appeared that the stimulus must travel through no less than from seventy to eighty cells. /

We may, at least, safely conclude that the antennae, which are characteristic of the genus Catasetum, are specially adapted to receive and convey the effects of a touch to the disc of the pollinium. This causes the membrane to rupture, and the pollinium is then ejected by the elasticity of its pedicel. If we required further proof, nature affords it in the case of the so-called genus Monathanthus, which, as we shall presently see, is the female of *Catasetum tridentatum*, and it does not possess pollinia which can be ejected, and the antennae are here entirely absent.

I have stated that in *C. saccatum* the right-hand antenna invariably hangs down, with the tip turned slightly outwards, and that it is almost paralysed. I ground my belief on five trials, in which I violently hit, bent, and pricked this antenna, and this produced no effect; but when immediately afterwards the left-hand antenna was touched with much less force, the pollinium was shot forth. In a sixth case a forcible blow on the right-hand antenna did cause the act of ejection, so that it is not completely paralysed. As this antenna does not guard the labellum, which in all orchids is the part attractive, that is to insects, its sensitiveness would be useless.

From the large size of the flower, more especially of the viscid disc, and from its wonderful power of adhesion, I formerly inferred that the flowers were visited by large insects, and this is now known to be the case. The viscid matter sticks so firmly after it has set hard, and the pedicel is so strong (though very thin and only one-twentieth of an inch in breadth at the hinge), that to my surprise a pollinium attached to an object supported for a few seconds a weight of 1,262 grains, or nearly three ounces; and it supported for a considerable time a slightly less weight. When / the pollinium is shot forth, the large spike-like anther is generally carried with it. If the disc strikes a flat surface like a table, the momentum from the weight of the anther often carries the pollen-bearing end beyond the disc, and the pollinium is thus affixed in a wrong direction for the fertilization of another flower, supposing it to have been attached to an insect's body. The flight of the pollinium is often rather crooked.[3] but it must not be forgotten that under nature the ejection is caused by the antennae being touched by a large insect standing on the labellum, which will thus have its head and thorax placed near to the anther. A rounded object thus held is always accurately struck in the middle, and when removed with the pollinium adhering to it, the weight of the anther depresses the hinge of the pollinium; and in this position the anther-case readily drops off, leaving the balls of pollen free, in a proper position for fertilizing the female flower. The utility / of so forcible an ejection no doubt is to drive the soft and viscid cushion of the disc against the hairy thorax of

---

[3] M. Baillon (*Bull. de la Soc. Bot. de France*, vol. i, 1854, p. 285) states that *Catasetum luridum* ejects its pollinia always in a straight line, and in such a direction that it sticks fast to the bottom of the concavity of the labellum; and he imagines that in this position it fertilizes the flower in a manner not clearly explained. In a subsequent paper in the same volume (p. 367) M. Ménière justly disputes M. Baillon's conclusion. He remarks that the anther-case is easily detached, and sometimes naturally detaches itself; the pollinia then swing downwards by the elasticity of the pedicel, the viscid disc still remaining attached to the roof of the stigmatic chamber. M. Ménière hints that, by the subsequent and progressive retraction of the pedicel, the pollen-masses might be carried into the stigmatic chamber. This is not possible in the three species which I have examined, and would be useless. But M. Ménière himself then goes on to show how important insects are for the fertilization of orchids; and apparently infers that their agency comes into play with Catasetum, and that this plant does not fertilize itself. Both M. Baillon and M. Ménière correctly describe the curved position in which the elastic pedicel lies before it is set free. Neither of these botanists seems to be aware that the species of Catasetum (at least the five which I have examined) are exclusively male plants.

the large hymenopterous insects which frequent the flowers. When once attached to an insect, assuredly no force which the insect could exert would remove the disc and pedicel; but the caudicles are ruptured without much difficulty, and thus the balls of pollen might readily be left on the adhesive stigma of the female flower.

Catasetum callosum. The flowers of this species[4] are smaller than those of the last, but resemble them in most respects. The edge of the labellum is covered with papillae; the cavity in the middle is small, and behind it there is an elongated anvil-like projection – facts which I mention from the resemblance in some of these points between the labellum of this species and that of *Myanthus barbatus*, the hermaphrodite form of *Catasetum tridentatum*, presently to be described. When either antenna is touched, the pollinium is ejected with much force. The yellow-coloured pedicel is much bowed, and is joined by a hinge to the extremely viscid disc. The two antennae stand symmetrically on each side of the anvil-like projection, with their tips lying within the small cavity of the labellum. The walls of this cavity have a pleasant nutritious taste. The antennae are remarkable, from their whole surface being roughened with papillae. The plant is a male, and the female form is at present unknown.

Catasetum tabulare. This species belongs to the same type as *C. saccatum*, but differs greatly from it in appearance. The central portion of the labellum consists of a narrow, elongated, table-like projection, of / an almost white colour and formed of a thick mass of succulent tissue, having a sweetish taste. Towards the base of the labellum there is a large cavity, which externally resembles the nectary of an ordinary flower, but apparently never contains nectar. The pointed extremity of the left-hand antenna lies within this cavity, and would infallibly be touched by an insect gnawing the bilobed and basal end of the medial projection of the labellum. The right-hand antenna is turned inwards, with the extreme part bent at right angles and pressed against the column; therefore I do not doubt that it is paralysed as in *C. saccatum*; but the flowers examined by me had lost almost all their sensitiveness.

Catasetum planiceps (?). This species does not differ much from the following one, so I will describe it briefly. The green and spotted labellum stands on the upper side of the flower; it is jar-shaped, with a small orifice. The two elongated and roughened antennae lie coiled up

---

[4] A fine spike of flowers of this species was kindly sent me by Mr Rucker, and was named for me by Dr Lindley.

some little way apart and parallel to one another, within the labellum. They are both sensitive to a touch.

Catasetum tridentatum. The general appearance of this species, which is very different from that of *C. saccatum, callosum* and *tabulare*, is represented in fig. 30, with a sepal on each side cut off.

The flower stands with the labellum uppermost, that is, in a reversed position compared with most orchids. The labellum is helmet-shaped, its distal portion being reduced to three small points. It cannot hold nectar from its position; but the walls are thick, and have, as in the other species, a pleasant nutritious taste. The stigmatic chamber, though functionless as a stigma, is of large size. The summit of the column, and the spike-like anther, are not so much elongated as in / *C. saccatum.* In other respects there is no important difference. The antennae are of greater length; their tips for about one-twentieth of their length are roughened by cells produced into papillae.

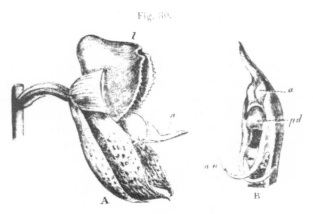

Fig. 30   *Catasetum tridentatum*
a. anther, *pd.* pedicel of pollinium, *an.* antennae, *l.* labellum
A. Side view of flower in its natural position, with two of the sepals cut off
B. Front view of column, in position reverse of fig. A

The pedicel of the pollinium is articulated as before by a hinge to the disc; it can move freely only in one direction owing to one end of the disc being upturned, and this restricted power of movement apparently comes into play when the pollinium is carried by an insect to the female flower. The disc is, as in the other species, of large size, and the end which when ejected first strikes any object, is much more viscid than the rest of the surface. This latter surface is drenched with a milky fluid, which, when exposed to the air, rapidly turns brown, and sets into a cheesy consistence. The upper surface of the disc consists of strong membrane / formed of polygonal cells, resting on and adhering to a thick cushion, formed of irregular rounded balls of brown matter, separated from each other and embedded in a transparent, structureless, highly elastic substance. This cushion towards the posterior end of the disc graduates into viscid matter, which when consolidated is brown, translucent, and homogeneous. Altogether the disc of Catasetum presents a much more complex structure than in the other Vandeae.

I need not further describe the present species, except as to the position of the antennae. They occupied exactly the same position in all the many flowers which were examined. Both lie curled within the helmet-like labellum; the left-hand one stands higher up, with its inwardly bowed extremity in the middle; the right-hand antenna lies lower down and crosses the whole base of the labellum, with the tip just projecting beyond the left margin of the base of the column. Both are sensitive, but apparently the one which is coiled within the middle of the labellum is the more sensitive of the two. From the position of the petals and sepals, an insect visiting the flower would almost certainly alight on the crest of the labellum; and it could hardly gnaw any part of the great cavity without touching one of the two antennae, for the left-hand one guards the upper part, and the right-hand one the lower part. When either of these is touched the pollinium is ejected and the disc will strike the head or thorax of the insect.

The position of the antennae in this Catasetum may be compared with that of a man with his left arm raised and bent so that his hand stands in front of his chest, and with his right arm crossing his body lower down so that the fingers project just beyond his left side. In *Catasetum callosum* both arms are held lower down, / and are extended symmetrically. In *C. saccatum* the left arm is bowed and held in front, as in *C. tridentatum*, but rather lower down; whilst the right arm hangs downwards paralysed, with the hand turned a little outwards. In every case notice will be given in an admirable manner, when an insect visits the labellum, and the time has arrived for the ejection of the pollinium, so that it may be transported to the female plant.

Catasetum tridentatum is interesting under another point of view.

137

Botanists were astonished when Sir R. Schomburgk[5] stated that he had seen three forms, believed to constitute three distinct genera, namely, *Catasetum tridentatum*, *Monachanthus viridis*, and *Myanthus barbatus*, all growing on the same plant. Lindley remarked[6] that 'such cases shake to the foundation all our ideas of the stability of genera and species'. Sir R. Schomburgk affirms that he has seen hundreds of plants of *C. tridentatum* in Essequibo without ever finding one specimen with seeds;[7] whereas / he was surprised at the gigantic seed-vessels of the Monachanthus; and he correctly remarks that 'here we have traces of sexual difference in Orchideous flowers'. Dr Crüger also informs me that in Trinidad he never saw capsules naturally produced by the flowers of this Catasetum;[8] nor when they were fertilized by him with their own pollen, as was done repeatedly. On the other hand, when he fertilized the flowers of the *Monachanthus viridis* with pollen from the Catasetum, the operation never failed. The Monachanthus also commonly produces fruit in a state of nature.

From what I had myself observed, I was led to examine carefully the female organs of *C. tridentatum*, *callosum*, and *saccatum*. In no case was the stigmatic surface viscid, as it is in all other orchids (except as we

[5] *Transactions of the Linnean Soc.*, vol. xvii, p. 522. Another account by Dr Lindley appeared in the *Botanical Register*, fol. 1851, of a distinct species of Myanthus and Monachanthus appearing on the same scape: he alludes also to other cases. Some of the flowers in these cases were in an intermediate condition, which is not surprising, seeing that in dioecious plants we sometimes have a partial resumption of the characters of both sexes. Mr Rodgers of Riverhill informs me that he imported from Demerara a Myanthus, and that when it flowered a second time it was metamorphosed into a Catasetum. Dr Carpenter (*Comparative Physiology*, 4th edit., p. 633) alludes to an analogous case which occurred at Bristol. Lastly Dean Herbert informed me many years ago that *Catasetum luridum* flowered and kept true for nine years in the Botanic Garden at York; it then threw up a scape of a Myanthus, which as we shall presently see is an hermaphrodite, intermediate in form between the male and female. M. Duchartre has given a full historical account of the appearance of these forms on the same plant, in *Bull. de la Soc. Bot. de France*, vol. ix, 1862, p. 113.

[6] The *Vegetable Kingdom*, 1853, p. 178.

[7] Brongniart states (*Bull. de la Soc. Bot. de France*, vol. ii, 1855, p. 20) that M. Neumann, a skilful fertilizer of orchids, could never succeed in fertilizing Catasetum.

[8] Dr Hance writes to me that he has in his collection a plant of *Catasetum tridentatum* from the West Indies bearing a fine capsule; but it does not appear to have been ascertained that this particular flower was that of Catasetum, and there is no great improbability in a single flower of Monachanthus being produced by a plant of Catasetum, as well as a whole scape, which we know has often occurred. J. G. Beer says (quoted by Irmisch, *Beiträge zu Biologie der Orchideen*, 1853, p. 22) that during three years he tried in vain to fertilize Catasetum, but on one occasion, by placing only the viscid disc of a pollinium within the stigma, a ripe fruit was produced; but it may be asked, Did the seeds contain embryos?

shall hereafter see in Cypripedium), and as is indispensable for securing the pollen-masses by the rupture of the caudicles. I carefully looked to this point both in young and old flowers of *C. tridentatum*. When the surface of the stigmatic chamber and of the stigmatic canal of the above-named three species is scraped off, after having been kept in spirits, it is found to be composed of utriculi (including nuclei of the proper shape), but not nearly so numerous as with ordinary orchids. The utriculi cohere more together / and are more transparent; I examined for comparison those of many kinds of orchids which had been kept in spirits, and in all found them much less transparent. In *C. tridentatum*, the ovarium is shorter, much less deeply furrowed, narrower at the base, and internally more solid than in Monachanthus. Again, in all three species of Catasetum the ovule-bearing cords are short; and the ovules present a considerably different appearance, in being thinner, more transparent, and less pulpy than in the numerous other orchids examined for the sake of comparison. Perhaps these bodies hardly ought to be called ovules, although they correspond closely in general appearance and position with true ovules, for I was unable in any case to make out the opening of the testa and the included nucleus; nor were the ovules ever inverted.

From these several facts, namely – the shortness, smoothness, and narrowness of the ovarium, the shortness of the ovule-bearing cords, the state of the ovules themselves, the stigmatic surface not being viscid, the transparent condition of the utriculi – and from neither Sir R. Schomburgk nor Dr Crüger having ever seen *C. tridentatum* producing seed in its native home, or when artificially fertilized, we may confidently look at this species, as well as the other species of Catasetum, as male plants.

With respect to *Monachanthus viridis* and *Myanthus barbatus*, the President of the Linnean Society has kindly permitted me to examine the spike bearing these two so-called genera, preserved in spirits, which was sent home by Sir R. Schomburgk. The flower of the Monachanthus (A, fig. 31) resembles pretty closely in external appearance that of *Catasetum tridentatum* (fig. 30). The labellum, which holds the same relative position to the other parts, is not nearly so deep, / especially on the sides, and its edge is crenated. The other petals and sepals are all reflexed, and are not so much spotted as in the Catasetum. The bract at the base of the ovarium is much larger. The whole column, especially the filament and the spike-like anther, are much shorter; and the rostellum is much less protuberant. The

139

antennae are entirely absent, and the pollen-masses are rudimentary. These are interesting / facts, from corroborating the view taken of the function of the antennae; for as there are no pollinia to eject, an organ adapted to convey the stimulus from the touch of an insect to the rostellum would be useless. I could find no trace of a viscid disc or pedicel, and no doubt they had been lost; for Dr Crüger says[9] that 'the

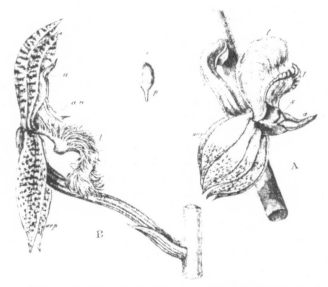

Fig. 31   B. *Myanthus barbatus*   A. *Monachanthus viridis*
a. anther, *an.* antennae, *l.* labellum, *p.* pollen-mass, rudimentary, *s.* stigmatic cleft, *sep* two lower sepals
A. Side view of *Monachanthus viridis* in its natural position (the shading in both drawings has been added from Mr Reiss' drawing in the *Linnean Transactions*)
B. Side view of *Myanthus barbatus* in its natural position

anther of the female flowers drops off immediately after the opening of the same, i.e. before the flower has reached perfection as regards colour, size, and smell. The disc does not cohere, or very slightly, to the pollen-masses, but drops off about the same time, with the anther;' leaving behind them the rudimentary pollen-masses.

Instead of a large stigmatic chamber, there is a narrow transverse

[9] *Journ. Linn. Soc. Bot.*, vol. viii, 1864, p. 127.

cleft close beneath the small anther. I was able to insert one of the pollen-masses of the male Catasetum into this cleft, which from having been kept in spirits was lined with coagulated beads of viscid matter, and with utriculi. The utriculi, differently from those in Catasetum, were charged (after having been kept in spirits) with brown matter. The ovarium is longer, thicker near the base, and more plainly furrowed than in Catasetum; the ovule-bearing cords are also much longer, and the ovules more opaque and pulpy, as in all common orchids. I believe that I saw the opening at the partially inverted end of the testa, with a large projecting nucleus; but as the specimens had been kept many years in spirits and were somewhat altered, I dare not speak positively. From these facts alone it is almost certain that Monachanthus is a female plant; and as already stated, Sir R. Schomburgk and Dr Crüger have both seen it seeding abundantly. Altogether the flower differs in a most / remarkable manner from that of the male *Catasetum tridentatum*, and it is no wonder that the two plants were formerly ranked as distinct genera.

The pollen-masses offer so curious and good an illustration of a structure in a rudimentary condition, that they are worth description; but I must first recur to the perfect pollen-masses of the male Catasetum. These may be seen at D and E, fig. 29, attached to the pedicel: they consist of a large sheet of cemented or waxy pollen-grains, folded over so as to form a sack, with an open slit along the lower surface, within which at the lower and produced end, a layer of highly elastic tissue, forming the caudicle, is attached; the other end being attached to the pedicel of the rostellum. The exterior grains of pollen are more angular, have thicker walls, and are yellower than the interior grains. In the early bud the two pollen-masses are enveloped in two conjoined membranous sacks, which are soon penetrated by the two produced ends of the pollen-masses and by their caudicles; and afterwards the extremities of the caudicles adhere to the pedicel. Before the flower expands the membranous sacks including the two pollen-masses open; and the pollen-masses are left resting naked on the back of the rostellum.

In Monachanthus, on the other hand, the two membranous sacks containing the rudimentary pollen-masses never open; but they easily separate from each other and from the anther. The tissue of which they are formed is thick and pulpy. Like most rudimentary parts, the pollen-masses vary much in size and form; they are only about one-tenth of the bulk of those of the male; they are flask-shaped (*p*, fig. 31), with the lower end greatly produced so as almost to penetrate the exterior or membranous sack. There is / no fissure along their lower surfaces for the protrusion of the caudicles. The exterior pollen-grains are square and have thicker walls than the interior grains, just as in the proper male pollen; and, what is very curious, each cell has its nucleus. Now, R. Brown states[10] that in the early stages of the formation of the pollen-grains of ordinary orchids (as with other plants) a minute nucleus is often visible; so that the rudimentary pollen-grains of Monachanthus apparently have retained – as is so general with rudiments in the animal kingdom – an embryonic character. Lastly, at the base, within each flask-shaped pollen-mass, there is a little mass of brown elastic tissue – that is, a vestige of a caudicle – which runs far up the pointed end of the flask, but does not (at least in some of the specimens) come to the surface, and could never be attached to any part of the pedicel. These rudimentary and enclosed caudicles are, therefore, utterly useless. Notwithstanding the small size and almost aborted condition of the female pollen-masses, when they were placed by Dr Crüger within the stigma of a female plant they emitted 'here and there a rudimentary tube'. The petals then faded and the ovarium enlarged, but after a week it turned yellow and finally dropped off without bringing any seeds to perfection. This appears to me a very curious instance of the slow and gradual manner in which structures are modified; for the female pollen-masses, which can never be naturally removed or applied to the stigma, still partially retain their former powers and function.

Thus every detail of structure which characterizes the male pollen-masses is represented in the female plant in a useless condition. Such cases are familiar to / every naturalist, but can never be observed without renewed interest. At a period not far distant, naturalists will hear with surprise, perhaps with derision, that grave and learned men formerly maintained that such useless organs were not remnants retained by inheritance, but were specially created and arranged in their proper places like dishes on a table (this is the simile of a distinguished botanist) by an Omnipotent hand 'to complete the scheme of nature'.

The third form, *Myanthus barbatus* (fig. 31, B), is sometimes borne on the same plant together with the two preceding forms. The flowers differ greatly in external appearance, but not in essential structure,

---

[10] *Transactions of the Linnean Soc.*, vol. xvi, p. 711.

from those of both the other forms. They generally stand in a reversed position, compared with those of *Catasetum tridentatum* and of *Monachanthus viridis*, that is, with the labellum downwards. The labellum is fringed in an extraordinary manner with long papillae; it has a quite insignificant medial cavity, at the hinder margin of which a curious curved and flattened horn projects, which represents the anvil-like projection on the labellum of the male *C. callosum*. The other petals and sepals are spotted and elongated, with the two lower sepals alone reflexed. The antennae are not so long as in the male *C. tridentatum*; they project symmetrically on each side of the horn-like process at the base of the labellum, with their tips, which are not roughened with papillae, almost entering the medial cavity. The stigmatic chamber is of nearly intermediate size between that of the male and female forms; it is lined with utriculi charged with brown matter. The straight and well-furrowed ovarium is nearly twice as long as that of the female Monachanthus, but not so thick where it joins the flower; the ovules are opaque and pulpy after having been kept / in spirits, and resemble those of the female in all respects, but are not so numerous. I believe that I saw the nucleus projecting from the testa, but dare not, as in the case of Monachanthus, speak positively. The pollinia are about a quarter of the size of those of the male Catasetum, but have a perfectly well developed disc and pedicel. The pollen-masses were lost in the specimens examined by me; but Mr Reiss has given, in the *Linnean Transactions*, a drawing of them, showing that they are of due proportional size and have the proper folded or cleft structure, within which the caudicles are attached. Thus as both the male and female organs are in appearance perfect, *Myanthus barbatus* may be considered as an hermaphrodite form of the same species, of which the Catasetum is the male and Monachanthus the female. Nevertheless, the intermediate forms, which are common in Trinidad, and which resemble more or less closely the above described Myanthus, have never been seen by Dr Crüger to produce seed-capsules.

It is a highly remarkable fact, that this sterile hermaphrodite form resembles in its whole appearance and structure the males of two other species, namely, *C. saccatum* and more especially *C. callosum*, much more closely than it does either the male or female form of the same species. As all orchids, with the exception of a few in the present small subfamily, as well as all the members of several allied groups of plants, are hermaphrodites, there can be no doubt that the common progenitor of the Orchideae was an hermaphrodite. We may therefore attribute the hermaphrodite condition and the general appearance of Myanthus to reversion to a former state; and if so, the ancestors of all the species of Catasetum must / have resembled the males of *C. saccatum* and *callosum*, for as we have just seen, it is to these two plants that Myanthus presents so many striking resemblances.[11]

Lastly I may be permitted to add that Dr Crüger, after having carefully observed these three forms in Trinidad, fully admits the truth of my conclusion that *Catasetum tridentatum* is the male and *Monachanthus viridis* the female of the same species. He further confirms my prediction that insects are attracted to the flowers for the sake of gnawing the labellum, and that they carry the pollen-masses from the male to the female plant. He says 'the male flower emits a peculiar smell about twenty-four hours after opening, and the antennae assume their greatest irritability at the same time. A large humble-bee, noisy and quarrelsome, is now attracted to the flowers by the smell, and a great number of them may be seen every morning for a few hours disputing with each other for a place in the interior of the labellum, for the purpose of gnawing off the cellular tissue on the side opposite to the column, so that they turn their backs to the latter. As soon as they touch the upper antenna of the male flower, the pollen-mass, with its disc and gland, is fixed on their back, and they are often seen flying about with this peculiar-looking ornament on them. I have never seen it attached except to the very middle of the / thorax. When the bee walks about, the pollen-mass lies flat on the back and wings; but when the insect enters a female flower, always with the labellum turned upwards, the pollinium, which is hinged to the gland by elastic tissue, falls back by its own weight and rests on the anterior face of the column. When the insect returns backwards from the flower, the pollinia are caught by the upper margin of the stigmatic cavity, which projects a little beyond the face of the column; and if the gland be then

---

[11] The male of the Indian antelope (*A. bezoartica*) after castration produces horns of a widely different shape from those of the perfect male; and larger and thicker than those occasionally produced by the female. We see something of the same kind in the horns of the common ox. I have remarked in my *Descent of Man*, 2nd edit., p. 506, that such cases may probably be attributed to reversion to a former state of the species; for we have good reason to believe that any cause which disturbs the constitution leads to reversion. Myanthus, though having the organs of both sexes apparently perfect, is sterile; it has therefore had its sexual constitution disturbed, and this seems to have caused it to revert in character to a former state.

detached from the back of the insect, or the tissues which connect the pollinia with the caudicle, or this with the gland, break, fecundation takes place.' Dr Crüger sent me specimens of the humble-bees which he caught gnawing the labellum, and these consist of *Euglossa nov. spec.*, *cajennensis* and *piliventris*.

Catasetum mentosum and a Monachanthus, according to Fritz Müller,[12] grow in the same district of South Brazil; and he easily succeeded in fertilizing the latter with pollen from the former. The pollen-masses could be inserted only partially into the narrow stigmatic cleft; but when this was done, a process of deglutition, as described under Cirrhaea, commenced and was slowly completed. On the other hand, Fritz Müller entirely failed in his attempts to fertilize the flowers of this Catasetum with its own pollen or with that from another plant. The pollinia of the female Monachanthus are very small; the pollen-grains are variable both in size and shape; the anther never opens, and the pollen-masses are not attached to the caudicle. Nevertheless, when these rudimentary pollen-masses, which can never naturally be removed from their cells, were placed on the slightly viscid / stigma of the male Catasetum, they emitted their tubes.

The genus Catasetum is interesting to an unusual degree in several respects. The separation of the sexes is unknown among other orchids, except perhaps in the allied genus Cycnoches. In Catasetum we have three sexual forms, generally borne on separate plants, but sometimes mingled together on the same plant; and these three forms are wonderfully different from one another, much more different than, for instance a peacock is from a peahen. But the appearance of these three forms now ceases to be an anomaly, and can no longer be viewed as an unparalleled instance of variability.

This genus is still more interesting in its manner of fertilization. We see a flower patiently waiting with its antennae stretched forth in a well-adapted position, ready to give notice whenever an insect puts its head into the cavity of the labellum. The female Monachanthus, not having true pollinia to eject, is destitute of antennae. In the male and hermaphrodite forms, namely *Catasetum tridentatum* and *Myanthus barbatus*, the pollinia lie doubled up, like a spring, ready to be instantly shot forth when the antennae are touched. The disc end is always projected foremost, and is coated with viscid matter which quickly sets hard and affixes the hinged pedicel firmly to the insect's body. The

---

[12] *Bot. Zeitung*, 1868, p. 630.

insect flies from flower to flower, till at last it visits a female plant: it then inserts one of the pollen-masses into the stigmatic cavity. As soon as the insect flies away the elastic caudicle, made weak enough to yield to the viscidity of the stigmatic surface, breaks, and leaves behind a pollen-mass; then the pollen-tubes slowly protrude, penetrate the stigmatic canal, and the act of fertilization is completed. Who would have / been bold enough to have surmised that the propagation of a species depended on so complex, so apparently artificial, and yet so admirable an arrangement?

I have examined three other genera placed by Lindley in the small subfamily of Catasetidae, namely, Mormodes, Cycnoches and Cyrto-podium. The latter plant was purchased by me under this name, and bore a flower stem about four feet in height with yellowish bracts spotted with red; but the flowers presented none of the remarkable peculiarities of the three other genera, with the exception that the anther was hinged to a point projecting from the summit of the column, as in Catasetum.

Mormodes ignea. To show how difficult it sometimes is to understand the manner in which an orchid is fertilized, I may mention that I carefully examined twelve flowers,[13] trying various experiments and recording the results, before I could at all make out the meaning and action of the several parts. It was plain that the pollinia were ejected, as in Catasetum, but how each part of the flower played its proper part I could not even conjecture. I had given up the case as hopeless, until summing up my observations, the explanation presently to be given, and subsequently proved by repeated experiments to be correct, suddenly occurred to me.

The flower presents an extraordinary appearance, and its mechanism is even more curious than its appearance (fig. 32). The base of the column is bent backwards, at right angles to the ovarium or footstalk, / and then resumes an upright position to near its summit, where it is again bent. It is, also, twisted in a unique manner, so that its front surface, including the anther, rostellum, and the upper part of the stigma faces one side of the flower; this being either to the / right or left, according to the position of the flower on the spike. The twisted stigmatic surface extends down to the base of the column and is

---

[13] I must express my cordial thanks to Mr Rucker, of West Hill, Wandsworth, for having lent me a plant of this Mormodes with two fine spikes, bearing an abundance of flowers, and for having allowed me to keep the plant for a considerable time.

hollowed out into a deep cavity at its upper end. The large viscid disc of the pollinium is lodged in this cavity close beneath the rostellum; and the rostellum is seen in the drawing (*pd.*) covered by the bowed pedicel.

The anther-case (*a* in the figure) is elongated and triangular, closely resembling that of Catasetum; but it does not extend up to the apex of

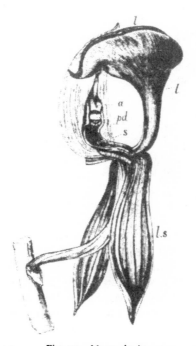

Fig. 32   *Mormodes ignea*
Lateral view of flower, with the upper sepal and the near upper petal cut off
N.B. The labellum in the drawing is a little lifted up, to show the depression on its under surface, which ought to be pressed close down on the bent summit of the column

a. anther, *pd.* pedicel of pollinium, *s.* stigma, *l.* labellum, *l.s.* lateral sepal

the column. The apex consists of a thin flattened filament, which from the analogy of Catasetum I suppose to be the produced filament of the stamen; but it may be a prolongation of some other element of the column. In the bud-state it is straight, but before the flower expands, it becomes much bent by the pressure of the labellum. A group of spiral vessels runs up the column as far as the summit of the anther-case;

they are then reflexed and run some way down the anther-case. The point of reflexion forms a short thin hinge by which the top of the anther-case is articulated to the column beneath its bent summit. The hinge, although smaller than a pin's head in size, is of paramount importance; for it is sensitive and conveys the stimulus from a touch to the disc of the pollinium, causing it to separate from its place of attachment. The hinge also serves to guide the pollinium during its ejection. As it has to convey the necessary stimulus to the disc, one may suspect that a portion of the rostellum, which lies in close contact with the filament of the anther, runs up to this point; but I could not here detect any difference in structure on comparing these parts with those of Catasetum. The cellular tissue round the hinge is gorged with fluid, and a large drop exudes when the anther is torn from the column during the ejection / of the pollinium. This gorged condition may perhaps facilitate the rupture of the hinge.

The pollinium does not differ much from that of Catasetum (see fig. 29, D, p. 183); and it lies in like manner curved round the rostellum, which is less protuberant than in that genus. The upper and broad end of the pedicel, however, extends beneath the pollen-masses within the anther; and these are attached by rather weak caudicles to a medial crest on its upper surface.

The viscid surface of the large disc lies in contact with the roof of the stigmatic cavity, so that it cannot be touched by an insect visiting the flower. The anterior end of the disc is furnished with a small dependent curtain (dimly shown in fig. 32); and this, before the act of ejection, is continuously joined on each side to the upper margins of the stigmatic cavity. The pedicel is united to the posterior end of the disc; but when the disc is freed, the lowermost part of the pedicel becomes doubly bent, so that it then appears as if attached by a hinge to the centre of the disc.

The labellum is a highly remarkable structure: it is narrowed at its base into a nearly cylindrical footstalk, and its sides are so much reflexed as almost to meet at the back, forming a folded crest on the summit of the flower. After rising up perpendicularly it arches over the apex of the column, against which it is firmly pressed down. The labellum at this point is hollowed out (even in the bud) into a slight cavity, which receives the bent summit of the column. This slight depression manifestly represents the large cavity, with thick fleshy walls, which insects gnaw, on the anterior surface of the labellum, in the several species of Catasetum. Here by a singular change of function, the cavity serves to keep the labellum in its proper position on the summit of the column, but is, perhaps, / likewise attractive to insects. In the drawing (fig. 32) the labellum has been forcibly raised a little up, so as to show the depression and the bent filament. In its natural position it may almost be compared to a huge cocked-hat, supported by a footstalk and placed on the head of the column.

The twisting of the column, which I have seen in no other orchid, causes all the important organs of fructification in the flowers on the left side of the spike to face to the left, and in all those on the right side to face to the right. So that two flowers taken from opposite sides of the same spike and held in the same relative position are seen to be twisted in opposite directions. One single flower, which was crowded by the others, was barely twisted, so that its column faced the labellum. The labellum is also slightly twisted: for instance, in the flower figured, which faced to the left, the midrib of the labellum was first twisted to the right-hand, and then to the left, but in a less degree, and being bent over it pressed on the posterior surface of the crooked summit of the column. The twisting of all the parts of the flower commences in the bud.

The position thus acquired by the several organs is of the highest importance; for if the column and labellum had not been twisted laterally, the pollinia, when shot forth, would have struck the overarching labellum and have then rebounded, as actually occurred with the single abnormal flower having a nearly straight column. If the organs had not been twisted in opposite directions on the opposite sides of the same crowded spike, so as always to face to the outside, there would not have been a clear space for the ejection of the pollinia and their adhesion to insects.

When the flower is mature the three sepals hang / down, but the two upper petals remain nearly upright. The bases of the sepals, and especially of the two upper petals, are thick and swollen and have a yellowish tint; when quite mature, they are so gorged with fluid, that, if punctured by a fine glass tube, the fluid rises by capillary attraction to some height in it. These swollen bases, as well as the footstalk of the labellum, have a decidedly sweet and pleasant taste; and I can hardly doubt that they are attractive to insects, for no free nectar is secreted.

I will now endeavour to show how all the parts of the flower are co-ordinated and act together. The pedicel of the pollinium is bowed round the rostellum, as in Catasetum; in this latter genus, when freed, it merely straightens itself with force, in Mormodes something more takes place. If the reader will look forward to fig. 34 (p. 157), he will see a section of the flower-bud of the allied genus of Cycnoches, which differs only in the shape of the anther and in the viscid disc having a much deeper dependent curtain. Now let him suppose the pedicel of the pollinium to be so elastic that, when freed, it not only straightens itself, but suddenly bends back on itself with a reversed curvature, so as to form an irregular hoop. The curved surface which was before in contact with the protuberant rostellum now forms the outside of the hoop. The exterior surface of the curtain, which depends beneath the disc, is not viscid; and it now lies on the anther-case, with the viscid surface of the disc on the outside. This is exactly what takes place with Mormodes. But the pollinium assumes with such force its reversed curvature (aided, apparently, by a transverse curling outwards of the margins of the pedicel), that it not only forms itself into a hoop, but suddenly springs away from the protuberant / face of the rostellum. As the two pollen-masses adhere, at first, rather firmly to the anther-case, the latter is torn off by the rebound; and as the thin hinge at the summit of the anther-case does not yield so easily as the basal margin, the pollinium together with the anther-case is instantly swung upwards like a pendulum. But in the course of the upward swing the hinge yields, and the whole body is projected perpendicularly up in the air, an inch or two above and close in front of the terminal part of the labellum. If no object is in the way, as the pollinium falls down, it generally alights and sticks, though not firmly, on the folded crest of the labellum, directly over the column. I witnessed repeatedly all that has been here described.

The curtain of the disc, which, after the pollinium has formed itself into a hoop, lies on the anther-case, is of considerable service in preventing the viscid edge of the disc from adhering to the anther, and thus permanently retaining the pollinium in the form of a hoop. This would have been fatal, as we shall presently see, to a subsequent movement of the pollinium which is necessary for the fertilization of the flower. In some of my experiments, when the free action of the parts was checked, this did occur, and the pollinium, together with the anther-case, remained permanently glued together in the shape of an irregular hoop.

I have already stated that the minute hinge by which the anther-case is articulated to the column, a little way beneath its bent filamentary apex, is sensitive to a touch. I tried four times and found that I could touch with some force any other part; but when I gently touched this point with the finest needle, instantly the membrane which unites the disc / to the edges of the stigmatic cavity where it is lodged, ruptured, and the pollinium was shot upwards and fell on the crest of the labellum as just described.

Now let us suppose an insect to alight on the folded crest of the labellum, and no other convenient landing-place is afforded, and then to lean over the front of the column so as to gnaw or suck the bases of the petals swollen with sweet fluid. The weight and movements of the insect would disturb the labellum and the bent underlying summit of the column; and the latter, pressing on the hinge in the angle, would cause the ejection of the pollinium, which would infallibly strike the head of the insect and adhere to it. I tried by placing my gloved finger on the summit of the labellum, with the tip just projecting beyond its margin, and then gently moving my finger it was really beautiful to see how instantly the pollinium was projected upwards, and how accurately the viscid surface of the disc struck my finger and firmly adhered to it. Nevertheless, I doubt whether the weight and movements of an insect would suffice to thus act indirectly on the sensitive point; but look at the drawing and see how probable it is that an insect leaning over would place its front legs over the edge of the labellum on the summit of the anther-case, and thus touch the sensitive point. The pollinium would then be ejected, and the viscid disc would certainly strike and adhere to the insect's head.

Before proceeding, it may be worth while to mention some of the early trials which I made. I pricked deeply the column in different parts, including the stigma, and cut off the petals, and even the labellum, without causing the ejection of the pollinium; this, however, once happened when I cut rather roughly through the thick footstalk of the labellum, the filamentary / summit of the column no doubt having been thus disturbed. When I gently prised up the anther-case at its base or on one side, the pollinium was ejected, but then the sensitive hinge would necessarily have been bent. When the flower has long remained expanded and is nearly ready for spontaneous ejection, a slight jar on any part of the flower causes the action. Pressure on the thin pedicel of the pollinium, and therefore on the underlying protuberant rostellum, is followed by the ejection of the pollen-masses; but this is not surprising, as the stimulus from a touch on the sensitive hinge has to be conveyed through this part of the rostellum to the disc. In Catasetum slight pressure on this point does not cause the act of ejection; but in this genus the protuberant part of the rostellum does not lie in the course along which the stimulus has to be conveyed from the antennae to the disc. A drop of chloroform, of spirits of wine, or of boiling water placed on this part of the rostellum produced no effect; nor, to my surprise, did exposure of the whole flower to vapour of chloroform.

Seeing that this part of the rostellum was sensitive to pressure, and that the flower was widely open on one side, and being preoccupied with the case of Catasetum, I at first felt convinced that insects entered the lower part of the flower and touched the rostellum. Accordingly I pressed the rostellum with variously shaped objects, but the viscid disc never once adhered in a proper manner to the object. If I used a thick needle, the pollinium, when ejected, formed a hoop round it with the viscid surface outside; if I used a broad flat object, the pollinium struggled against it and sometimes coiled itself up spirally, but the disc either did not adhere at all, or very imperfectly. At the close of the twelfth trial I was in despair. The / strange position of the labellum, perched on the summit of the column, ought to have shown me that here was the place for experiment. I ought to have rejected the notion that the labellum was thus placed for no good purpose. This plain guide was overlooked, and for a long time I completely failed to understand the structure of the flower.

We have seen that when the pollinium is ejected and swings upwards, it adheres by the viscid surface of the disc to any object projecting beyond the edge of the labellum directly over the column. When thus attached, it forms an irregular hoop, with the torn-off anther-case still covering the pollen-masses which are close to the disc, but protected from adhering to it by the dependent curtain. Whilst in this position the projecting and bowed part of the pedicel would effectually prevent the pollen-masses from being placed on the stigma, even supposing the anther-case to have fallen off. Now let us suppose the pollinium to be attached to an insect's head, and observe what takes place. The pedicel, when first separated from the rostellum, is damp; as it dries, it slowly straightens itself, and when perfectly straight the anther-case readily drops off. The pollen-masses are now naked, and they are attached to the end of the pedicel by easily ruptured caudicles, at the right distance and in a proper position for their insertion into the adhesive stigma, as soon as the insect visits another flower. Thus every detail of structure is now perfectly adapted for the act of fertilization.

When the anther-case drops off, if has performed its triple function;

namely, its hinge as an organ of sense, its weak attachment to the column as a guide causing the pollinium at first to swing perpendicularly upwards, and its lower margin, together with the curtain of the / disc, as a protection to the pollen-masses from being permanently glued to the viscid disc.

From observations made on fifteen flowers, it was ascertained that the straightening of the pedicel does not occur until from twelve to fifteen minutes have elapsed. The first movement causing the act of ejection is due to elasticity, and the second slow movement to the drying of the outer and convex surface; but this latter movement differs from that observed in the pollinia of so many Vandeae and Ophreae, for, when the pollinium of this Mormodes was placed in water, it did not recover the hoop-like form which it had at first acquired by elasticity.

The flowers are hermaphrodites. The pollinia are perfectly developed. The elongated stigmatic surface is extremely viscid and abounds with innumerable utriculi, the contents of which shrink and become coagulated after immersion for less than an hour in spirits of wine. When placed in spirits for a day, the utriculi were so acted on that they disappeared, and this I have not noticed in any other orchid. The ovules, after exposure to spirits for a day or two, presented the usual semi-opaque, pulpy appearance common to all hermaphrodite and female orchids. From the unusual length of the stigmatic surface I expected that, if the pollinia were not ejected from the excitement of a touch, the anther-case would have detached itself, and the pollen-masses would have swung downwards and fertilized the stigma of the same flower. Accordingly, I left four flowers untouched; after they had remained expanded from eight to ten days, the elasticity of the pedicel conquered the force of attachment and the pollinia were spontaneously ejected, but they did not fall on the stigma and were subsequently wasted. /

Although *Mormodes ignea* is an hermaphrodite, yet it must be as truly dioecious in function as Catasetum; for as it takes from twelve to fifteen minutes before the pedicel of an ejected pollinium straightens itself and the anther-case drops off, it is almost certain that within this time an insect with a pollinium attached to its head would have left one plant and flown to another.

Mormodes luxata. This rare and fine species is fertilized in the same manner as *Mormodes ignea*, but differs in several important points of structure. The right and left sides of the same flower differ from one another even in a greater degree than in the last species. One of the petals and one of the sepals project at right angles to the column, while the corresponding ones stand upright and surround it. The upturned and twisted labellum is furnished with two large lateral lobes: of these one embraces the column, while the other stands partly open on the side where the one petal and sepal lie flat. Insects can thus easily enter the flower on this latter side. All the flowers on the left side of the spike are open on their left sides, while those on the right side are open on this side. The twisted column with all the important accessory parts, together with the rectangularly bent apex, closely resemble the corresponding parts in *M. ignea*. But the underside of the labellum does not rest on and press against the rectangularly bent apex of the column. This stands free in the middle of a cup formed by the extremity of the labellum.

I did not obtain many flowers fit for examination, as three had ejected their pollinia owing to the shocks received during their journey. I pricked deeply the labellum, column and stigma of some of the flowers without any effect; but when I lightly touched with a / needle, not the anther-hinge as in the last species, but the apex of the column of one flower, the pollinium was instantly ejected. The bases of the petals and sepals are not swollen and succulent like those of *M. ignea*; and I have little doubt that insects gnaw the labellum, which is thick and fleshy, with the same peculiar taste as in Catasetum. If an insect were to gnaw the terminal cup, it could hardly fail to touch the apex of the column, and then the pollinium would swing upwards and adhere to some part of the insect's body. The pedicels of the pollinia straighten themselves and the anther-cases are cast off, in about fifteen minutes after the act of ejection. We may therefore confidently believe that this species is fertilized in the same peculiar manner as *Mormodes ignea*.

Cycnoches ventricosum. Mr Veitch was so kind as to send me on two occasions several flowers and flower-buds of this extraordinary plant. A sketch of a flower in its natural position, with one sepal cut off, is shown at fig. 33 (p. 156), and a longitudinal section through a young bud at fig. 34 (p. 157).

The labellum is thick and fleshy, with the usual taste of this organ in the Catasetidae; it resembles in shape a shallow basin turned upside down. The two other petals and the three sepals are reflexed. The column is almost cylindrical, thin, flexible, elastic and of extraordinary length. It curves round so as to bring the stigma and anther opposite to and beneath the convex surface of the labellum. The apex of the column is not nearly so much produced as in Mormodes and Catasetum. The pollinia closely resemble those of Mormodes; but the disc is larger, and its curtain, which is fringed, is so large that it covers the whole entrance into the stigmatic chamber. The structure of these parts is best seen in the section, / fig. 34; in which the pedicel of the pollinium has not as yet become separate from the rostellum, but the figure line of separation is shown by a line (dotted in the figure) of hyaline tissue. The filament of the anther (*f*, fig. 34) has not as yet grown to its full length. When fully developed it bears two little leaf-like appendages which lie on the anther. Lastly, on the sides of the stigma there are two slight protuberances (fig. 33), which apparently represent the antennae of Catasetum, but have not the same function.

Neither the labellum nor the protuberances on the sides of the stigma are at all sensitive; but when on three occasions I momentarily touched the filament, between the little leaf-like appendages, the pollinium was ejected in the same manner and through the same mechanism as in Mormodes; but it was thrown only to the distance of about an inch. If the filament had been touched by an object which had not been quickly removed, or if by an insect, the viscid disc would certainly have adhered to it. Mr Veitch informs me that he has often touched the end of the column, and the pollinium has adhered to his finger. When the pollinium is ejected, the pedicel forms a hoop, with the exterior surface of the curtain of the disc resting on and covering the anther. In about fifteen minutes the pedicel straightens itself, and the anther-case drops off; and now the pollinium is in a right position for fertilizing another flower. As soon as the viscid matter on the under surface of the disc is exposed to the air it quickly changes colour and sets hard. It then adheres with surprising force to any object. From these various facts and from the analogy of the other Catasetidae, we may conclude that insects visit the flowers for the sake of gnawing the labellum: / but it cannot be predicted whether they alight on the surface which is uppermost in the drawing (fig. 33) and then crawl over the margin so as to gnaw the convex surface, and in doing so touch with their abdomens / the extremity of the column, or whether they first alight on this part of the column; but in either case they would cause the ejection of the pollinia, which would adhere to some part of their bodies.

The specimens which I examined were certainly male plants, for the pollinia were well developed. The stigmatic cavity was lined with a thick layer of pulpy matter which was not adhesive. But as the flowers cannot possibly be fertilized until the pollinia have been ejected, together with the great curtain which covers the whole stigmatic surface, it may be that / this surface becomes at a later period adhesive so as to secure the pollen-masses. The ovules when kept for some time in alcohol were filled with brownish pulpy matter, as is always the case

Fig. 33   *Cycnoches ventricosum*
Flower viewed in its natural dependent position
c. column, after the ejection of the pollinium together with the anther, *f.* filament of anther, *s.* stigmatic cavity, *L.* labellum, *pet.* the two lateral petals, *sep.* sepals

with perfect ovules. Therefore it appears that this Cycnoches must be an hermaphrodite; and Mr Bateman, in his work on the Orchideae, says that the present species produces seeds without being, as I understand, artifically fertilized; but how this is possible is unintelligible to me. On the other hand, Beer says[14] that the stigma of

[14] Quoted by Irmisch, *Beiträge zur Biologie der Orchideen*, 1853, p. 22.

156

Cycnoches is dry, and that the plant never sets seeds. According to Lindley *C. ventricosum* produces on the same scape flowers with a simple labellum, others with a much segmented and differently coloured labellum (viz., the so-called *C. egertonianum*), and others in an intermediate condition. From the analogous differences in the flowers of Catasetum, we are tempted to believe that we here have male, female, and hermaphrodite forms of the same species of Cycnoches.[15]

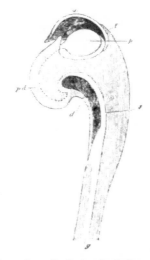

Fig. 34   Diagrammatic section of a flower-bud, the column placed upright
a. anther, *f.* filament of anther, *p.* pollen-mass, *pd.* pedicel of pollinium, barely separated as yet from the rostellum, *d.* disc of pollinium with the dependent curtain, *s.* stigmatic chamber, *g.* stigmatic canal leading to the ovarium

I have now finished my description of the Catasetidae as well as of many other Vandeae. The study of these wonderful and often beautiful productions, with all their many adaptations, with parts capable of movement, and other parts endowed with something so like, though no doubt different from, sensibility, has been to me most

[15] Lindley's *Vegetable Kingdom*, 1853, p. 177. He has also published in the *Botanical Register*, fol. 1951, a case of two forms appearing on the same scape of another species of Cycnoches. Mr Bateman also says that *C. egertonianum* has been known to produce in Guatemala and once in England scapes of a purple-flowered and widely different species of Cycnoches; but that it generally produces in England scapes of the common yellow *C. ventricosum.*

interesting. The flowers of orchids, in their strange and endless diversity of shape, may be compared / with the great vertebrate class of fish, or still more appropriately with tropical homopterous insects, which appear to us as if they had been modelled in the wildest caprice, but this no doubt is due to our ignorance of their requirements and conditions of life. /

CHAPTER VIII

CYPRIPEDEAE – HOMOLOGIES OF THE FLOWERS OF ORCHIDS

Cypripedium, differs much from all other orchids – Labellum in the form of a slipper with two small orifices by which insects can escape – Manner of fertilization by small bees of the genus Andrena – Homological nature of the several parts of the flowers of the Orchideae – Wonderful amount of modification which they have undergone.

We have now arrived at Lindley's last and seventh tribe, including, according to most botanists, only a single genus, Cypripedium, which differs from all other orchids far more than any other two of these do from one another. An enormous amount of extinction must have swept away a multitude of intermediate forms, and has left this single genus, now widely distributed, as a record of a former and more simple state of the great Orchidean order. Cypripedium possesses no rostellum; for all three stigmas are fully developed, though confluent. The single anther, which is present in all other orchids, is here rudimentary, and is represented by a singular shield-like projecting body, deeply notched or hollowed out on its lower margin. There are two fertile anthers which belong to an inner whorl, represented in ordinary orchids by various rudiments. The grains of pollen are not united together by threes or fours, as in so many other genera, nor are they tied together by elastic threads, nor furnished with a caudicle, nor cemented into waxy masses. The labellum is of / large size, and is a compound organ as in all other orchids.

The following remarks apply only to the six species which I have examined, namely, C. *barbatum, purpuratum, insigne, venustum, pubescens* and *acaule*; though I have casually looked at some other kinds. The basal part of the labellum is folded round the short column, so that its edges nearly meet along the dorsal surface; and the broad extremity is folded over in a peculiar manner, forming a sort of shoe, which closes up the end of the flower. Hence arises the English name of Ladies'-slipper. The overarching edges of the labellum are inflected or sometimes only smooth and / polished internally; and this is of much importance, as it prevents insects which have once entered the labellum from escaping through the great opening in the upper surface. In the position in which the flower grows, as here represented, the dorsal surface of the column is uppermost. The stigmatic surface is slightly protuberant, and is not adhesive; it stands nearly parallel to the lower surface of the labellum. With a flower in its natural state, the margin of the dorsal surface of the stigma can be barely distinguished between the edges of the labellum and through the notch in the

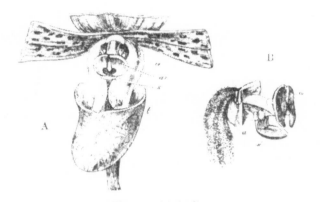

Fig. 35 *Cypripedium*

a. anther, a'. rudimentary, shield-like anther, s. stigma, l. labellum

A. Flower viewed from above, with the sepals and petals, excepting the labellum, partly cut off. The labellum has been slightly depressed, so that the dorsal surface of the stigma is exposed; the edges of the labellum have thus become a little separated and the toe or extremity stands lower than is natural

B. Side view of column, with all the sepals and petals removed

rudimentary, shield-like anther (a'); but in the drawing (s, fig. A) the margin of the stigma has been brought outside the edges of the depressed labellum, and the toe is a little bent downwards, so that the flower is represented as rather more open than it really is. The edges of the pollen-masses of the two lateral anthers (a) can be seen through the two small orifices or open spaces in the labellum (fig. A) on each side, close to the column. These two orifices are essential for the fertilization of the flower.

The grains of pollen are coated by and immersed in viscid fluid, which is so glutinous that it can be drawn out into short threads. As the two anthers stand behind and above the lower convex surface (see fig. B) of the stigma, it is impossible that the glutinous pollen can without some mechanical aid get on to this, the efficient surface of the stigma. The economy here shown by nature in her manner of gaining the same end is surprising. In all the other orchids seen by me, the stigma is viscid and more or less concave, by which means the dry pollen, transported by means of the viscid matter secreted by the rostellum or modified stigma, is retained. In Cypripedium the pollen is glutinous, and assumes the function of viscidity, which / in all other orchids except Vanilla belongs exclusively to the rostellum and the two confluent stigmas. These latter organs, on the other hand, in Cypripedium entirely lose their viscidity, and at the same time become slightly convex, so as more effectually to rub off the glutinous pollen adhering to the body of an insect. Moreover in several of the North American species, as in *C. acaule* and *pubescens*, the surface of the stigma is beset, as Professor Asa Gray remarks,[1] 'with minute, rigid, sharp-pointed papillae, all directed forwards, which are excellently adapted to brush off the pollen from an insect's head or back'. There is one partial exception to the above rule of the pollen of Cypripedium being viscid while the stigma is not viscid and is not convex; for in *C. acaule* the pollen is more granular and less viscid, according to Asa Gray, than in the other American species, and in *C. acaule* alone the stigma is slightly concave and viscid. So that here the exception almost proves the truth of the general rule.

I have never been able to detect nectar within the labellum, and Kurr[2] makes the same remark with resepct to *C. calceolus*. The inner surface of the labellum, however, in those species which I examined, is clothed with hairs, the tips of which secrete little drops of slightly viscid fluid. And these if sweet or nutritious would suffice to attract insects. The fluid when dried forms a brittle crust on the summits of the hairs. Whatever the attraction may be, it is certain that small bees frequently enter the labellum.

Formerly I supposed that insects alighted on the labellum and inserted their proboscides through either / of the orifices close to the anthers; for I found that when a bristle was thus inserted the glutinous pollen adhered to it, and could afterwards be left on the stigma; but this latter part of the operation was not well effected. After the

[1] *American Journal of Science*, vol. xxxiv, 1862, p. 428.
[2] *Bedeutung der Nektarien*, 1833, p. 29.

publication of my book Professor Asa Gray wrote to me[3] that he was convinced from an examination of several American species that the flowers were fertilized by small insects entering the labellum through the large opening on the upper surface, and crawling out by one of the two small orifices close to the anthers and stigma. Accordingly I first introduced some flies into the labellum of *C. pubescens*, though the large upper opening, but they were either too large or too stupid, and did not crawl out properly. I then caught and placed within the labellum a very small bee which seemed of about the right size, namely, *Andrena parvula*, and this by a strange chance proved, as we shall presently see, to belong to the genus on which in a state of nature the fertilization of *C. calceolus* depends. The bee vainly endeavoured to crawl out again the same way by which it had entered, but always fell backwards, owing to the margins being inflected. The labellum thus acts like one of those conical traps with the edges turned inwards, which are sold to catch beetles and cockroaches in the London kitchens. It could not creep out through the slit between the folded edges of the basal part of the labellum, as the elongated, triangular, rudimentary stamen here closes the passage. Ultimately it forced its way out through one of the small orifices close to one of the anthers, and was found when caught to be smeared with the glutinous pollen. I then put the same bee back into the labellum; and again it crawled out through one of the small / orifices, always covered with pollen. I repeated the operation five times, always with the same result. I afterwards cut away the labellum, so as to examine the stigma, and found its whole surface covered with pollen. It should be noticed that an insect in making its escape must first brush past the stigma and afterwards one of the anthers, so that it cannot leave pollen on the stigma, until being already smeared with pollen from one flower it enters another; and thus there will be a good chance of cross-fertilization between two distinct plants. Delpino[4] with much sagacity foresaw that some insect would be discovered to act in this manner; for he argued that if an insect were to insert its proboscis, as I had supposed, from the outside through one of the small orifices close to one of the anthers, the stigma would be liable to be fertilized by the plant's own pollen; and in this he did not believe, from having confidence in what I have often insisted on – namely, that all the

[3] See also *American Journal of Science*, vol. xxxiv, 1862, p. 427.
[4] *Fecondazione nelle Piante Antocarpee*, 1867, p. 20.

contrivances for fertilization are arranged so that the stigma shall receive pollen from a distinct flower or plant. But these speculations are now all superfluous; for, owing to the admirable observations of Dr H. Müller,[5] we know that *Cypripedium calceolus* in a state of nature is fertilized in the manner just described by bees belonging to five species of Andrena.

Thus the use of all the parts of the flower – namely, the inflected edges, or the polished inner sides of the labellum – the two orifices and their position close to the anthers and stigma – the large size of the medial rudimentary stamen – are rendered intelligible. An / insect which enters the labellum is thus compelled to crawl out by one of the two narrow passages, on the sides of which the pollen-masses and stigma are placed. We have seen that exactly the same end is gained in the case of Coryanthes by the labellum being half filled with secreted fluid; and in the case of Pterostylis and some other Australian orchids by the labellum being irritable, so that when touched by an entering insect it shuts up the flower, with the exception of a single narrow passage.[6]

HOMOLOGICAL NATURE OF THE SEVERAL PARTS OF THE FLOWERS OF THE ORCHIDEAE

The theoretical structure of few flowers has been so largely discussed as that of the Orchideae; nor is this surprising, seeing how unlike they are to common flowers; and here will be a convenient place for considering this subject. No group of organic beings can be well understood until their homologies are made out; that is, until the general pattern, or, as it has often been called, the ideal type, of the several members of the group is intelligible. No one member may now exist exhibiting the full pattern; but this does not make the subject less important to the naturalist – probably makes it more important for the full understanding of the group.

[5] *Verh. d. Nat. Ver. für Pr. Rheinland und Westfal.*, Jahrg. xxv, III. Folge, v. Bd. p. 1: see also *Befruchtung der Blumen*, 1873, p. 76.

[6] *Selenipedium palmifolium* is one of the Cypripedeae, and according to Dr Crüger (*Journ. Linn. Soc. Bot.*, vol. viii, 1864, p. 134) bears very fragrant flowers, which 'in all probability are always impregnated by insects. The labellum is, like some Aristolochia-flowers, constructed after the fish-pot system, i.e. a funnel-shaped opening conducts into it, and insects find it difficult to escape through the same. The only other opening near the base of the labellum is partly closed by the sexual apparatus, and the insect has to force its way out there.'

The homologies of any being, or group of beings, / can be most surely made out by tracing their embryological development when that is possible; or by the discovery of organs in a rudimentary condition; or by tracing, through a long series of beings, a close gradation from one part to another, until the two parts or organs, though employed for widely different functions and most unlike each other, can be joined by a succession of short links. No instance is known of a close gradation between two organs, unless they are homologically one and the same organ.

The importance of the science of homology rests on its giving us the keynote of the possible amount of difference in plan within any group; it allows us to class under proper heads the most diversified organs; it shows us gradations which would otherwise have been overlooked, and thus aids us in classification; it explains many monstrosities; it leads to the detection of obscure and hidden parts, or mere vestiges of parts, and shows us the meaning of rudiments. Besides these uses, homology clears away the mist from such terms as the scheme of nature, ideal types, archetypal patterns or ideas, etc.; for these terms come to express real facts. The naturalist, thus guided, sees that all homologous parts or organs, however much they may be diversified, are modifications of one and the same ancestral organ; in tracing existing gradations he gains a clue in tracing, as far as that is possible, the probable course of modification through which beings have passed during a long line of generations. He may feel assured that, whether he follows embryological development, or searches for the merest rudiment, or traces gradations between the most different beings, he is pursuing the same object by different routes, and is tending towards the knowledge of the actual progenitor of the group, as it once grew and / lived. Thus the subject of homology gains largely in interest.

Although this subject, under whatever aspect it be viewed, will always be most interesting to the student of nature, it is very doubtful whether the following details on the homological nature of the flowers of orchids will possess any interest for the general reader. If, indeed, he cares to see how much light an acquaintance with homology, though far from perfect, throws on a subject, this will, perhaps, be nearly as good an instance as could be given. He will see how curiously a flower may be moulded out of many separate organs – how perfect the cohesion of primordially distinct parts may become – how organs may be used for purposes widely different from their proper uses –

how other organs may be entirely suppressed, or leave mere useless emblems of their former existence. Finally, he will see how enormous has been the amount of change which these flowers have undergone from their parental or typical form.

Robert Brown first clearly discussed the homologies of orchids,[7] and left, as might be expected, little to be done. Guided by the general structure of monocotyledonous plants and by various considerations, he propounded the doctrine that the flower properly consists of three sepals, three petals, six anthers in two whorls or circles (of which only one anther belonging to the outer whorl is perfect in all the common forms), and of three pistils, with one of them modified into the rostellum. These fifteen organs are arranged as usual, alternately, three within three, in five whorls. Of the existence of three of the anthers in two of / the whorls, R. Brown offers no sufficient evidence, but believes that they are combined with the labellum, whenever that organ presents crests or ridges. In these views Brown is followed by Lindley.[8]

Brown traced the spiral vessels in the flower by making transverse sections,[9] and only occasionally, as far as it appears, by longitudinal sections. As spiral vessels are developed at a very early period of growth, and this circumstance always gives much value to a part in making out homologies; and as they are apparently of high functional importance, though their function is not well known, it appeared to me, guided also by the advice of Dr Hooker, to be worth while to trace upwards all the spiral vessels from the six groups surrounding the ovarium. Of the six ovarian groups of vessels, I will call (though not correctly) that under the labellum the anterior group; that under the

---

[7] I believe his latest views are given in his celebrated paper read 1–15 November, 1831, and published in the *Linnean Transactions*, vol. xvi, p. 685.

[8] Professor Asa Gray has described in the *American Journal of Science*, July, 1866, a monstrous flower of *Cypripedium candidum*, and remarks on it, 'here we have (and perhaps the first direct) demonstration that the orchideous type of flower has two staminal verticils, as Brown always insisted'. Dr Crüger also advances evidence (*Journ. Linn. Soc. Bot.*, vol. viii, 1864, p. 132) in favour of the presence of five whorls of organs; but he denies that the homologies of the parts can be deduced from the course of the vessels, and he does not admit that the labellum is formed by the union of one petal with two petaloid stamens.

[9] *Linn. Transact.*, vol. xvi, p. 696–701. Link in his 'Bemerkungen über der Bau der Orchideen' (*Botanische Zeitung*, 1849, p. 745) seems to have also trusted to transverse sections. Had he traced the vessels upwards I cannot believe that he would have disputed Brown's view of the nature of the two anthers in Cypripedium. Brongniart in his admirable paper (*Annales des Sciences Nat.*, vol. xxiv, 1831) incidentally shows the course of some of the spiral vessels.

upper sepal the posterior group; and the two groups on the two sides of the ovarium the antero-lateral and postero-lateral groups.

The result of my dissections is given in the following diagram (fig. 36). The fifteen little circles represent / so many groups of spiral vessels, in every case traced down to one of the six large ovarian groups. They alternate in five whorls, as represented; but I have not attempted to give the actual distances at which they stand apart. In order to guide the eye, the three central groups running to the three pistils are connected by a triangle.

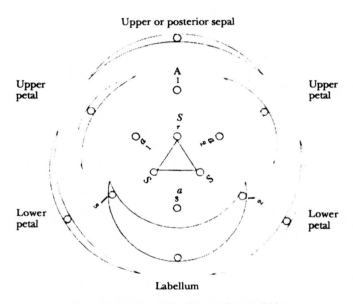

Fig. 36   Section of the flower of an orchid
The little circles show the position of the spiral vessels

S S. *Stigmas;* S_r, stigma modified into the rostellum
A_1. Fertile anther of the outer whorl; A_2 A_3, anthers of the same whorl combined with the lower petal, forming the labellum
a_1, a_2. Rudimentary anthers of the inner whorl (fertile in Cypripedium), generally forming the clinandrum; a_3, third anther of the same whorl, when present, forming the front of the column

Five groups of vessels run into the three sepals together with the two upper petals; three enter the / labellum; and seven run up the great central column. These vessels are arranged, as may be seen, in rays proceeding from the axis of the flower; and all on the same ray invariably run into the same ovarian group; thus the vessels supplying the upper sepal, the fertile anther (A_1), and the upper pistil or stigma (i.e. the rostellum S_r), all unite and form the posterior ovarian group. Again, the vessels supplying, for instance, the left lower sepals, the corner of the labellum and one of the two stigmas (S) on the same side, unite and form the antero-lateral group; and so with all the other vessels.

Hence, if the existence of groups of spiral vessels can be trusted, the flower of an orchid certainly consists of fifteen organs, in a much modified and confluent condition. We see three stigmas, with the two lower ones generally confluent, and with the upper one modified into the rostellum. We see six stamens, arranged in two whorls, with generally one alone (A_1) fertile. In Cypripedium, however, two stamens of the inner whorl (a_1 and a_2) are fertile, and in other orchids these two are represented more plainly in various ways than the remaining stamens. The third stamen of the inner whorl (a_3), when its vessels can be traced, forms the front of the column: Brown thought that it often formed a medial excrescence, or ridge, cohering to the labellum; or, in the case of Glossodia,[10] a filamentous organ, freely projecting in front of the labellum. The former conclusion does not agree with my dissections; about Glossodia I know nothing. The two infertile stamens of the outer whorl (A_2, A_3) were believed by Brown to be only occasionally represented, and then by lateral excrescences / on the labellum; but I find the corresponding vessels invariably present in the labellum of every orchid examined – even when the labellum is very narrow or quite simple, as in Malaxis, Herminium, or Habenaria.

We thus see that an orchid-flower consists of five simple parts, namely, three sepals and two petals; and of two compounded parts, namely, the column and labellum. The column is formed of three pistils, and generally of four stamens, all completely confluent. The labellum is formed of one petal with two petaloid stamens of the outer whorl, likewise completely confluent. I may remark, as making this fact more probable, that in the allied Marantaceae the stamens, even the fertile stamens, are often petaloid, and partially cohere. This view of the nature of the labellum explains its large size, its frequently tripartite form, and especially the manner of its coherence to the column, unlike that of the other petals.[11] As rudimentary organs vary

[10] See Brown's observations under Apostasia in Wallich's *Plantae Asiaticae rariores*, 1830, p. 74.
[11] Link remarks on the manner of coherence of the labellum to the column in his 'Bemerkungen' in *Bot. Zeitung*, 1849, p. 745.

much, we can thus perhaps understand the variability, which as Dr
Hooker informs me is characteristic of the excrescences on the
labellum. In some orchids which have a spur-like nectary, the two sides
are apparently formed by the two modified stamens; thus in
Gymnadenia conopsea (but not in *Orchis pyramidalis*), the vessels,
proceeding from the two antero-lateral ovarian groups, run down the
sides of the nectary; those from the single anterior group run down
the exact middle of the nectary, then returning up the opposite side
form the midrib of the labellum. The sides of the nectary being thus
formed of two distinct organs, apparently explains the tendency / as in
Calanthe, *Orchis morio*, etc., to the bifurcation of its extremity.

The number, position, and course of all the spiral vessels exhibited
in the diagram (fig. 36) were observed in some Vandeae and
Epidendreae.[12] In the Malaxeae / all were observed excepting a_3,

---

[12] It may be advisable to give a few details on the flowers which I dissected; but I
looked to special points, such as the course of the vessels in the labellum, in many
cases not worth here giving. In the Vandeae I traced all the vessels in *Catasetum
tridentatum* and *saccatum*; the great group of vessels going to the rostellum separate
(as likewise in *Mormodes*) from the posterior ovarian group, beneath the
bifurcation supplying the upper sepal and fertile anther; the anterior ovarian group
runs a little way along the labellum before it bifurcates and sends a group (a_3) up the
front of the column; the vessels proceeding from the postero-lateral group run up
the back of the column, on each side of those running to the fertile anther, and do
not go to the edges of the clinandrum. In *Acropera luteola* the base of the column,
where the labellum is attached, is much produced, and the vessels of the whole
anterior ovarian group are similarly produced; those (a_3) going up the front of the
column are abruptly reflected back; the vessels at the point of reflexion are curiously
hardened, flattened, and produced into odd crests and points. In an *Oncidium* I
traced the vessels S_r to the viscid gland of the pollinium. Among the Epidendreae I
traced all the vessels in a *Cattleya*; and all in *Evelyna carivata* except a_3, which I did
not search for. In the Malaxeae I traced all in *Liparis pendula* except a_3, which I do
not believe is present. In *Malaxis paludosa* I traced nearly all the vessels. In
Cypripedium barbatum and *purpuratum* I traced all except a_3, which I am nearly sure
does not exist. In the Neotteae I traced in *Cephalanthera grandiflora* all the vessels,
excepting that to the aborted rostellum and those to the two auricles a_1 and a_2,
which were certainly absent. In *Epipactis* I traced all excepting a_1, a_2, and a_3, which
are certainly absent. In *Spiranthes autumnalis* the vessel S_r runs to the bottom of the
fork of the rostellum: there are no vessels to the membranes of the clinandrum in
this orchid nor in *Goodyera*. In none of the Ophreae do the vessels a_1, a_2, and a_3
occur. In *Orchis pyramidalis* I traced all the others, including two to the two separate
stigmas: in this species the contrast between the vessels of the labellum and of the
other sepals and petals is striking, as in the latter the vessels do not branch, whilst
the labellum has three vessels, the lateral ones running of course into the antero-
lateral ovarian group. In *Gymnadenia conopsea* I traced all the vessels; but I am not
sure whether the vessels supplying *the sides* of the upper sepal do not, as in the allied
Habenaria, wander from their proper course and enter the postero-lateral ovarian
group: the vessel S_r, going to the rostellum, enters the little folded crest of

which is the most difficult one to trace, and apparently is oftenest absent. In the Cypripedeae, again, all were traced except a_3,[13] which, I feel pretty sure, was here really absent: in this tribe the stamen (A_1) is represented by a conspicuous shield-like rudiment, and a_1 and a_2 are developed into two fertile anthers. In the Ophreae and Neotteae all were traced, with the important exception of the vessels belonging to the three stamens (a_1, a_2, and a_3) of the inner whorl. In *Cephalanthera grandiflora*, I clearly saw a_3 proceeding from the anterior ovarian group, and running up the front of the column. This anomalous orchid has no rostellum, and the vessel marked S, in the diagram was entirely absent, though seen in every other species.

Although the two anthers (a_1 and a_2) of the inner whorl are not fully and normally developed in any orchid, excepting Cypripedium, their rudiments are generally present and are often utilized; for they often form the membranous sides of the cup-like clinandrum on the summit of the column, which includes and protects the pollen-masses. These rudiments thus aid their fertile brother-anther. In the young flower-bud / of *Malaxis paludosa*, the close resemblance between the two membranes of the clinandrum and the fertile anther, in shape, texture, and in the height to which the spiral vessels extended, was most striking: it was impossible to doubt that in these two membranes we had two rudimentary anthers. In Evelyna, one of the Epidendreae, the clinandrum was similarly formed, as were the horns of the clinandrum in Masdevallia, which serve in addition to keep the labellum at the proper distance from the column. In *Liparis pendula* and some other species, these two rudimentary anthers form not only

---

membrane, which projects between the bases of the anther-cells. Lastly, in *Habenaria chlorantha* I traced all the vessels, excepting as in the other Ophreae the three of the inner staminal whorl, and I looked carefully for a_3: the vessel / supplying the fertile anther runs up the connective membrane between the two anther-cells, but does not bifurcate: the vessel to the rostellum runs up to the top of the shoulder or ledge beneath the connective membrane of the anther, but does not bifurcate and extend to the two widely separated viscid discs.

[13] From Irmisch's (*Beiträge zur Biologie der Orchideen*, 1853, pp. 78 and 42) description of the development of the flower-bud of Cypripedium, it would appear that there is a tendency to the formation of a free filament in front of the labellum, as in the case of Glossodia before mentioned; and this will perhaps account for the absence of spiral vessels, proceeding from the anterior ovarian group and coalescing with the column. In Uropedium, a genus which A. Brongniart (*Annal. des. Sc. Nat.*, 3rd series, Bot. vol. xiii, p. 114) considers closely allied to, and even perhaps a monstrosity of, Cypripedium, a third fertile anther occupies this same position.

the clinandrum, but likewise wings, which project on each side of the entrance into the stigmatic cavity, and serve as guides for the insertion of the pollen-masses. In Acropera and Stanhopea, as far as I could make out, the membranous borders of the column, down to its base, were also thus formed; but in other cases, as in Cattleya, the wing-like borders of the column seem to be simple developments of the two pistils. In this latter genus, as well as in Catasetum, these same two rudimentary stamens, judging from the position of the vessels, serve chiefly to strengthen the back of the column; and the strengthening of the front of the column is the sole function of the third stamen of the inner whorl (a_3), in those cases in which it was observed. This third stamen runs up the middle of the column to the lower edge, or lip, of the stigmatic cavity.

I have said that in the Ophreae and Neotteae the spiral vessels of the inner whorl, marked a_1, a_2, a_3 in the diagram, are entirely absent, and I looked carefully for them; but in nearly all the members of these two tribes, two small papillae, or auricles as they have been often called, stand in exactly the position which the two first of these three anthers would have occupied, / had they been developed. Not only do they stand in this position, but the column in some cases, as in Cephalanthera, has on each side a prominent ridge, running from them to the bases or midribs of the two upper petals; that is, in the proper position of the filaments of these two stamens. It is, again, impossible to doubt that the two membranes of the clinandrum in Malaxis are formed by these two anthers in a rudimentary and modified condition. Now, from the perfect clinandrum of Malaxis, through that of Spiranthes, Goodyera, *Epipactis latifolia*, and *E. palustris* (see fig. 16, p. 71 and fig. 15, p. 66), to the minute and slightly flattened auricles in the genus Orchis, a perfect gradation can be traced. Hence I conclude that these auricles are doubly rudimentary; that is they are rudiments of the membranous sides of the clinandrum, these membranes themselves being rudiments of the two anthers so often referred to. The absence of spiral vessels running to the auricles is by no means sufficient to overthrow the views here advocated as to the much disputed nature of these structures; that such vessels may quite disappear, we have proof in *Cephalanthera grandiflora*, in which the rostellum and its vessels are completely aborted.

Finally, then, with respect to the six stamens which ought to be represented in every orchid; the three belonging to the outer whorl are always present, the upper one being fertile (except in Cypripedium), and the two lower ones invariably petaloid and forming part of the labellum. The three stamens of the inner whorl are less plainly developed, especially the lower one, a_3, which, when it can be detected, serves only to strengthen the column, and, in some rare cases, according to Brown, forms a separate projection or filament; the two upper anthers of this inner whorl are fertile / in Cypripedium, and in other cases are generally represented either by membranous expansions, or by minute auricles without spiral vessels. These auricles, however, are sometimes quite absent, as in some species of Ophrys.

On this view of the homologies of orchid-flowers, we can understand the existence of the conspicuous central column – the large size, generally tripartite form, and peculiar manner of attachment of the labellum – the origin of the clinandrum – the relative position of the single fertile anther in most of the genera, and of the two fertile anthers in Cypripedium – the position of the rostellum, as well as of all the other organs – and lastly, the frequent occurrence of a bilobed stigma, and the occasional occurrence of two distinct stigmas. I have encountered only one case of difficulty, namely in Habenaria and the allied genus, Bonatea. The flowers have undergone such an extraordinary amount of distortion, owing to the wide separation of their anther-cells and of the two viscid discs of the rostellum, that any anomaly in them is the less surprising. The anomaly relates only to the vessels supplying the sides of the upper sepal and of the two upper petals; for the vessels running into their midribs and into all the other more important organs pursue the same identical course as in the other Ophreae. The vessels which supply the sides of the upper sepal, instead of uniting with the midrib and entering the posterior ovarian group, diverge and enter the postero-lateral groups. Again, the vessels on the anterior side of the two upper petals, instead of uniting with those of the midrib and entering the postero-lateral ovarian groups, diverge, or wander from their proper course, and enter the antero-lateral groups.

This anomaly is so far of importance, as it throws / some doubt on the view that the labellum is always an organ compounded of one petal and two petaloid stamens; for if any one were to assume that from some unknown cause the lateral vessels of the lower petals had diverged in an early progenitor of the Orchidean order from their proper course into the antero-lateral ovarian groups, and that this structure had been inherited by all existing orchids, even by those with the smallest and simplest labellums, I could answer only as follows; but the answer is, I think, satisfactory. From the analogy of other monocotyledonous plants, we might expect the hidden presence of fifteen organs in the flowers of the Orchideae, arranged alternately in five whorls; and in these flowers we find fifteen groups of vessels exactly thus arranged. Hence there is a strong probability that the vessels, A_2 and A_3, which enter the sides of the labellum, not in one or two cases, but in all the orchids seen by me, and which occupy the precise position which they would have occupied had they supplied two normal stamens, do really represent modified and petaloid stamens, and are not lateral vessels of the labellum which have wandered from their proper course. In Habenaria and Bonatea,[14] on the other hand, the vessels proceeding / from the sides of the upper sepal and of the two upper petals, which enter the wrong ovarian groups, cannot possibly represent any lost but once distict organs.

We have now finished with the general homologies of the flowers of orchids. It is interesting to look at one of the magnificent exotic species, or, indeed, at one of our humblest forms, and observe how profoundly it has been modified, as compared with all ordinary flowers – with its great labellum, formed of one petal and two petaloid stamens – with its singular pollen-masses, hereafter to be referred to – with its column formed of seven cohering organs, of which three alone perform their proper function, namely, one anther and two generally confluent stigmas – with the third stigma modified into the rostellum and incapable of being fertilized – and with three of the anthers no longer functionally active, but serving either to protect the pollen of the fertile anther, or to strengthen the column, or existing as mere rudiments, or entirely suppressed. What an amount of modification, cohesion, abortion, and change of function do we here see! Yet hidden

---

[14] In *Bonatea speciosa*, of which I have examined only dry specimens sent me by Dr Hooker, the vessels from the sides of the upper sepal enter the postero-lateral ovarian group, exactly as in Habenaria. The two upper petals are divided down to their bases, and the vessels supplying the anterior segment and those supplying the *anterior portion* of the posterior segment unite and then run, as in Habenaria, into the antero-lateral (and therefore wrong) group. The anterior segments of the two upper petals cohere with the labellum, causing it to have five segments, which is a most unusual fact. The two wonderfully protuberant stigmas also cohere to the upper surface of the labellum; and the lower sepals apparently also cohere to its underside. Consequently a section of the base of the labellum divides one lower petal, two petaloid anthers, portions of the two upper petals, and apparently of the two lower sepals and the two stigmas: altogether the section passes through the whole of or through portions of either seven or nine organs. The base of the labellum is here as complex an organ as the column of other orchids.

in that column, with its surrounding petals and sepals, we know that there are fifteen groups of vessels, arranged three within three, in alternate order, which probably have been preserved to the present time from being developed at a very early period of growth, before the shape or existence of any part of the flower is of importance for the well-being of the plant.

Can we feel satisfied by saying that each orchid was created, exactly as we now see it, on a certain 'ideal type'; that the omnipotent Creator, having fixed on one plan for the whole order, did not depart from this / plan; that he, therefore, made the same organ to perform diverse functions – often of trifling importance compared with their proper function – converted other organs into mere purposeless rudiments, and arranged all as if they had to stand separate, and then made them cohere? Is it not a more simple and intelligible view that all the Orchideae owe what they have in common, to descent from some monocotyledonous plant, which, like so many other plants of the same class, possessed fifteen organs, arranged alternately three within three in five whorls; and that the now wonderfully changed structure of the flower is due to a long course of slow modification – each modification having been preserved which was useful to the plant, during the incessant changes to which the organic and inorganic world has been exposed? /

CHAPTER IX

GRADATION OF ORGANS, ETC.
CONCLUDING REMARKS

Gradation of organs, of the rostellum, of the pollen-masses – Formation of the caudicle – Genealogical affinities – Secretion of nectar – Mechanism of the movement of the pollinia – Uses of the petals – Production of seed – Importance of trifling details of structure – Cause of the great diversity of structure in the flowers of orchids – Cause of the perfection of the contrivances – Summary on insect-agency – Nature abhors perpetual self-fertilization.

This chapter will be devoted to the consideration of several miscellaneous subjects which could not well have been introduced elsewhere.

On the gradation of certain organs. The rostellum, the pollinia, the labellum, and, in a lesser degree, the column, are the most remarkable points in the structure of orchids. The formation of the column and labellum, by the confluence and partial abortion of several organs, has been discussed in the last chapter. With respect to the rostellum, no such organ exists in any other group of plants. If the homologies of orchids had not been pretty well made out, those who believe in the separate creation of each organism might have advanced this as an excellent instance of a perfectly new organ having been specially created, and which could not have been developed by successive slow modifications of any pre-existing part. But, as Robert Brown long ago remarked, it is not a new organ. It is impossible to look at the two groups of spiral vessels (fig. 36) running from the bases of / the midribs of the two lower sepals to the two lower stigmas, which are sometimes quite distinct, and then to look at the third group of vessels running from the base of the midrib of the upper sepal to the rostellum, which occupies the exact position of a third stigma, and doubt its homological nature. There is every reason to believe that the whole of this upper stigma, and not merely a part, has been converted into the rostellum; for there are plenty of cases of two stigmas, but not one of three stigmatic surfaces being present in those orchids which have a rostellum. On the other hand, in Cypripedium and Apostasia (the latter ranked by Brown in the Orchidean order), which are destitute of a rostellum, the stigmatic surface is trifid.

As we know only those plants which are now living, it is impossible to follow all the gradations by which the upper stigma has been converted into the rostellum; but let us see what are the indications of such a change having been effected. With respect to function the change has not been so great as it at first appears. The function of the rostellum is to secrete viscid matter, and it has lost the capacity of being penetrated by the pollen-tubes. The stigmas of orchids, as well as of most other plants, secrete viscid matter, the use of which is to retain the pollen when brought to them by any means, and to excite the growth of the pollen-tubes. Now if we look to one of the simplest rostellums – for instance, to that of Cattleya or Epidendrum – we find a thick layer of viscid matter, not distinctly separated from the viscid surface of the two confluent stigmas: its use is simply to affix the pollen-masses to a retreating insect, which are thus dragged out of the anther and transported to another flower, where they are retained by the almost equally viscid stigmatic surface. So that the office of the rostellum is still to / secure the pollen-masses, but indirectly by means of their attachment to an insect's body.

The viscid matter of the rostellum and of the stigma appear to have nearly the same nature; that of the rostellum generally has the peculiar property of quickly drying or setting hard; that of the stigma, when removed from the plant, apparently dries more quickly than gum-water of about equal density or tenacity. This tendency to dry is the more remarkable, as Gärtner[1] found that drops of the stigmatic secretion from Nicotania did not dry in two months. The viscid matter of the rostellum in many orchids when exposed to the air changes colour with remarkable quickness, and becomes brownish-purple; and I have noticed a similar but slower change of colour in the viscid secretion of the stigmas of some orchids, as of *Cephalanthera grandiflora*. When the viscid disc of an Orchis, as Bauer and Brown have observed, is placed in water, minute particles are expelled with violence in a peculiar manner; and I have observed exactly the same fact in the layer of viscid matter covering the stigmatic utriculi in an unopened flower of *Mormodes ignea*.

In order to compare the minute structure of the rostellum and

---

[1] *Beiträge zur Kenntniss der Befruchtung*, 1844, p. 236.

stigma, I examined young flower-buds of *Epidendrum cochleatum* and *floribundum*, which, when mature, have a simple rostellum. The posterior parts of both organs were quite similar. The whole of the rostellum at this early age consisted of a mass of nearly orbicular cells, containing spheres of brown matter, which resolve themselves into the viscid fluid. The stigma was covered with a thinner layer of similar cells, and beneath them were the coherent spindle-formed / utriculi. These are believed to be connected with the penetration of the pollen-tubes; and their absence in the rostellum probably accounts for its not being penetraed. If the structure of the rostellum and of the stigma is as here described, their only difference consists in the layer of cells which secrete the viscid matter being thicker in the rostellum than in the stigma, and in the utriculi having disappeared from the former. There is therefore no great difficulty in believing that the upper stigma, whilst still in some degree fertile or capable of penetration by the pollen-tubes, might have gradually acquired the power of secreting a larger amount of viscid matter, losing at the same time its capacity for fertilization; and that insects smeared with this viscid matter removed and transported the pollen-masses in a more and more effective manner to the stigmas of other flowers. In this case an incipient rostellum would have been formed.

In the several tribes, the rostellum presents a marvellous amount of diversity of structure; but most of the differences can be connected without very wide breaks. One of the most striking differences is, that either the whole anterior surface to some depth, or only the internal parts become viscid; and in this latter case the surface retains, as in Orchis, a membranous condition. But these two states graduate into each other so closely, that it is scarcely possible to draw any line of separation between them: thus, in Epipactis, the exterior surface undergoes a vast change from its early cellular condition, for it becomes converted into a highly elastic and tender membrane, which is in itself slightly viscid, and allows the underlying viscid matter readily to exude; yet it acts as a membrane, and its under surface is lined with much / more viscid matter. In *Habenaria chlorantha* the exterior surface is highly viscid, but still closely resembles, under the microscope, the exterior membrane of Epipactis. Lastly, in some species of Oncidium, etc., the exterior surface, which is viscid, differs, as far as appearance under the microscope goes, from the underlying viscid layer only in colour; but it must have some essential difference, for I find that, until this very thin exterior layer is disturbed, the underlying matter remains viscid; but, after it has been disturbed, the underlying matter rapidly sets hard. The gradation in the state of the surface of the rostellum is not surprising, for in all cases the surface is cellular in the bud; so that an early condition has only to be retained more or less perfectly.

The nature of the viscid matter differs remarkably in different orchids: in Listera it sets hard almost instantly, more quickly than plaster of Paris; in Malaxis and Angraecum it remains fluid for several days; but these two states pass into each other by many gradations. In an Oncidium I have observed the viscid matter to dry in a minute and a half; in some species of Orchis in two or three minutes; in Epipactis in ten minutes; in Gymnadenia in two hours; and in Habenaria in over twenty-four hours. After the viscid matter of Listera has set hard, neither water nor weak spirits of wine has any effect on it; whereas that of *Habenaria bifolia*, after having been dried for several months, when moistened became as adhesive as ever it was. The viscid matter in some species of Orchis, when remoistened, presented an intermediate condition.

One of the most important differences in the state of the rostellum is, whether or not the pollinia are permanently attached to it. I do not allude to those / cases in which the upper surface of the rostellum is viscid, as in Malaxis and some Epidendrums, and simply adheres to the pollen-masses; for these cases present no difficulty. But I refer to the so-called congenital attachment of the pollinia by their caudicles to the rostellum or viscid disc. It is not, however, strictly correct to speak of congenital attachment, for the pollinia are invariably free at an early period, and become attached either earlier or later in different orchids. No actual gradation is at present known in the process of attachment; but it can be shown to depend on very simple conditions and changes. In the Epidendreae the pollinia consist of a ball of waxy pollen, with a long caudicle (formed of elastic threads with adherent pollen-grains), which never becomes spontaneously attached to the rostellum. In some of the Vandeae, as in *Cymbidium giganteum*, on the other hand, the caudicles are congenitally (in the above sense) attached to the pollen-masses, but their structure is the same as in the Epidendreae, with the sole difference, that the extremities of the elastic threads adhere to, instead of merely lying on, the upper lip of the rostellum.

In a form allied to Cymbidium, namely, *Oncidium unguiculatum*, I studied the development of the caudicles. At an early period the pollen-masses are enclosed in membranous cases, which soon rupture at one point. At this early period, a layer of rather large cells, including remarkably opaque matter, may be detected within the cleft of each pollen-mass. This matter can be traced as it gradually changes into a translucent substance which forms the threads of the caudicles. As the change progresses, the cells themselves disappear. Finally the threads at one end adhere to the waxy pollen-masses, and at the other end / after protruding through a small opening in the membranous case in a semi-developed state, they adhere to the rostellum, against which the anther is pressed. So that the adhesion of the caudicle to the back of the rostellum seems to depend solely on the early rupturing of the anther-case, and on a slight protrusion of the caudicles, before they have become fully developed and hardened.

In all the Orchideae a portion of the rostellum is removed by insects when the pollinia are removed; for the viscid matter, though conveniently spoken of as a secretion, is in fact part of the rostellum in a modified condition. But in those species which have their caudicles attached at an early period to the rostellum, a membranous or solid portion of its exterior surface in an unmodified condition is likewise removed. In the Vandeae this portion is sometimes of considerable size (forming the disc and pedicel of the pollinium), and gives to their pollinia their remarkable character; but the differences in the shape and size of the removed portions of the rostellum can be finely graduated together, even within the single tribe of the Vandeae; and still more closely by commencing with the minute oval atom of membrane to which the caudicle of Orchis adheres, passing thence to that of *Habenaria bifolia*, to that of *H. chlorantha* with its drum-like pedicel, and thence through many forms to the great disc and pedicel of Catasetum.

In all the cases in which a portion of the exterior surface of the rostellum is removed together with the caudicles of the pollen-masses, definite and often complicated lines of separation are formed, so as to allow of the easy separation of the removed portions. But the formation of these lines of separation does not differ much from the process by which certain portions / of the exterior surface of the rostellum assume a condition intermediate between that of unaltered membrane and of viscid matter, which has been already alluded to. The actual separation of portions of the rostellum depends in many cases on the excitement from a touch; but how a touch thus acts is at present inexplicable. Such sensitiveness in the stigma to a touch (and the rostellum, as we know, is a modified stigma), and indeed in almost every other part, is by no means a rare quality in plants.

In Listera and Neottea, if the rostellum is touched, even by a human hair, two points rupture and the loculi containing the viscid matter instantly expel it. Here we have a case towards which as yet no gradation is known. But Dr Hooker has shown that the rostellum is at first cellular, and that the viscid matter is developed within the cells, as in other orchids.

The last difference which I will mention in the state of the rostellum of various orchids is the existence in many Ophreae of two widely separated viscid discs, sometimes included in two separate pouches. Here it appears at first sight as if there were two rostella; but there is never more than one medial group of spiral vessels. In the Vandeae we can see how a single viscid disc and a single pedicel might become divided into two; for in some Stanhopeas the heart-shaped disc shows a trace of a tendency to division; and in Angraecum we have two distinct discs and two pedicels, either standing close together or removed only a little way apart.

It might be thought that a similar gradation from a single rostellum into what appears like two distinct rostella was shown still more plainly in the Ophreae; for we have the following series – in *Orchis pyramidalis* a single disc enclosed in a single pouch – in Aceras two / discs touching and affecting each other's shapes, but not actually joined – in *Orchis latifolia* and *maculata* two quite distinct discs but with the pouch still showing plain traces of division; and, lastly, in Ophrys we have two perfectly distinct pouches, including of course two perfectly distinct discs. But this series does not indicate the former steps by which a single rostellum became divided into two distinct organs; on the contrary, it shows how the rostellum, after having been anciently divided into two organs, has now in several cases been reunited into a single organ.

This conclusion is founded on the nature of the little medial crest, sometimes called the rostellate process, between the bases of the two anther-cells (see fig. 1, B and D, p. 7). In both divisions of the Ophreae – namely the species having naked discs and those having discs enclosed in a pouch – whenever the two discs come into close juxtaposition, this medial crest or process appears.[2] On the other

[2] Professor Babington (*Manual of British Botany*, 3rd edit.) uses the existence of this 'rostellate process' as a character to separate Orchis, Gymnadenia, and Aceras from the other genera of Ophreae. The group of spiral vessels, properly belonging to the rostellum, runs up and even into, the base of this crest or process.

hand, when the two discs stand widely apart, the summit of the rostellum between them is smooth, or nearly smooth. In the Frog Orchis (*Peristylus viridis*) the overarching summit is bent like the roof of a house; and here we see the first stage in the formation of the folded crest. In *Herminium monorchis*, however, which has two separate and large discs, a crest, or solid ridge, is rather more plainly developed than might have been expected. In *Gymnadenia conopsea, Orchis maculata*, and others, the crests consists of a hood of thin membrane; in / *O. mascula* the two sides of the hood partly adhere; and in *O. pyramidalis* and in Aceras it is converted into a solid ridge. These facts are intelligible only on the view, that, whilst the two discs were gradually brought together, during a long series of generations, the intermediate portion or summit of the rostellum became more and more arched, until a folded crest, and finally a solid ridge was formed.

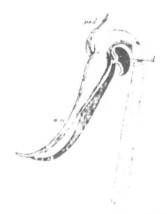

Fig. 37   Rostellum of Catasetum
an. antennae of rostellum, *d.* viscid disc, *ped.* pedicel of rostellum, to which the pollen-masses are attached

Whether we compare together the state of the rostellum in the various tribes of the Orchideae, or compare the rostellum with the pistil and stigma of an ordinary flower, the differences are wonderfully great. A simple pistil consists of a cylinder surmounted by a small viscid surface. Now, see what a contrast the rostellum of Catasetum, when dissected from all the other elements of the column, presents; and as I traced all the vessels in this orchid, the drawing may be trusted as approximately accurate. The whole organ / has lost its normal function of being fertilized. Its shape is most singular, with the upper end thickened, bent over and produced into two long tapering and sensitive antennae, each of these being hollow within, like an adder's fang. Behind and between the bases of these antennae we see the large viscid disc, attached to the pedicel; the latter differs in structure from the underlying portion of the rostellum, and is separated from it by a layer of hyaline tissue, which spontaneously dissolves when the flower is mature. The disc, attached to the surrounding parts by a membrane which ruptures as soon as it is excited by a touch, consists of strong upper tissue, with an underlying elastic cushion, coated with viscid matter; and this again in most orchids is overlaid by a film of a different nature. What an amount of specialization of parts do we here behold! Yet in the comparatively few orchids described in this volume, so many and such plainly-marked gradations in the structure of the rostellum have been described, and such plain facilities for the conversion of the upper pistil into this organ, that, we may well believe, if we could see every orchid which has ever existed throughout the world, we should find all the gaps in the existing chain, and every gap in many lost chains, filled up by a series of easy transitions.

We now come to the second great peculiarity in the Orchideae, namely their pollinia. The anther opens early, and often deposits the naked masses of pollen on the back of the rostellum. This action is prefigured in Canna, a member of a family nearly related to the Orchideae, in which the pollen is deposited on the pistil, close beneath the stigma. In the state of the pollen there is great diversity: in Cypripedium and Vanilla / single grains are embedded in a glutinous fluid; in all the other orchids seen by me (except the degraded Cephalanthera) the grains are united three or four together.[3] These compound grains are

[3] In several cases I have observed four tubes emitted from the four grains which form one of the compound grains. In some semi-monstrous flowers of *Malaxis paludosa*, and of *Aceras anthropophora*, and in perfect flowers of *Neottia nidus-avus*, I have observed tubes emitted from the pollen-grains, whilst still within the anther and not in contact with the stigma. I have thought this worth mentioning, as R. Brown (*Linn. Transact.*, vol. xvi, p. 729) states, apparently with some surprise, that the pollen-tubes were emitted from the pollen, whilst still within the anther, in a decaying flower of Asclepias. These cases show that the protruding tubes are at least at first, formed exclusively at the expense of the contents of the pollen-grains.

Having alluded to the monstrous flowers of the Aceras, I will add that I examined several (always the lowest on the spike) in which the labellum was hardly developed, and was pressed close against the stigma. The rostellum was not developed, so that the pollinia did not possess viscid discs; but the most curious feature was, that the

tied one to the other by elastic threads, but they often form packets which are tied together in like manner, or they are cemented into the so-called waxy masses. The waxy masses graduate in the Epidendreae and Vandeae from eight to four, to two, and, by the cohesion of the two, into a single mass. In some of the Epidendreae we have both kinds of pollen within the same anther, namely, large waxy masses, and caudicles formed of elastic threads with numerous compound grains adhering to them.

I can throw no light on the nature of the cohesion of the pollen in the waxy masses; when they are placed in water for three or four days, the compound grains readily fall apart; but the four grains of which each is formed still firmly cohere; so that the nature of the cohesion in the two cases must be different. The elastic threads by which the packets of pollen are / tied together in the Ophreae, and which run far up inside the waxy masses of the Vandeae, are also of a different nature from the cementing matter; for the threads are acted on by chloroform and by long immersion in spirits of wine; whilst these fluids have no particular action on the cohesion of the waxy masses. In several Epidendreae and Vandeae the exterior grains of the pollen-masses differ from the interior grains, in being larger, and in having yellower and much thicker walls. So that in the contents of a single anther-cell we see a surprising degree of differentiation in the pollen, namely, grains cohering by fours, then being either tied together by threads or cemented together into solid masses, with the exterior grains different from the interior ones.

In the Vandeae, the caudicle, which is composed of fine coherent threads, is developed from the semi-fluid contents of a layer of cells. As I find that chloroform has a peculiar and energetic action on the caudicles of all orchids, and likewise on the glutinous matter which envelopes the pollen-grains in Cypripedium, and which can be drawn out into threads, we may suspect that in this latter genus – the least differentiated in structure of all the Orchideae, – we see the primordial condition of the elastic threads by which the pollen-grains are tied together in other and more highly developed species.[4] /

---

two anther-cells had become, apparently in consequence of the position of the rudimentary labellum, widely separated, and were joined by a connective membrane, almost as broad as that of *Habenaria chlorantha*!

[4] August de Saint Hilaire (*Leçons de Botanique*, etc., 1841, p. 447) says that the elastic threads exist in the early bud, after the pollen-grains have been partly formed, as a thick creamy fluid. He adds that his observations on *Ophrys apifera* have

The caudicle, when largely developed and destitute of pollen-grains, is the most striking of the many peculiarities presented by the pollinia. In some Neotteae, especially in Goodyera, we see it in a nascent condition, projecting just beyond the pollen-mass, with the threads only partially coherent. In the Vandeae by tracing the gradation from the ordinary naked condition of the caudicle, through Lycaste in which it is almost naked, through Calanthe, to *Cymbidium giganteum*, in which it is covered with pollen-grains, it seems probable that its ordinary condition has been arrived at by the modification of a pollinium like that of one of the Epidendreae; namely, by the abortion of the pollen-grains which primordially adhered to separate elastic threads, and afterwards by the cohesion of these threads.

In the Ophreae we have better evidence than is afforded by gradation, that their long, rigid and naked caudicles have been developed, at least partially, by the abortion of the greater number of the lower pollen-grains and by the cohesion of the elastic threads by which these grains were tied together. I had often observed a cloudy appearance in the middle of the translucent caudicles in certain species; and on carefully opening several caudicles of *Orchis pyramidalis*, I found in their centres, fully halfway down between the packets of pollen and the viscid disc, many pollen-grains (consisting, as usual, of our united grains), / lying quite loose. These grains, from their embedded position, could never by any possibility have been left on the stigma of a flower, and were absolutely useless. Those who can persuade themselves that purposeless organs have been specially created, will think little of this fact. Those on the contrary, who believe in the slow modification of organic beings, will feel no surprise that the changes have not always been perfectly effected – that, during and after the many inherited states of the abortion of the lower pollen-

---

shown him that this fluid is secreted by the rostellum, and is slowly forced drop by drop into the anther. Had not so eminent an authority made this statement, I should not have noticed it. It is certainly erroneous. In buds of *Epipactis latifolia* I opened the anther, whilst perfectly closed and free from the rostellum, and found the pollen-grains united by elastic threads. *Cephalanthera grandiflora* has no rostellum to secrete the above thick fluid, yet the pollen-grains are thus united. In a monstrous specimen of *Orchis pyramidalis* the auricles, or rudimentary anthers on each side of the proper anther, had become partly developed, and they stood quite on one side of the rostellum and stigma; yet I found in one of these auricles a distinct caudicle (which necessarily had no disc at its extremity), and this caudicle could not possibly have been secreted by the rostellum or stigma. I could advance additional evidence, but it would be superfluous.

grains and of the cohesion of the elastic threads, there should still exist a tendency to the production of a few grains where they were originally developed; and that these should consequently be left entangled within the now united threads of the caudicle. They will look at the little clouds formed by the loose pollen-grains within the caudicles of *Orchis pyramidalis*, as good evidence that an early progenitor of this plant had pollen-masses like those of Epipatis or Goodyera, and that the grains slowly disappeared from the lower parts, leaving the elastic threads naked and ready to cohere into a true caudicle.

As the caudicle plays an important part in the fertilization of the flower, it might have been developed from one in a nascent condition, such as we see in Epipactis, to any required length merely by the continued preservation of varying increments in its length, each beneficial in relation to other changes in the structure of the flower, and without any abortion of the lower pollen-grains. But we may conclude from the facts just given, that this has not been the sole means – that the caudicle owes much of its length to such abortion. That in some cases it has subsequently been largely increased in length by Natural Selection, is highly probable; for in *Bonatea speciosa* / the caudicle is actually more than thrice as long as the elongated pollen-masses; and it is highly improbable that so lengthy a mass of grains, slightly cohering together by the aid of elastic threads, should ever have existed, as an insect could not have safely transported and applied a mass of this shape and size to the stigma of another flower.

We have hitherto considered gradations in the state of the same organ. To anyone with more knowledge than I possess, it would be an interesting subject to trace the gradations between the several species and groups of species in this great and closely connected order. But to make a perfect gradation, all the extinct forms which have ever existed, along many lines of descent converging to the common progenitor of the group, would have to be called back into life. It is due to their absence, and to the consequent wide gaps in the series, that we are enabled to divide the existing species into definable groups, such as genera, families, and tribes. If there had been no extinction, there would still have been great lines or branches of special development – the Vandeae, for instance, would still have been distinguishable as a great body, from the great body of the Ophreae; but ancient and intermediate forms, very different probably from their present descendants, would have rendered it utterly impossible to separate by distinct characters the one great body from the other.

I will venture on only a few more remarks. Cypripedium, in having three stigmas developed, and therefore in not possessing a rostellum, in having two fertile anthers with a large rudiment of a third, and in the state of its pollen, seems a remnant of the order whilst in a simpler or more generalized condition. Apostasia / is a related genus, placed by Brown among the Orchideae, but by Lindley in a small distinct family. These broken groups do not indicate to us the structure of the common parent-form of all the Orchideae, but they serve to show the probable state of the order in ancient times, when none of the forms had become so widely differentiated from one another and from other plants, as are the existing orchids, especially the Vandeae and Ophreae; and when, consequently, the order made a nearer approach in all its characters, than it does at present, to such allied groups as the Marantaceae.

With respect to other orchids, we can see that an ancient form, like one of the subtribe of the Pleurothallidae, some of which have waxy pollen-masses with a minute caudicle, might have given rise, by the entire abortion of the caudicle, to the Dendrobiae, and by an increase of the caudicle to the Epidendreae. Cymbidium shows us how simply a form like one of our present Epidendreae could be modified into one of the Vandeae. The Neotteae stand in nearly similar relation to the higher Ophreae, which the Epidendreae do to the higher Vandeae. In certain genera of the Neotteae we have compound pollen-grains cemented into packets and tied together by elastic threads, which project and thus form a nascent caudicle. But this caudicle does not protrude from the lower end of the pollinium as in the Ophreae, nor does it always protrude from the extreme upper end in the Neotteae, but sometimes at an intermediate level; so that a transition in this respect is far from impossible. In Spiranthes, the back of the rostellum, lined with viscid matter, is alone removed: the front part is membranous, and ruptures like the pouch-formed rostellum of the Ophreae. An ancient form combining most of the characters, but in a less / developed state, of Goodyera, Epipactis, and Spiranthes, all members of the Neotteae, could by further slight modifications have given birth to the tribe of the Ophreae.

Hardly any question in Natural History is more vague and difficult to answer than what forms ought to be considered as the highest in a large group;[5] for all are well adapted to their conditions of life. If we look to successive modifications, with differentiation of parts and consequent complexity of structure, as the standard of comparison, the Ophreae and Vandeae will stand the highest among the Orchideae. Are we to lay much stress on the size and beauty of the flower, and on the size of the whole plant? if so, the Vandeae are pre-eminent. They have, also, rather more complex pollinia, with the pollen-masses often reduced to two. The rostellum, on the other hand, has apparently been more modified from its primordial stigmatic nature in the Ophreae, than in the Vandeae. In the Ophreae the stamens of the inner whorl are almost entirely suppressed, the auricles – mere rudiments of rudiments – being alone retained; and even these are sometimes lost. These stamens, therefore, have suffered extreme reduction; but can this be considered as a sign of highness? I should doubt whether any member of the Orchidean order has been more profoundly modified in its whole structure than *Bonatea speciosa*, one of the Ophreae. So again, within this same tribe, nothing can be more perfect than the contrivances in *Orchis pyramidalis* for its fertilization. Yet an ill-defined feeling tells me to rank the magnificent Vandeae as the highest. When we look within this tribe at the / elaborate mechanism for the ejection and transportal of the pollinia of Catasetum, with the sensitive rostellum so wonderfully modified, with the sexes borne on distinct plants, we may perhaps give the palm of victory to this genus.

SECRETION OF NECTAR

Many orchids, both our native species and the exotic kinds cultivated in our hothouses, secrete a copious supply of nectar. I have found the horn-like nectaries of Aerides filled with fluid; and Mr Rodgers, of Sevenoaks, informs me that he has taken crystals of sugar of considerable size from the nectary of *A. cornutum*. The nectar-secreting organs of the Orchideae present great diversities of structure and position in the various genera; but are almost always situated towards the base of the labellum. In Disa, however, the posterior sepal alone, and in Dispersis the two lateral sepals together with the labellum,

[5] The fullest and the most able discussion on this difficult subject is by Professor H. G. Bronn in his *Entwickelungs-Gesetze der Organischen Welt*, 1858.

secréte nectar. In *Dendrobium chrysanthum* the nectary consists of a shallow saucer; in Evelyna, of two large united cellular balls; and in *Bolbophyllum cupreum*, of a medial furrow. In Cattleya the nectary penetrates the ovarium. In *Angraecum sesquipedale* it attains the astonishing length of above eleven inches; but I need not enter on further details. The fact, however, should be recalled, that in Coryanthes the nectar-secreting glands pour forth an abundance of almost pure water, which drips into a bucket formed by the distal part of the labellum; and this secretion serves to prevent the bees which come to gnaw the surface of the labellum from flying away, and thus compels them to crawl out through the proper passage.

Although the secretion of nectar is of the highest / importance to orchids by attracting insects, which are indispensable for the fertilization of most of the species, yet good reasons can be assigned for the belief[6] that nectar was aboriginally an excretion for the sake of getting rid of superfluous matter during the chemical changes which go on in the tissue of plants, especially whilst the sun shines. The bracteae of some orchids have been observed[7] to secrete nectar, and this cannot be of any use to them for their fertilization. Fritz Müller informs me that he has seen such secretion from the bracteae of an Oncidium in its native Brazilian home, as well as from the bracteae and from the *outside* of the upper sepal of a Notylia. Mr Rodgers has observed a similar and copious secretion from the base of the flower-peduncles of Vanilla. The column of Acropera and Gongora likewise secretes nectar, as previously stated, but only after the flowers have been impregnated, and when such secretion could be of no use by attracting insects. It is in perfect accordance with the scheme of nature, as worked out by Natural Selection, that matter excreted to free the system from superfluous or injurious substances should be utilized for highly useful purposes. To give an example in strong contrast with our present subject, the larvae of certain beetles (Cassidae, etc.) use their own excrement to make an umbrella-like protection for their tender bodies.

It may be remembered that evidence was given in the first chapter proving that nectar is never found within the spur-like nectaries of several species of Orchis, but that various kinds of insects penetrate / the tender inner coat with the proboscides, and suck the fluid

[6] This subject has been fully discussed in my work *On the Effects of Cross and Self-fertilization in the Vegetable Kingdom*, 1876, p. 402.

[7] Kurr, *Ueber die Bedeutung der Nektarien*, 1833, p. 28.

contained in the inter-cellular spaces. This conclusion has been confirmed by Hermann Müller, and I have further shown that even Lepidoptera are able to penetrate other and tougher tissues. It is an interesting case of co-adaptation that in all the British species, in which the nectary does not contain free nectar, the viscid matter of the disc of the pollinium requires a minute or two in order to set hard; and it would be an advantage to the plant if insects were delayed thus long in obtaining the nectar by having to puncture the nectary at several points. On the other hand, in all the Ophreae which have nectar ready stored within the nectary, the discs are sufficiently viscid for the attachment of the pollinia to insects, without the matter quickly setting hard; and there would therefore be no advantage to these plants in insects being delayed for a few minutes whilst sucking the flowers.

In the case of cultivated exotic orchids which have a nectary, without any free nectar, it is of course impossible to feel absolutely sure that it would not contain any under more natural conditions. Nor have I made many comparative observations on the rate of the setting hard of the viscid matter of the disc in exotic forms. Nevertheless it seems that some Vandeae are in the same predicament as our British species of Orchis; thus *Calanthe masuca* has a very long nectary, which in all the specimens examined by me was quite dry internally, and was inhabited by powdery Cocci; but in the intercellular spaces between the two coats there was much fluid; and in this species the viscid matter of the disc, after its surface had been disturbed, entirely lost its adhesiveness in two minutes. In an Oncidium the disc, similarly disturbed, became dry in / one minute and a half; in an Odontoglossum in two minutes; and in neither of these orchids was there any free nectar. On the other hand, in *Angraecum sesquipedale*, which has free nectar stored within the lower end of the nectary, the disc of the pollinium, when removed from the plant and with its surface disturbed, was strongly adhesive after forty-eight hours.

Sarcanthus teritifolius offers a more curious case. The disc quite lost in its viscidity and set hard in less than three minutes. Hence it might have been expected that no fluid would have been found in the nectary, but only in the intercellular spaces; nevertheless there was fluid in both places, so that here we have both conditions combined in the same flower. It is probable that insects would sometimes rapidly suck the free nectar and neglect that beween the two coats; but even in this case I strongly suspect that they would be delayed by a totally different means in sucking the free nectar, so as to allow the viscid matter to set hard. In this plant, the labellum with its nectary is an extraordinary organ. I wished to have had a drawing made of its structure; but found that it was as hopeless as to give a drawing of the wards of a complicated lock. Even the skilful Bauer, with numerous figures and sections on a large scale, hardly makes the structure intelligible. So complicated is the passage, that I failed in repeated attempts to pass a bristle from the outside of the flower into the nectary; or in a reversed direction from the cut-off end of the nectary to the outside. No doubt an insect with a voluntarily flexible proboscis could pass it through the passages, and thus reach the nectar; but in effecting this, some delay would be caused; and time would be thus allowed for the / curious square viscid disc to become securely cemented to an insect's head or body.

As in Epipactis the cup at the base of the labellum serves as a nectar-receptacle, I expected to find that the analogous cups in Stanhopea, Acropera, etc., would serve for the same purpose; but I could never find a drop of nectar in them. According, also, to M. Ménière and Mr Scott[8] this is never the case in these genera, or in Gongora, Cirrhaea, and many others. In *Catasetum tridentatum*, and in the female form Monachanthus, we see that the upturned cup cannot possibly serve as a nectar-receptacle. What then attracts insects to these flowers? That they must be attracted is certain; more especially in the case of Catasetum, in which the sexes stand on separate plants. In many genera of Vandeae there is no trace of any nectar-secreting organ or receptacle; but in all these cases (as far as I have seen), the labellum is either thick and fleshy, or is furnished with extraordinary excrescences, as in the genera Oncidium and Odontoglossum. In *Phalaenosis grandiflora* there is a curious anvil-shaped projection on the labellum, with two tendril-like prolongations from its extremity which turn backwards and apparently serve to guard the sides of the anvil, so that insects would be forced to alight on its crown. Even in our British *Cephalanthera grandiflora*, the labellum of which never contains nectar, there are orange-coloured ribs and papillae on the inner surface which faces the column. In Calanthe (fig. 26) a cluster of odd little spherical warts projects from the labellum, and there is an extremely long nectary, which does not include nectar; in *Eulophia viridis* the short nectary is equally destitute of nectar, and the labellum / is covered with longitudinal, fimbriated ridges. In several species of Ophrys, there are

---

[8] *Bulletin Bot. Soc. de France*, vol. ii, 1855, p. 352.

two small shining protuberances, at the base of the labellum, beneath the two discs. Innumerable other cases could be added of the presence of singular and diversified excrescences on the labellum; and Lindley remarks that their use is quite unknown.

From the position, relatively to the viscid discs, which these excrescences occupy, and from the absence of any free nectar, it formerly seemed to me highly probable that they afforded food and thus attracted either Hymenoptera or flower-feeding Coleoptera. There is no more inherent improbability in a flower being habitually fertilized by an insect coming to feed on the labellum, than in seeds being habitually disseminated by birds attracted by the sweet pulp in which they are embedded. But I am bound to state that Dr Percy, who had the thick and furrowed labellum of a Warrea analysed for me by fermentation over mercury, found that it gave no evidence of containing more saccharine matter than the other petals. On the other hand, the thick labellum of Catasetum and the bases of the upper petals of *Mormodes ignea*, have a slightly sweet, rather pleasant, and nutritious taste. Nevertheless, it was a bold speculation that insects were attracted to the flowers of various orchids in order to gnaw the excrescences or other parts of their labella; and few things have given me more satisfacton than the full confirmation of this view by Dr Crüger, who[9] has repeatedly witnessed in the West Indies humble-bees of the genus Euglossa gnawing the labellum of Catasetum, Coryanthes, Gongora, and Stanhopea. Fritz Müller also has often found, in / South Brazil, the prominences on the labellum of Oncidium gnawed. We are thus enabled to understand the meaning of the various extraordinary crests and projections on the labellum of many orchids; for they invariably stand in such a position that insects, whilst gnawing them, would be almost sure to touch the viscid discs of the pollinia and thus remove them, afterwards effecting the fertilization of another flower.

MOVEMENTS OF THE POLLINIA

The pollinia of many orchids undergo a movement of depression, after they have been removed from their places of attachment and have been exposed for a few seconds to the air. This is due to the

---

[9] *Journ. Linn. Soc. Bot.*, 1864, vol. viii, p. 129.

contraction of a portion, sometimes to an exceedingly minute portion, of the exterior surface of the rostellum, which retains a membranous condition. This membrane, as we have seen, is likewise sensitive to a touch, so as to rupture in certain definite lines. In a Maxillaria the middle part of the pedicel, and in Habenaria the whole drum-like pedicel contracts. The point of contraction in all the other cases seen by me, is either close to the surface of attachment of the caudicle to the disc, or at the point where the pedicel is united to the disc; but both the disc and pedicel are parts of the exterior surface of the rostellum. in these remarks I do not refer to the movements which are simply due to the elasticity of the pedicel, as in the Vandeae.

The long strap-formed disc of *Gymnadenia conopsea* is well adapted to show the mechanism of the movement of depression. The whole pollinium, both in its upright and depressed (but not closely depressed) position, has been shown (p. 45) in fig. 10. The disc, in its uncontracted condition with the caudicle removed, / is seen from above highly magnified in the upper of the two adjoining figures; and in the lower figure we have a longitudinal section of the uncontracted disc, together with the base of the attached and upright caudicle. At the broad end of the disc there is a deep crescent-shaped depression, bordered by a slight ridge formed of longitudinally elongated cells.

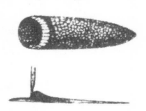

Fig. 38   Disc of *Gymnadenia conopsea*

The end of the caudicle is attached to the steep sides of this depression and ridge. When the disc is exposed to the air for about thirty seconds, the ridge contracts and sinks flat down; in sinking, it drags with it the caudicle, which then lies parallel to the elongated tapering part of the disc. If placed in water the ridge rises, re-elevating the caudicle, and when re-exposed to the air it sinks again, but each time with somewhat enfeebled power. During each sinking and rising of the caudicle, the whole pollinium is of course depressed and elevated.

That the power of movement lies exclusively in the surface of the disc is well shown in the case of the saddle-shaped disc of *Orchis pyramidalis*; for whilst it was held under water I removed the attached caudicles and the layer of viscid matter from the inferior surface, and immediately that the disc was exposed to the air the proper contraction ensued. The disc is formed of several layers of minute cells, which are best seen in specimens that have been kept in spirits of wine, for their contents are thus rendered more opaque. The cells in the flaps of the saddle are a little elongated. As long as the saddle is kept damp, its upper surface is nearly flat, but when exposed to the air (see fig. 3, / E, p. 13) the two flaps or sides contract and curl inwards; and this causes the divergence of the pollinia. By a kind of contraction two valleys are likewise formed in front of the caudicles, so that the latter are thrown forwards and downwards, almost in the same way as if trenches were dug in front of two upright poles, and then carried on so as to undermine them. As far as I could perceive, an analogous contraction causes the depression of the pollinia in *Orchis mascula.* With *O. hircina* both pollinia are attached to a single rather large square disc, the whole front of which, after exposure to the air, sinks down and is then separated from the hinder part by an abrupt step. By this contraction both pollinia are carried forwards and downwards.

Some pollinia which had been gummed on card for several months, when placed in water, rose up and afterwards underwent the movement of depression. A fresh pollinium, on being alternately damped and exposed to the air, rises and sinks several times alternately. Before I had ascertained these facts, which show that the movement is simply hygrometric, I thought that it was a vital action, and tried vapour of chloroform and of prussic acid, and immersion in laudanum; but these reagents did not check the movement. Nevertheless, there are some difficulties in understanding how the movement can be simply hygrometric. The flaps of the saddle in *Orchis pyramidalis* (see fig. 3, D, p. 13) curl completely inwards in nine seconds, which is a surprisingly short time for mere evaporation to produce an effect;[10] and the / movement is apparently due to the drying of the under surface, although this is covered with a thick layer of viscid matter. The edges, however, of the saddle might become slightly dry in the nine seconds. When the saddle-formed disc is placed in spirits of wine it contracts energetically; and this is probably due to the attraction of alcohol for water. When replaced in water it opens again. Whether or not the contraction is wholly hygrometric, the movements are admirably regulated in each species,

---

[10] This fact does not now appear to me so surprising as it formerly did, for my son Francis has shown (*Transact,. Linn. Soc.*, 2nd series, Bot. vol. i, 1876, p. 149) with what extraordinary quickness the awn of Stipa twists and untwists when exposed to dry and damp air. These movements being due, as he has shown, to the twisting and untwisting of the separate cells.

so that the pollen-masses, when transported by insects from flower to flower, assume a proper position for striking the stigmatic surface.

These various movements would be quite useless, unless the pollinia were attached in a uniform position to the insects which visit the flowers so as to be always directed in the same manner after the movement of depression; and this necessitates that the insects should be forced to visit the flowers of the same species in a uniform manner. Hence I must say a few words on the sepals and petals. Their primary function, no doubt, is to protect the organs of fructification in the bud. After the flower is fully expanded, the upper sepal and two upper petals often continue the same office. We cannot doubt that this protection is of service, when we see in Stelis the sepals so neatly reclosing and reprotecting the flower some time after its expansion; in Masdevallia the sepals are permanently soldered together, with two little windows alone left open; and in the open and exposed flowers of Bolbophyllum, the mouth of the stigmatic chamber after a time closes. Analogous facts with respect to Malaxis, Cephalanthera, etc., could be given. But the hood formed by the upper sepal and two upper petals, besides affording protection, evidently forms a guide, / compelling insects to visit the flowers in front. Few persons now doubt the correctness of C. K. Sprengel's view,[1] that the bright and conspicuous colours of flowers serve to attract insects from a distance. Nevertheless some orchids have singularly inconspicuous and greenish flowers, perhaps in order to escape some danger; but many of these are strongly scented, which would equally well serve to attract insects.

The labellum is by far the most important of the external envelopes of the flower. It not only secretes nectar, but is often modelled into variously shaped receptacles for holding this fluid, or is itself rendered attractive so as to be gnawed by insects. Unless the flowers were by some means rendered attractive, most of the species would be cursed with perpetual sterility. The labellum always stands in front of the rostellum, and its outer portion often serves as a landing-place for the necessary visitors. In *Epipactis palustris* this part is flexible and elastic, and apparently compels insects in retreating to brush against the

[1] This author's curious work, with its quaint title of *Das Entdeckte Geheimniss der Natur*, until lately was often spoken lightly of. No doubt he was an enthusiast, and perhaps carried some of his ideas to an extreme length. But I feel sure, from my own observations, that his work contains an immense body of truth. Many years ago Robert Brown, to whose judgment all botanists defer, spoke highly of it to me, and remarked that only those who knew little of the subject would laugh at him.

rostellum. In Cypripedium the distal portion is folded over like the end of a slipper, and compels insects to crawl out of the flower by one of two special passages. In Pterostylis and a few other orchids the labellum is irritable, so that when touched it shuts the flower, leaving only a single passage by which an insect can escape. In Spiranthes, when the flower is fully mature, the column moves from the labellum, space being thus left for / the introduction of the pollen-masses attached to the proboscis of a humble-bee. In *Mormodes ignea* the labellum is perched on the summit of the column, and here insects alight and touch a sensitive point, causing the ejection of the pollen-masses. The labellum is often deeply channelled, or has guiding ridges, or is pressed closely against the column; and in a multitude of cases it approaches closely enough to render the flower tubular. By these several means insects are forced to brush against the rostellum. We must not, however, suppose, that every detail of structure in the labellum is of use: in some instances, as with Sarcanthus, its extraordinary shape seems to be partly due to its development in close apposition to the curiously shaped rostellum.

In *Listera ovata* the labellum stands far from the column, but its base is narrow, so that insects are led to stand exactly beneath the middle of the rostellum. In other cases, as in Stanhopea, Phalaenopsis, Gongora, etc., the labellum is furnished with upturned basal lobes, which manifestly act as lateral guides. In some cases, as in Malaxis, the two upper petals are curled backwards so as to be out of the way; in other cases as in Acropera, Masdevallia, and some Bolbophyllums, these upper petals plainly serve as lateral guides, compelling insects to visit the flowers directly in front of the rostellum. In other cases, wings formed by the margins of the clinandrum or of the column, serve as lateral guides, both in the withdrawal of the pollinia and in their subsequent insertion into the stigmatic cavity. So that there can be no doubt that the petals, sepals, and rudimentary anthers do good service in several ways, besides affording protection to the bud.

The final end of the whole flower, with all its parts, is the production of seed; and these are produed by / orchids in vast profusion. Not that such profusion is anything to boast of; for the production of an almost infinite number of seeds or eggs, is undoubtedly a sign of lowness or organization. That a plant, not being an annual, should escape extinction, chiefly by the production of a vast number of seeds or seedlings, shows a poverty of contrivance, or a want of some fitting protection against other dangers. I was curious to estimate the number of seeds produced by some few orchids; so I took a ripe capsule of *Cephalanthera grandiflora*, and arranged the seeds on a long ruled line as equably as I could in a narrow hillock; and then counted the seeds in an accurately measured length of one-tenth of an inch. In this way the contents of the capsule were estimated at 6,020 seeds, and very few of these were bad; the four capsules borne by the same plant would have therefore contained 24,080 seeds. Estimating in the same manner the smaller seeds of *Orchis maculata*, I found the number nearly the same, viz., 6,200; and, as I have often seen above thirty capsules on the same plant, the total amount would be 186,300. As this orchid is perennial, and cannot in most places be increasing in number, one seed alone of this large number yields a mature plant once in every few years.

To give an idea what the above figures really mean, I will briefly show the possible rate of increase of *O. maculata*: an acre of land would hold 174,240 plants, each having a space of six inches square, and this would be just sufficient for their growth; so that, making the fair allowance of 400 bad seeds in each capsule, an acre would be thickly clothed by the progeny of a single plant. At the same rate of increase, the grandchildren would cover a space slightly exceeding the island of Anglesea; and the great grandchildren / of a single plant would nearly (in the ratio of 47 to 50) clothe with one uniform green carpet the entire surface of the land throughout the globe. But the number of seeds produced by one of our common British orchids is as nothing compared to that of some of the exotic kinds. Mr Scott found that the capsule of an Acropera contained 371,250 seeds; and judging from the number of flowers, a single plant would sometimes yield about seventy-four millions of seeds. Fritz Müller found 1,756,440 seeds in a single capsule of a Maxillaria; and the same plant sometimes bore half-a-dozen such capsules. I may add that by counting the packets of pollen (one of which was broken up under the microscope) I estimated that the number of pollen-grains, each of which emits its tube, in a single anther of *Orchis mascula* was 122,400. Amici[12] estimated the number in *O. morio* at 120,300. As these two species apparently do not produce more seed than the allied *O. maculata*, a capsule of which contained 6,200 seeds, we see that there are about twenty pollen-grains for each ovule. According to this standard, the number of pollen-grains in the anther of a single flower of the Maxillaria which yielded 1,756,440 seeds must be prodigious.

[12] Mohl, *The Vegetable Cell*, translated by Henfrey, p. 133.

What checks the unlimited multiplication of the Orchideae throughout the world is not known. The minute seeds within their light coats
are well fitted for wide dissemination; and I have several times
observed seedlings springing up in my orchard and in a newly planted
wood, which must have come from a considerable distance. This was
especially the case with *Epipactis latifolia*; and an instance has been
recorded by a good observer[13] of seedlings of this plant / appearing at
the distance of between eight and ten miles from any place where it
grew. Notwithstanding the astonishing number of seeds produced by
orchids, it is notorious that they are sparingly distributed; for instance,
Kent appears to be the most favourable county in England for the
order, and within a mile of my house nine genera, including thirteen
species, grow; but of these one alone, *Orchis morio*, is sufficiently
abundant to make a conspicuous feature in the vegetation; as is *O.
maculata* in a lesser degree in open woodlands. Most of the other
species, though not deserving to be called rare, are sparingly
distributed; yet, if their seeds or seedlings were not largely destroyed,
any one of them would immediately cover the whole land. In the
tropics the species are very much more numerous; thus Fritz Müller
found in South Brazil more than thirteen kinds belonging to several
genera growing on a single Cedrela tree. Mr Fitzgerald has collected
within the radius of one mile of Sydney in Australia no less than sixty-
two species, of which fifty-seven were terrestrial. Nevertheless the
number of individuals of the same species is, I believe, in no country
nearly so great as that of very many other plants. Lindley formerly
estimated that there were in he world about 6,000 species of
Orchideae, included in 433 genera.[14]

The number of the individuals which come to maturity does not
seem to be at all closely determined by the number of seeds which each
species produces; and this holds good when closely related forms are
compared. Thus *Ophrys apifera* fertilizes itself and every flower
produces a capsule; but the individuals of this species are not so
numerous in some parts of / England as those of *O. muscifera*, which
cannot fertilize itself and is imperfectly fertilized by insects, so that a
large proportion of the flowers drop off unimpregnated. *Ophrys
aranifera* is found in large numbers in Liguria, yet Delpino estimates
that not more than one out of 3,000 flowers produces a capsule.[15] Mr

[13] Mr Bree, in *Loudon's Mag. of Nat. Hist.*, vol. ii, 1829, p. 70.
[14] *Gardener's Chron.*, 1862, p. 192.
[15] *Ult. Osservaz. sulla Dicogamia*, part i, p. 177.

Cheeseman says[16] that with the New Zealand *Pterostylis trullifolia* much less than a quarter of the flowers, which are beautifully adapted for cross-fertilization, yield capsules; whereas with the allied *Acianthus sinclairii*, the flowers of which equally require insect-aid for their fertilization, seventy-one capsules were produced by eighty-seven flowers; so that this plant must produce an extraordinary number of seeds; nevertheless in many districts it is not at all more abundant than the Pterostylis. Mr Fitzgerald, who in Australia has particularly attended to this subject, remarks that every flower of *Thelymitra carnea* fertilizes itself and produces a capsule; yet it is not nearly so common as *Acianthus fornicatus*, 'the majority of the flowers of which are unproductive. *Phajus grandifolius* and *Calanthe veratrifolia* grow in similar situations. Every flower of the Phajus produces seeds, only occasionally one of the Calanthe, yet Phajus is rare and Calanthe common.'

The frequency with which throughout the world members of various orchideous tribes fail to have their flowers fertilized, though these are excellently constructed for cross-fertilization, is a remarkable fact. Fritz Müller informs me that this holds good in the luxuriant forests of South Brazil with most of the Epidendreae, and with the genus Vanilla. For instance, / he visited a site where Vanilla creeps over almost every tree, and although the plants had been covered with flowers, yet only two seed-capsules were produced. So again with an Epidendrum, 233 flowers had fallen off unimpregnated and only one capsule had been formed; of the still remaining 136 flowers, only four had their pollinia removed. In New South Wales Mr Fitzgerald does not believe that more than one flower out of a thousand of *Dendrobium speciosum* sets a capsule; and some other species there are very sterile. In New Zealand over 200 flowers of *Coryanthes triloba* yielded only five capsules; and at the Cape of Good Hope only the same number were produced by 78 flowers of *Disa grandiflora*. Nearly the same result has been observed with some of the species of Ophrys in Europe. The sterility in these cases is very difficult to explain. It manifestly depends on the flowers being constructed with such elaborate care for cross-fertlization, that they cannot yield seeds without the aid of insects. From the evidence which I have given elsewhere[17] we may conclude that it would be far more profitable to most plants to yield a few cross-

[16] *Transact. New Zealand Inst.*, vol. vii, 1875, p. 351.
[17] *The Effects of Cross and Self-fertilization in the Vegetable Kingdom*, 1876.

fertilized seeds, at the expense of many flowers dropping off unimpregnated, rather than produce many self-fertilized seeds. Profuse expenditure is nothing unusual under nature, as we see with the pollen of wind-fertilized plants, and in the multitude of seeds and seedlings produced by most plants in comparison with the few that reach maturity. In other cases the paucity of the flowers that are impregnated may be due to the proper insects having become rare under the incessant changes to which the world is subject; or to other plants which are more / highly attractive to the proper insects having increased in number. We know that certain orchids require certain insects for their fertilization, as in the cases before given of Vanilla and Sarcochilus. In Madagascar *Angraecum sesquipedale* must depend on some gigantic moth. In Europe *Cypripedium calceolus* appears to be fertilized only by small bees of the genus Andrena, and *Epipactis latifolia* only by wasps. In those cases in which only a few flowers are impregnated owing to the proper insects visiting only a few, this may be a great injury to the plant; and many hundred species throughout the world have been thus exterminated; those which survive having been favoured in some other way. On the other hand, the few seeds which are produced in these cases will be the product of cross-fertilization, and this as we now positively know is an immense advantage to most plants.

I have now nearly finished this volume, which is perhaps too lengthy. It has, I think, been shown that the Orchideae exhibit an almost endless diversity of beautiful adaptations. When this or that part has been spoken of as adapted for some special purpose, it must not be supposed that it was originally always formed for this sole purpose. The regular course of events seems to be, that a part which originally served for one purpose, becomes adapted by slow changes for widely different purposes. To give an instance: in all the Ophreae, the long and nearly rigid caudicle manifestly serves for the application of the pollen-grains to the stigma, when the pollinia are transported by insects to another flower; and the anther opens widely in order that the pollinium should be easily withdrawn; but in the Bee Ophrys, the caudicle, by a slight increase in length and decrease in its thickness, and by / the anther opening a little more widely, becomes specially adapted for the very different purpose of self-fertilization, through the combined aid of the weight of the pollen-mass and the vibration of the flower when moved by the wind. Every gradation between these two states is possible – of which we have a partial instance in *O. aranifera*.

Again, the elasticity of the pedicel of the pollinium in some Vandeae is adapted to free the pollen-masses from their anther-cases; but by a further slight modification, the elasticity of the pedicel becomes specially adapted to shoot out the pollinium with considerable force so as to strike the body of the visiting insect. The great cavity in the labellum of many Vandeae is gnawed by insects and thus attracts them; but in *Mormodes ignea* it is greatly reduced in size, and serves in chief part to keep the labellum in its new position on the summit of the column. From the analogy of many plants we may infer that a long spur-like nectary is primarily adapted to secrete and hold a store of nectar; but in many orchids it has so far lost this function, that it contains fluid only in the intercellular spaces. In those orchids in which the nectary contains both free nectar and fluid in the intercellular spaces, we can see how a transition from the one state to the other could be effected, namely, by less and less nectar being secreted from the inner membrane, with more and more retained within the intercellular spaces. Other analogous cases could be given.

Although an organ may not have been originally formed for some special purpose, if it now serves for this end, we are justified in saying that it is specially adapted for it. On the same principle, if a man were to make a machine for some special purpose, but were / to use old wheels, springs, and pulleys, only slightly altered, the whole machine, with all its parts, might be said to be specially contrived for its present purpose. Thus throughout nature almost every part of each living being has probably served, in a slightly modified condition, for diverse purposes, and has acted in the living machinery of many ancient and distinct specific forms.

In my examination of orchids, hardly any fact has struck me so much as the endless diversities of structure – the prodigality of resources – for gaining the very same end, namely, the fertilization of one flower by pollen from another plant. This fact is to a large extent intelligible on the principle of Natural Selection. As all the parts of a flower are co-ordinated, if slight variations in any one part were preserved from being beneficial to the plant, then the other parts would generally have to be modified in some corresponding manner. But these latter parts might not vary at all, or they might not vary in a fitting manner, and these other variations, whatever their nature might be, which tended to bring all the parts into more harmonious action with one another, would be preserved by Natural Selection.

To give a simple illustration: in many orchids the ovarium (but sometimes the foot stalk) becomes for a period twisted, causing the labellum to assume the position of a lower petal, so that insects can easily visit the flower; but from slow changes in the form or position of the petals, or from new sorts of insects visiting the flowers, it might be advantageous to the plant that the labellum should resume its normal position on the upper side of the flower, as is actually the case with *Malaxis paludosa*, and some species of Catasetum, etc. This change, it is obvious, might be simply effected by the continued selection of varieties / which had their ovaria less and less twisted; but if the plant only afforded varieties with the ovarium more twisted, the same end could be attained by the selection of such variations, until the flower was tuned completely round on its axis. This seems to have actually occurred with *Malaxis paludosa*, for the labellum has acquired its present upward position by the ovarium being twisted twice as much as is usual.

Again, we have seen that in most Vandeae there is a plain relation between the depth of the stigmatic chamber and the length of the pedicel, by which the pollen-masses are inserted; now if the chamber became slightly less deep from any change in the form of the column or other unknown cause, the mere shortening of the pedicel would be the simplest corresponding change; but if the pedicel did not happen to vary in shortness, the slightest tendency to its becoming bowed from elasticity as in Phalaenopsis, or to a backward hygrometric movement as in one of the Maxillarias, would be preserved, and the tendency would be continually augmented by selection; thus the pedicel, as far as its action is concerned, would be modified in the same manner as if it had been shortened. Such processes carried on during many thousand generations in various ways, would create an endless diversity of co-adaped structures in the several parts of the flower for the same general purpose. This view affords, I believe, the key which partly solves the problem of the vast diversity of structure adapted for closely analogous ends in many large groups of organic beings.

The more I study nature, the more I become impressed with ever-increasing force, that the contrivances and beautiful adaptations slowly acquired through each part occasionally varying in a slight / degree but in many ways, with the preservation of those variations which were beneficial to the organism under complex and ever-varying conditions of life, transcend in an incomparable manner the contrivances and adaptations which the most fertile imagination of man could invent.

The use of each trifling detail of structure is far from a barren search to those who believe in Natural Selection. When a naturalist casually takes up the study of an organic being, and does not investigate its whole life (imperfect though that study will ever be), he naturally doubts whether each trifling point can be of any use, or indeed whether it be due to any general law. Some naturalists believe that numberless structures have been created for the sake of mere variety and beauty – much as a workman would make different patterns. I, for one, have often and often doubted whether this or that detail of structure in many of the Orchideae and other plants could be of any service; yet, if of no good, these structures could not have been modelled by the natural preservation of useful variations; such details can only be vaguely accounted for by the direct action of the conditions of life, or the mysterious laws of correlated growth.

To give nearly all the instances of trifling details of structure in the flowers of orchids, which are certainly of high importance, would be to recapitulate almost the whole of this volume. But I will recall to the reader's memory a few cases. I do not here refer to the fundamental framework of the plant, such as the remnants of the fifteen primary organs arranged alternately in the five whorls; for almost everyone who believes in the gradual evolution of species will admit that their presence is due to inheritance from a remote parent-form. Innumerable facts with respect to the / uses of the variously shaped and placed petals and sepals have been given. So again, the importance of as light difference in the shape of the caudicle of the pollinium of the Bee Ophrys, compared with that of the other species of the same genus, has likewise been referred to; to this might be added the doubly-bent caudicle of the Fly Ophrys. Indeed, the important relation of the length and shape of the caudicle, with reference to the position of the stigma, might be cited throughout many whole tribes. The solid projecting knob of the anther in *Epipactis palustris*, which does not include pollen, liberates the pollen-masses when it is moved by insects. In *Cephalanthera grandiflora*, the upright position of the almost closed flower protects the slightly coherent pillars of pollen from disturbance. The length and elasticity of the filament of the anther in certain species of Dendrobium apparently serves for self-fertilization, if insects fail to transport the pollen-masses. The slight forward inclination of the crest of the rostellum in Listera prevents the anther-case being caught as soon as the viscid matter is ejected. The elasticity of the lip of the rostellum in Orchis causes it to spring up again when only one of the pollen-masses has been removed, thus keeping the second viscid disc ready for action, which otherwise would be wasted. No one who had not studied orchids would have suspected that these and very many other small details of structure were of the highest importance to each species; and that consequently, if the species were exposed to new conditions of life, and the structure of the several parts varied ever so little, the smallest details of structure might readily be acquired though Natural Selection. These cases afford a good lesson of caution with respect to the importance of apparently trifling particulars of structure in other organic beings. /

It may be naturally enquired, Why do the Orchideae exhibit so many perfect contrivances for their fertilization? From the observations of various botanists and my own, I am sure that many other plants offer analogous adaptations of high perfection; but it seems that they are really more numerous and perfect with the Orchideae than with most other plants. To a certain extent this enquiry can be answered. As each ovule requires at least one, probably several, pollen-grains,[18] and as the seeds produced by orchids are so inordinately numerous, we can see that it is necessary that large masses of pollen should be left on the stigma of each flower. Even in the Neotteae, which have granular pollen, with the grains tied together by weak threads, I have observed that considerable masses of pollen are generally left on the stigmas. This circumstance apparently explains why the grains cohere in packets or large waxy masses, as they do in so many tribes, namely, to prevent waste in the act of transportal. The flowers of most plants produce pollen enough to fertilize several flowers, so as to allow of or to favour cross-fertilization. But with the many orchids which produce only two pollen-masses, and with some of the Malaxeae which produce only one, the pollen from a single flower cannot possibly fertilize more than two flowers or only a single one; and cases of this kind do not occur, as I believe, in any other group of plants. If the Orchideae had elaborated as much pollen as is produced by other plants, relatively to the number of seeds which they yield, they would have had to produce a most extravagant amount, and this would have caused exhaustion. Such exhaustion is avoided by pollen not being produced

[18] Gärtner, *Beiträge zur Kenntniss der Befruchtung*, 1844, p. 135.

in any great / superfluity owing to the many special contrivances for its safe transportal from plant to plant, and for placing it securely on the stigma. Thus we can understand why the Orchideae are more highly endowed in their mechanism for cross-fertilization, than are most other plants.

In my work on the *Effects of Cross and Self Fertilisation in the Vegetable Kingdom*, I have shown that when flowers are cross-fertilized they generally receive pollen from a distinct plant and not that from another flower on the same plant; a cross of this latter kind doing little or no good. I have further shown that the benefits derived from a cross between two plants depends altogether on their differing somewhat in constitution; and there is much evidence that each individual seedling possesses its own peculiar constitution. The crossing of distinct plants of the same species is favoured or determined in various ways, as described in the above work, but chiefly by the prepotent action of pollen from another plant over that from the same flower. Now with the Orchideae it is highly probable that such prepotency prevails, for we know from the valuable observations of Mr Scott and Fritz Müller,[19] that with several orchids pollen from their own flower is quite impotent, and is even in some cases poisonous to the stigma. Besides this prepotency, the Orchideae present various special contrivances – such as the pollinia not assuming a proper position for striking the stigma until some time has elapsed after their removal from the anthers – the slow curving forwards and then backwards of the rostellum in Listera and Neottia – the / slow movement of the column from the labellum in Sprianthes – the dioecious condition of Catasetum – the fact of some species producing only a single flower, etc. – all render it certain or highly probable that the flowers are habitually fertilized with pollen from a distinct plant.

That cross-fertilization, to the complete exclusion of self-fertilization, is the rule with the Orchideae, cannot be doubted from the facts already given in relation to many species in all the tribes throughout the world. I could almost as soon believe the flowers in general were not adapted for the production of seeds, because there are a few plants which have never been known to yield seed, as that the flowers of the Orchideae are not as a general rule adapted so as to ensure

---

[19] A full abstract of these observations is given in my *Variation of Animals and Plants under Domestication*, ch. xvii, 2nd edit., vol. ii, p. 114.

cross-fertilization. Nevertheless, some species are regularly or often self-fertilized; and I will now give a list of all the cases hitherto observed by myself and others. In some of these the flowers appear often to be fertilized by insects, but they are capable of fertilizing themselves without aid, though in a more or less incomplete manner; so that they do not remain utterly barren if insects fail to visit them. Under this head may be included three British species, namely, *Cephalanthera grandiflora*, *Neottia nidus-avis*, and perhaps *Listera ovata*. In South Africa *Disa macrantha* often fertilizes itself; but Mr Weale believes that it is likewise cross-fertilized by moths. Three species belonging to the Epidendreae rarely open their flowers in the West Indies; nevertheless these flowers fertilize themselves, but it is doubtful whether they are fully fertilized, for a large proportion of the seeds spontaneously produced by some members of this tribe in a hothouse were destitute of an embryo. Some species of Dendrobium, judging from their structure and from their / occasionally producing capsules under cultivation, likewise come under this head.

Of species which regularly fertilize themselves without any aid and yield full-sized capsules, hardly any case is more striking than that of *Ophrys apifera*, which was advanced by me in the first edition of this work. To this case may now be added two other European plants, *Orchis* or *Neotinea intacta* and *Epipactis viridiflora*. Two North American species, *Gymnadenia tridentata* and *Platanthera hyperborea* appear to be in the same predicament, but whether when self-fertilized they yield a full complement of capsules containing good seeds has not been ascertained. A curious Epidendrum in South Brazil which bears two additional anthers fertilizes itself freely by their aid; and *Dendrobium cretaceum* has been known to produce perfect self-fertilized seeds in a hothouse in England. Lastly, *Spiranthes australis* and two species of Thelymitra, inhabitants of Australia, come under this same head. No doubt other cases will hereafter be added to this short list of about ten species which it appears can fertilize themselves fully, and of about the same number of species which fertilize themselves imperfectly when insects are excluded.

It deserves especial attention that the flowers of all the above-named self-fertile species still retain various structures which it is impossible to doubt are adapted for insuring cross-fertilization, though they are now rarely or never brought into play. We may therefore conclude that all these plants are descended from species or varieties which were formerly fertilized by insect-aid. Moreover, several of the genera to which these self-fertile species belong, include other species, which are incapable of self-fertilization. Thelymitra offers indeed the only instance known to me of two / species within the same genus which regularly fertilize themselves. Considering such cases as those of Ophrys, Disa, and Epidendrum, in which one species alone in the genus is capable of complete self-fertilization, whilst the other species are rarely fertilized in any manner owing to the rarity of the visits of the proper insects; bearing also in mind the large number of species in many parts of the world which from this same cause are seldom impregnated, we are led to believe that the above-named self-fertile plants formerly depended on the visits of insects for their fertilization, and that from such visits failing they did not yield a sufficiency of seed and were verging towards extinction. Under these circumstances it is probable that they were gradually modified, so as to become more or less completely self-fertile; for it would manifestly be more advantageous to a plant to produce self-fertilized seeds rather than none at all or extremely few seeds. Whether any species which is now never cross-fertilized will be able to resist the evil effects of long-continued self-fertilization, so as to survive for as long an average period as the other species of the same genera which are habitually cross-fertilized, cannot of course be told. But *Ophrys apifera* is still a highly vigorous plant, and *Gymnadenia tridentata* and *Platanthera hyperborea* are said by Asa Gray to be common plants in North America. It is indeed possible that these self-fertile species may revert in the course of time to what was undoubtedly their pristine condition, and in this case their various adaptations for cross-fertilization would be again brought into action. We may believe that such reversion is possible, when we hear from Mr Moggridge that *Ophrys scolopax* fertilizes itself freely in one district of Southern France without the aid of insects, and / is completely sterile without such aid in another district.

Finally, if we consider how precious a substance pollen is, and what care has been bestowed on its elaboration and on the accessory parts in the Orchideae – considering how large an amount is necessary for the impregnation of the almost innumerable seeds produced by these plants – considering that the anther stands close behind or above the stigma, self-fertilization would have been an incomparably safer and easier process than the transportal of pollen from flower to flower. Unless we bear in mind the good effects which have been proved to follow in most cases from cross-fertilization, it is an astonishing fact that the flowers of the Orchideae should not have been regularly self-fertilized. It apparently demonstrates that there must be something injurious in this latter process, of which fact I have elsewhere given direct proof. It is hardly an exaggeration to say that Nature tells us, in the most emphatic manner, that she abhors perpetual self-fertilization. /

INDEX

Aceras anthropophora, 26; pollen-tubes, 258
  longibracteata, 26
  monstrous flowers, 255
Acianthus exsertus, 90
  fornicatus, 90, 280
  sinclairii, 90; fertilized by insects, 280
Acontia luctuosa with pollen-masses, 31
Acropera, pollinia of, 154, 156; upper petals, 276
  loddigesii, 166
  luteola, 166; vessels of, 239
Adaptations, how far special, 267; diversity of, 282
Aerides, movement of pollinia, 156; secretion of nectar, 265
  cornutum, 265
  odorata, 158
  virens, 156
Amici, on number of pollen-grains in *Orchis morio*, 278
Anderson, Mr, on Dendrobium, 142; on the Epidendrea, 147
Angraecum, viscid matter in, 251
  distichum, 154
  eburneum, 155
  sesquipedale, 154, 162, 282; nectary of, 265
Antennae of the rostellum of Catasetum, 184, 187
Anthers, rudimentary, 240
Apostasia, 248
Arethuseae, 80
Auricles, or papillae, rudimentary, 241, 242

Babington, Professor, on the rostellum, 255

Baillon, M., on Catasetum, 191
Barkeria, 146
Bateman, Mr, obligations to, 105, 162; on Cycnoches, 224
Battersby, Dr, obligations to, 106
Bauer, Mr, on pollen-grains in Cephalanthera, 80, 82; on pollen-masses of Bletia, 143
Bee Ophrys, 52
Beer, J. G., on Catasetum, 197; on Cycnoches, 224
Bees with attached pollinia, 30
Belt, Mr, on *Angraecum sesquipedale*, 165
Bentham on monstrous flowers of *Orchi pyramidalis*, 38
Bird's-nest Orchis, 125
Bolbophyllum, 274; upper petals, 376
  barbigerum, 138
  cocoinum, 137
  cupreum, 137; nectary of, 265
  rhizophorae, 137
Bonatea speciosa, 71, 76; vessels of, 244; modified structure, 264; caudicle, 361
Bond, Mr F., on moths with attached pollinia, 30; obligations to, 72, 75
Bracteae, secreting nectar, 266
Brassia, movement of pollinia, 156
Bree, Mr, on seed of *Epipactis latifolia*, 278
Bronguiart, M., on secretion of nectar, 41; on *Catasetum*, 196; spiral vessels in orchids, 235; on Uropedium, 240
Bronn, Professor, on *Stanhopea devoniensis*, 171; classification of organic beings, 264
Brown, C., on *Sobralia macrantha*, 91

Brown, Robert, on the fertilization of orchids, 3; viscidity of stigma, 13; *Ophrys apifera*, 54; utriculi of the stigma, 202; homologies of orchids, 234, 235, 237; rostellum of orchids, 247; Apostasia, 248; / pollen-tubes, 258; Sprengel's work, 275

Butterflies with attached pollinia, 31

Butterfly orchis, 69
    lesser, 73

Caladenia dimorpha, 89

Calaena, 89

Calanthe dominii, 161
    masuca, structure of flower, 161; long nectary, 267, 269
    veratrifolia, 280
    vestita, 162

Carpenter, Dr, on Myanthus and Catasetum, 196

Catasetidae, 178

Catasetum, peculiar rostellum, 256; labellum, 270
    callosum, 192, 195
    luridum, 191
    mentosum, 206
    planiceps, 193
    saccatum, structure of flower, 180–5; vessels of, 239
    tabulare, 192
    tridentatum, structure of flower, 191; three forms on the same plant, 196; a male orchid, 197; vessels of, 239; peculiar form of rostellum, 256; nectar-receptacle, 269

Cattleya, sructure of flower, 143–8; vessels of, 239; nectary, 265
    crispa, 147

Caudicles of pollinia in the Vandeae, 152; development of, 252; structure, 260, 261

Cephalanthera, number of seeds, 277
    ensifolia, 86
    grandiflora, structure of flower, 80–6; vessels, 239, 242; change of colour in viscid secretions, 249; pollen, 259; labellum, 269;

number of seed, 277; upright position of flower, 287; partially self-fertile, 290

Cheeseman, Mr, on *Pterostylis trullifolia*, 88; *Acianthus sinclairii*, 90; imperfect fertilization of Pterostylis, 280

Chysis, 146

Cirrhaea, contracted stigma, 171

Clinandrum, the, 241

Coelogyne cristata, 146

Coryanthes, 90, 173; nectary, 232; secretion of nectar, 265
    fieldingii, 175
    macrantha, 175
    speciosa, structure of flower, 174
    triloba, partially self-sterile, 281

Crüger, Dr, on the Epidendreae, 147; *Gongora maculata*, 168; Stanhopea, 171; Coryanthes, 173; *C. macrantha*, 175; Catasetum, 197, 200; female pollen-masses, 202; *Selenipedium palmifolium*, 232; homologies in orchids, 235; bees gnawing the labellum, 270

Cycnoches egertonianum, 224
    ventricosum, structure of flower, 220–4

Cymbidium giganteum, 155; pollinia, 252, 260; modification of form, 263

Cypripedium, structure of flower, 226; secretion from, 229; pollen, 262; labellum, 275
    acaule, 229
    barbatum, vessels of, 239
    calceolus, 229–31; fertilized only by small bees, 282
    candidum, 235
    pubescens, 229, 230
    purpuratum, vessels of, 239

Cyrtostylis, 90

Darwin, Francis, on the movement of the awn of Stipa, 273
    George, insects fertilizing *Herminium monorchis*, 61; *Gymnadenia conopsea*, 67
    William, on *Epipactis palustris*, 99, 100

Delpino on insects being deceived by the presence of a nectary not containing nectar, 41; sterility of Spider Ophrys, 50, 51; *Cephalanthera ensifolia*, 86; movements of pollinia, 155; fertilization of *Cypripedium calceolus*, 231; imperfect fertilization of *Ophrys aranifera* in Liguria, 280

Dendrobium, length of anther, 287
  bigibbum, 142
  cretaceum, 142, 291 /
  chrysanthemum, structure of, 138–42; nectary, 265
  formosum, 142
  speciosum, partially sterile, 281
  tortile, 142

Descent, lines of, 262–5

Dickie, Professor, obligations to, 124

Disa, secretion of nectar, 265
  cornuta, 78
  grandiflora, 77; partially self-sterile, 281
  macrantha, 78; partially self-fertile, 290

Disc, viscidity of, in the *Ophreae*, 43; in *Catasetum*, 190; double in the *Ophreae*, 254; of *Gymnadenia conopsea*, 272

Disperis, secretion of nectar, 265

Duchartre, M., on Catasetum and Myanthus, 196

Dyer, Mr Thiselton, obligations to, 175

Epidendreae, 142; few seed capsules produced, 281
Epidendrum cochleatum, viscid secretion of, 249
  floribundum, 146; viscid secretion, 249
  glaucum, 146
Epipactis, vessels of, 239; viscid matter, 251
  latifolia, 100, 101; pollen, 259; fertilized only by wasps, 282; use of knob of anther, 287
  microphylla, 102

palustris, structure of flower, 93–100; labellum, 275
purpurata, 102
rubiginosa, 102
viridiflora, 102; self-fertile, 291
Epipogium gmelini, 103
Eulophia viridis, 156; nectary of, 269
Evelyna, nectary of, 265
  carivata, 146; vessels of, 239; clinandrum, 241

Farrer, T. H., obligations to, 46; on Bee Ophrys, 55; *Peristylis viridis*, 63
Fertilization, summary on, 290
Fertility of English orchids, 33
Fitzgerald, R. D., on *Pterostylis longifolia*, 89; *Caladenia dimorpha*, 89; *Acianthus fornicatus*, and *exsertus*, 90; *Vanilla aromatica*, 91; *Spiranthes australis*, 115; *Thelymitra carnea* and *longifolia*, 127; numbers of Orchideae collected near Sydney, 279; self-fertilization of *Thelymitra carnea*, 280; *Dendrobium speciosum*, 281
Flowers, use of external envelopes, 274
Fly Ophrys, 46
Frog Orchis, structure of flower, 62; secretion of nectar, 63

Galeandra funkii, 155
Gärtner on viscid matter of stigma, 249; pollen-grains in orchids, 288
Gerard, M. M., pollinia adhering to longicorn beetle, 16
Glossodia, 237
Gongora, labellum of, 276
  atro-purpurea, 169
  maculata, 168
  truncata, 169
Goodyera, vessels of, 239; caudicle in a nascent condition, 260
  discolor, 105
  pubescens, 105
  repens, 103, 105
Gordon, Rev. G., obligations to, 103
Gosse, Mr, on self-fertilized seeds of Epidendreae, 147, 148

Gradation of organs, 247
Gray, Professor Asa, on *Gymnadenia tridentata*, 68; *Platanthera*, 75; *Goodyera repens*, 105; *Spiranthes gracilis* and *cernua*, 111; *Cypripedium*, 229, 230, 235
Gymnadenia, viscid matter, 251
    albida, 43, 68
    conopsea, transplanted, 32; secretion of nectar, 40, 43; structure of flower, 65; vessels, 238, 239; rostellum, 255; movements of pollinia, 271; disc, 272
    odoratissima, 68
    tridentata, 68; self-fertile, 291

Habenaria bifolia, 78; secretion of nectar, 40, 43; viscid matter, 251 / *chlorantha*, 43, 69; vessels of, 239, 244; viscidity of exterior surface, 251
Hance, Dr, on Catasetum, 197
Herbert, Dean, on *Catasetum luridum* and Myanthus, 196
Herminium monorchis, 59; fertilized by insects, 61; rostellum, 255
Hildebrand, F., on the ovules in orchids, 172
Homologies of orchids, 232
Hooker, Dr, on *Listera*, 3, 115; labellum of *Calaena*, 89; obligations to, 115, 128, 244; spiral vessels in orchids, 235; variability of the labellum of orchids, 238; on the rostellum, 254
Horwood, Mr, assistance from, 129

Insects, frequency of visits to orchids, 33; attracted by bright colours, 275
Irmisch on Epipogium, 204; *Neottia nidus-avis*, 125; flower-bud of *Cypripdium*, 240

Krünitz, secretion of nectar by Orchis, 36
Kurr, on orchids secreting nectar, 38; secretion from hairs in *Cypripedium calceolus*, 229; nectar secreted from bracteae, 266

Labellum easily vibratile, 138; cup of, not secreting nectar in the Vandeae 269; excrescences on, 269; gnawed by insects, 270; its importance to the flower, 275; of Sarcanthus, 276
Ladies' slipper, 227
    tresses, 106
Laelia, 146
    cinnabarina, 148
Lepidoptera with attached pollinia, 30, 31
Leptotes, 146
Lindley, Dr, obligations to, 129; arrangement of orchids, 128; on forms of Catasetum, 197; of Cycnoches, 224; homologies of orchids, 235; on the number of genera and species, 279
Link on homologies of orchids, 235, 238
Liparis pendula, vessels of, 239; clinandrum, 241
Listera, viscid matter, 251; crest of rostellum, 287
    cordata, 124
    ovata, structure of, 115–24; labellum, 276
Lycaste skinnerii, 155; pollen of, 260

Malaxeae, 128
Malaxis, viscid matter, 251; upper petals, 276
    paludosa, transplanted, 32; structure of flower, 129–35; vessels, 239, 241; clinandrum, 241; pollen-tubes, 258; position of labellum affected by ovarium, 284
Malden, Rev. B. S., obligations to, 35, 64
Male flowers of Catasetum, 198
Marantaceae, 238
Marshall, Mr, on sterility of transplanted orchids, 32; *Habenaria chlorantha*, 72
Masdevallia, clinandrum of, 241; sepals, 274; upper petals, 276
    fenestrata, 135, 136, 142

Maxillaria, movements of pollinia, 156; number of pollen-grains in anther, 278
ornithorhyncha, movement of pollinia, 157, 159
Megaclinium falcatum, labellum of, 138
Ménière, M., on insects visiting orchids, 30; secretion of nectar by Coryanthes, 173; movement of Catasetum, 187, 191; the nectar-receptacle, 269
Microstylus rhedii, 132, 135
Miltonia clowesii, pollinia of, 154, 155
Modifications in orchids, 246
Moggridge, J. Traherne, on Ophrys scolopax, 52, 292; Ophrys apifera, 56, 58, 59; flowering of the Ophreae, 59
Monachanthus viridis, 196, 197, 198, 201
More, Mr A. G., on fertility of Bee Ophrys, 55; Epipactis palustris, 39, 97, 99; obligations to, 106 /
Mormodes ignea, structure of flower, 208–19; viscid secretion, 249; use of labellum, 276, 283
luxata, 219
Morren, on Vanilla aromatica, 91
Moths with attached pollinia, 21, 30, 31; intellect of, 37
Movements of pollinia, 271
Müller, Fritz, on Epidendreae, 148; pollinium of Ornithocephalus, 159, 160; Sphinx moth, 163; contracted stigma, 171, 172; ovules of Epidendreae and Vandeae, 173; Catasetum mentosum, 206; bracteae of the Oncidium secreting nectar, 266; labellum gnawed by insects, 271; number of seeds in capsule of Maxillaria, 278; number of Orchideae in South Brazil, 279; the orchideous tribes failing to be fertilized, 280; prepotency of pollen, 289
Müller, Hermann, on fertilization of Orchis mascula, 13; bees visiting the flowers of Orchis latifolia, 16; Nigritela angustifolia, 27; fertilization of orchids, 29; insects puncturing laburnum flowers, 41; Gymnadenia odorasissima, 68; Habenaria bifolia and chlorantha, 74; Epipactis rubiginosa, microphylla, and viridiflora, 102; Neottia nidus-avis, 125; Cypripedium calceolus, 231; secretion of nectar, 267
Musk Orchis, structure of flower, 59
Myanthus barbatus, 192, 199, 203; quite sterile, 205

Nectar, secretion of, by British Ophreae, 37, 39; in foreign orchids, 229; from bracteae, 229
Nectary cut off to test the intellect of moths, 37; length of, in Angraecum sesquipedale, 265
Neotinia intacta, 27, 291
Neotteae, 93; vessels of, 241
Neottia nidus-avis, 125; pollen-tubes, 258; partially self-fertile, 290
Nevill, Lady Dorothy, obligations to, 129
Nicotiana, stigma of, 249
Nigritella angustifolia, 27
Notylia, contracted stigma, 171

Odontoglossu, 156
Oliver, Professor, obligations to, 129
Oncidium, pollinia, 153, 156, 158; vessels of, 239; viscidity, 251; bracteae secreting nectar, 266
unguiculatum, development of caudicles, 252
Ophreae, 6; vessels of, 241
Ophrys apifera, structure of flower, 52; fertility of, 54–8; pollen, 259; self-fertilization, 279, 291
arachnites, 51
aranifera, 50; imperfect fertilization, 280
muscifera, transplanted, 32; structure, 45; fertility, 49; self-sterile, imperfectly fertilized by insects, 280
scolopas, 52, 292
Orchideae, modifications in, 246

Orchis fusca, 15; imperfect fertilization, 35; secretion of nectar, 37
  hircina, 25; nectary, 39; movement of pollinia, 273
  latifolia, 15; imperfect fertilization, 35; secretion of nectar, 37; two distinct discs, 255
  maculata, 15, 34; transplanted, 32; imperfect fertilization, 35; secretion of nectar, 37, 39; two distinct discs, 255; rostellum, 255; number of seeds, 277, 278;
Orchis mascula, structure of flower, 6; movement of pollinia, 273; number of pollen-grains, 278
  militaris, sterility of, 36; secretion of nectar, 37
  morio, 15, 128; fertility of, in cold season, 33; secretion of nectar, 37, 39; number of pollen-grains, 278
  pyramidalis, structure of flower, 16; movements of pollinia, 21, 272, 273; fertility in different stations, 34; secretion of nectar, 37, 39; monstrous flowers, 38; single disc, 254; rostellum, 256; pollen-grains, 260, 261; contrivances for its fertilization, 264
  ustulata, 25
Organs, gradation of, 247 /
Ornithocephalus, 160
Ovaria of orchids, 284
Oxenden, Mr G. C., obligations to, 25; on *Epipactis purpurata*, 102

Parfitt, Mr, on attached pollinia, 31
Parker, Mr R., obligations to, 129
Pedicel of pollinium, 253; elasticity of, 283
Percy, Dr, analysis of labellum of Warrea, 270
Peristylus viridis, secretion of nectar, 43, 63; rostellum, 255
Petals, uses of, 274
Phaius, 146
  grandifolius, 280

Phalaenopsis, viscidity of stigma, 153; movement of pollinia, 159; labellum, 276
  amabilis, 159
  grandiflora, 159; projection of labellum, 269
Platanthera, 75
  chlorantha, 69
  dilatata, 77
  flava, 76, 77
  hookeri, 75
  hyperborea, 76; self-fertile, 291
Pleurothallis ligulata, 135
  prolifera, 135
Pogonia ophioglossoides, 86
Pollen-masses, rudimentary in Monochanthus, 201; gradation of, 257, 288
Pollen-tubes emitted from anther, 258
Pollinia, movements of, in *Orchis mascula*, 12–15; in *O. pyramidalis*, 21; of the Vandeae, 154; of Catasetum, ejection of, 184; attachment to rostellum, 251; gradation, 257; movements, 271
Pterostylis, nectary of, 232
  longiflora, 87, 89
  trullifolia, 86, 88; imperfect fertilization in New Zealand, 280

Rodgers, Mr, obligations to, 129; on Myanthus and Monochanthus, 196; secretion of nectar in orchids, 265; in Vanilla, 266
Rodriguezia secunda, 159
  suaveolens, movement of pollinia, 156, 159
Rohrbach, Dr, on *Epipogium gmelini*, 103
Rostellum, a single organ in the Ophreae, 45; of the Vandeae, 150; aborted, 242; gradation of, 247; of Apostasia, 248; diversity of structure, 250; crest of, in the Ophreae, 255; in Catasetum, 256
Rucker, Mr, obligations to, 129, 180, 192, 208

Saccolabium, viscidity of stigma, 153, 156
Saint-Hilaire, A. de, on pollen of orchids, 259
Sarcanthus, labellum of, 276
  parishii, 142
  teretifolius, pollinia of, 154, 156; viscidity, 268
Scheinsaftblumen, 37
Schomburgk, Sir R., on Catasetum, 196
Scott, Mr, on flowers of Acropera, 168, 172; of Gongora, 169; nectar-receptacle, 269; number of seeds in capsule of Acropera, 278; prepotency of pollen, 289
Scudder, Mr, on *Pogonia ophioglossoides*, 86
Secretion of nectar, 36, 229, 265
Seeds, production and number of, 276, 277
Selenipedium palmifolium, 232
Self-fertilization, summary on, 293
Sepals, uses of, 274
Serapias cordigera, 27
Sexes of orchids, 196
Smith, Sir James, on position of flowers in Malaxis, 129
Smith, Mr G. E., on bees visiting the Bee Ophrys, 55
Sobralia macrantha, 91
Sophronitis, 146
Spider Ophrys, 50
Spiranthes australis, 114; labellum, 275; self-fertile, 291
  autumnalis, structure of flower, 106–14; vessels of, 239
  cernua, 111
  gracilis, 111
Sprengel, C. K., on fertilization of *Orchi militaris*, 36; secretion of nectar by Orchis, 36; on *Epipactis / latifolia*, 101; Listera, 115, 123; colours attracting insects, 275; value of his work, 275
Stamens in orchids, 242
Stanhopea, pollinia of, 155; labellum, 276

devoniensis, 171
oculata, 171
Stelis, use of the sepals, 274
  racemiflora, 135
Sterility of English orchids, 35
Stigma, viscidity of, in the Vandeae, 152; utriculi, 197; gradation, 248; structure, 249
Stipa, movements of, 273
Structure, diversity of, 282, 285
Structure, importance of trifling details, 286, 287

Thelymitra, self-fertile, 291
  carnea, 127; self-fertile, 280
  longiflora, 127
Thomson, R. B., on *Goodyera repens*, 105
Tilley, H. A., on *Vanilla aromatica*, 91
Trevelyan, Sir C., on Bombus with attached pollen-masses from Cattleya, 145
Treviranus on the secretion of nectar, 41; on Bee Ophrys, 56
Trimen, R., obligations to, 40; on *Bonatea speciosa*, 76, 77; *Disa grandiflora*, 77, 78
Turnbull, Mr, obligations to, 129
Tway-blade, 115

Uropedium, 240
Utriculi of stigma, 197, 218

Vandeae, 156
  structure of, 149; pollinia, 253, 258
Vanilla aromatica, 90
Vanillideae, 90; few seed capsules produced, 281
Veitch, Mr J., obligations to, 129, 180, 220
Vessels, spiral, of orchids, 235
Viscidity of disc in British Ophreae, 35; in Catasetum, 190
  of rostellum and stigma, 248, 249

Waetcher on fertilization of the orchids, 2
Walker, Mr F., obligations to, 100

Wallis, Mr, obligations to, 129
Warrea, 155; analysis of labellum, 270
Weale, J. Mansell, on Habenaria, 76; Bonatea, 77; Disa and Disperis, 78; *Disa macrantha*, 290

Weddell, Dr, on hybrids of Aceras, 26
Wright, Mr C, on the movement of pollinia, 156

Zygopetalum mackai, 155 /

Lightning Source UK Ltd.
Milton Keynes UK
UKOW050809171111

182203UK00003B/116/P